YAMANI

THE INSIDE STORY

Jeffrey Robinson

A MORGAN ENTREKIN BOOK
THE ATLANTIC MONTHLY PRESS
NEW YORK
•

First published in Great Britain in 1988 by Simon & Schuster Limited

First Atlantic Monthly Press edition, May 1989

Printed in the United States of America

Library of Congress Cataloging-in-Publication Data

Robinson, Jeffrey.
    Yamani : the inside story / Jeffrey Robinson.
    "A Morgan Entrekin book."
    Includes index.
    ISBN 0-87113-323-7
    1. Yamani, Ahmed Zaki, 1930–   . 2. Organization of Petroleum Exporting Countries—Officials and employees—Biography. 3. Saudi Arabia—Officials and employees—Biography. 4. Petroleum industry and trade—Government policy—History—20th century. I. Title.
HD9000.5.Y34R63   1989   341.7'5472282'0924—dc19   89-109

The Atlantic Monthly Press
19 Union Square West
New York, NY 10003

First printing

Contents

Contents

For my wife Aline

with love

Acknowledgements

A BOOK is always a team effort, even if my name is the only one appearing on the cover. I wish to express my sincerest thanks to the team. That includes my agents, Leslie Gardner and Robert Ducas, plus my now long-standing and ever-faithful editor, Nick Brealey.

The idea for this book came from David Thieme, always a risk-taker, always a treasured friend. I am greatly indebted to him.

Also a very special thank you for guidance, advice and a reading to Wanda Jablonski, founder and editor of *Petroleum Intelligence Weekly*. She has for many years been one of the most influential people in the oil industry. I am therefore both proud and flattered that she took the time to help me with this.

Much appreciation is also due to the following companies, institutions and offices:

The Arab-British Chamber of Commerce, the Arabian American Oil Corporation (Aramco), Associated Press, Bechtel, the Boeing Corp., British Aerospace, the British Museum Library, British Petroleum, the Brookings Institute, the Carter Presidential Center, the Center for Strategic and International Studies, the Central Intelligence Agency, the Chase Manhattan Bank, the European-Atlantic Group, Exxon, the Group of 30, the Gulf Oil Trading Company, Harvard University, the Hudson Institute, the Institute of Petroleum, the International Energy Agency, the International Monetary Fund, the Kuwait Petroleum Company, the Latsis Oil Company, the London Embassies of Nigeria, Saudi Arabia, the United Arab Emirates and the United States of America; the London School of Economics, the Middle East Institute, the Mobil Oil Corporation, the National Commercial Bank of Saudi Arabia, the National Iranian Oil Corporation, the Netherlands School of Economics, New York University, the Organization of Arab Petroleum

Acknowledgements

Exporting Countries (OAPEC), the Organization of Petroleum Exporting Countries (OPEC), the Oxford Institute for Energy Studies, Oxford University, the Petroleum Industry Research Foundation, Petroleum Information International, Petromin, the Press Association, Reuters, Royal Dutch/Shell, the Royal Institute for International Affairs, the Saudi Arabian Ministry of Information, the Saudi Arabian Monetary Agency, the Saudi Information Centre (London), the Saudi Press Agency, Socal, the Telegraph Information Service, Texaco, the United Kingdom Department of Energy, United Press International, the United States Department of Energy, the United States Department of Justice, the United States Department of State, the United States Information Service, the United States Library of Congress, the University of London's Middle East Centre and the University of Wales.

Also, the United States Senate: Committee on Foreign Relations, Subcommittee on Multinational Corporations, Subcommittee on International Economic Policy and Subcommittee on Near-Eastern and South Asian Affairs, Committee on Energy and Natural Resources; and the United States House of Representatives, Committee on International Relations, Subcommittee on Europe and the Middle East.

There were so many people who were gracious to me, whether through interviews, correspondence or, in the case of authors, journalists and academics, their own writings, I owe my heartfelt thanks to:

Belaid Abdesselam, George Abed, Professor M. A. Adelman, Gholamreza Agazadeh, the Marquess of Anglesey, Ambassador James Akins, Yasin Ali, Mohammed Almana, Mike Ameen, Dr Jamshid Amouzegar, Jack Anderson, Jules Arbose, Mohammed Asad, Dr Ali Ahmed Atiga, Robert Azzi, George Ballou, Richard Barker, Professor William Baxter, Hayyan ibn Bayyan, James Bedore, André Benard, Willard Beling, Rt Hon. Tony Benn MP, Lord Bessborough, Peter Bild, Linda Blandford, Rt Hon. Willy Brandt, Ambassador Kingman Brewster, William Brown, Harold Brownman, Rt Hon. John Bruton MP, John Bulloch, Emile Bustani, Lord Carrington, Elliott R. Cattarulla, J. Rives Childs, Bart Collins, Sir James Craig, Mr Daeiyan, Tony DiNigro, Christopher Dobson, Dr James B. Edwards, Steven Emerson, Robert Engler, Sheikh Saleh al Fadl, Fouad al Farsy, Joe Fitchett, the office of President Gerald Ford, Donald Fox, Herman Franssen, Edward Fried, Lawrence J. Goldstein, Gregory Good, Herbert Goodman, Dean Erwin Griswald, J. S. Habib, Paul Hallwood, Adrian Hamilton, Marvin Hamlisch, Rt Hon. Edward Heath, Said Hitti, Peter Hobday, Sir Julian Hodge, the late David Holden, David Holland, Lord Home, Wally Hopkins, Mr Houssanipour, Ambassador John Irwin II, Dr Hussama Jamaili, Richard Johns, Richard Johnstone, Graham Jones, Mr Kabir,

Acknowledgements

Majid Khadduri, Senator Edward M. Kennedy, Nemir Kirdar, the office of Henry Kissinger, Dr Juanita Kreps, Rt Hon. Kaare Kristiansen MP, Robert Lacey, the office of Chancellor Nigel Lawson, Lord Layton, Walter J. Levy, John Lichtblau, Abdelkader Maachou, Dr Robert Mabro, Ali Mahamadi, Peter Mansfield, Abdul Kasim Mansur, Onnic Marashian, Dr Ashraf Marwan, John J. McCloy, A. J. Meyer, Bijan Mossavar Rahmani, R. Narayanan, James Ashley Nasmyth, Rosemary Niehuss, the office of President Richard Nixon, M. Noble, Professor Peter Odell, Tony Ogden, William Owens, Princess Sarvenaz Pahlavi, Liz Paton, Ronald Payne, George Piercy, Ambassador William Porter, Chris Price, William Quandt, Arthur Reynolds, Ameen Rihani, David Rockefeller, William Rogers, Sir Alan Rothnie, Sheikh Ali Khalifa al-Sabah, Kemal Saiki, Anthony Sampson, Dr James Schlesinger, G. Henry Schuler, Professor Bernard Schwartz, Ian Seymour, S. Shamma, Jack Shaw, Mark Sheehan, Larry Shushan, William E. Simon, Stuart Sinclair, Colin Smith, Lord Strathalmond, Ambassador Mahdi al-Tajir, James Tanner, Abdullah Tariki, Zakhr Tariki, William Tavoulareas, Pierre Terzian, Lord Tonypandy, Louise Turner, Dr Luis Vallenilla, Ken Vaughan, Hafiz Wahba, Lionel Walsch, Ambassador John West, Dr Johannes Witteveen, Oscar Wyatt, Professor Gareth Wyn Jones, Mr Zabbal, Hamed Zaheri, R. S. Zahlan and Hatim Zu'bi.

My sincerest thanks as well to various unnamed friends and colleagues from:

Al-Ahram, Al-Arab, Al-Ittihad, Al-Madina, Al-Qabas, Arabic Weekly Report, Aramco World, the *Armed Forces Journal, Asian Affairs, Atlantic Monthly, Business Week, Commentary, Director Magazine, The Economist, Euromoney Magazine*, the *Financial Times, Forbes, Foreign Affairs, Fortune*, the *Guardian, Harpers, In Business, International Affairs, International and Comparative Law Quarterly*, the *International Herald Tribune*, the *International Journal of Middle East Studies, International Management, International Studies*, the *Los Angeles Times*, the *Middle East Economic Digest*, the *Middle East Economic Survey*, the *Middle East Journal, Middle East Money Magazine, Middle East Times*, the *Nation*, the *New Republic, Newsweek*, the *New York Times*, the *Observer, Petroleum Argus, Petroleum Economics, Petroleum Intelligence Weekly, Petroleum Times, Platts Oilgram News, Readers Digest*, the *Sunday Telegraph*, the *Sunday Times*, the *Daily Telegraph, Time, The Times, US News and World Report*, the *Wall Street Journal* the *Washington Post*, the *Wilson Quarterly, World Affairs Magazine* and *World Today*.

A fair amount of information used in this book has come to me in confidence. There are a number of people who agreed to speak with me only after I gave my solemn word that their identities would never be revealed. That includes several prominent Saudi businessmen, certain Middle Eastern diplomats and one member of the Saudi royal family. I will of course continue to protect their identities. I merely hope that each of these unnamed sources knows how grateful I am.

On the other hand, there were, I'm sorry to say, a small handful of people who were too self-important to give me a few minutes, either in person or on the phone.

Maybe, with a little luck, naming names will help to open those previously closed doors to the next serious request that comes along.

Among the people in Europe who denied me access to information were:

Sir Kit McMahon, a Deputy Governor of the Bank of England and now Chairman of the Midland Bank, who as a member of the Group of 30 sat on a committee with Sheikh Yamani in 1983 to produce a report called *The Future of the International Oil Market*. I am grateful to the other members of that seminar who did grant me some time.

Peter Walker, UK Minister for Wales and former Minister of Energy.

And Nigel Lawson, Chancellor of the Exchequer.

In the United States, one-term President Jimmy Carter steadfastly refused even to answer written questions. So too did former Secretary of State Cyrus Vance, former National Security Advisor Zbigniew Brzezinski, former special assistant Hamilton Jordan and former press aide Jody Powell.

It is my contention that access to information is one of the stanchions of a free society. I also contend that people who are or have been in a position to provide information have a responsibility to do so.

There is however hope.

A great deal of information for this book came into my possession because in the United States there is a Freedom of Information Act (FOIA).

Through this act, the Congress of the United States specifically provides for the release of government records to anyone who wants them, with the exception of items maintained in confidence for reasons such as national security.

Anyone asking for information may do so without stating why they want the information. The burden of proof that the information should be withheld rests with the government. A procedure for appeals is provided for by Congress specifically to prevent the government from needlessly withholding information, even if such information proves to be an embarrassment to the government.

In its present form, now more than ten years old, the American Freedom of Information Act is unique in the world.

Acknowledgements

But then, it might just be that democracy, as defined by the US Constitution and supported in spirit through the FOIA, is equally unique.

*   *   *   *

Finally a word to Sheikh Yamani.

When we began this book, I assured you that I would do my best to be fair, accurate, honest, thorough and unemotional.

I also made a point of insisting that the chips would have to fall where they may.

You in turn insisted that we confine ourselves to history, to Opec and the oil embargo, to stories about the people you've met over the years, to stories about your own childhood and background.

And, if my memory serves correctly, which it does, you very strongly advised me not to write about the period immediately preceding your departure from office.

I'm sorry, but I have respectfully declined that advice.

I am now certain that a number of things I've uncovered and written about will displease you.

I apologize to you if they do.

But I will not apologize to my readers for this.

That you refused to discuss your last few years in government and the reasons for your sudden dismissal was your right.

That I needed to discover the truth was my responsibility.

JR
Spring 1988

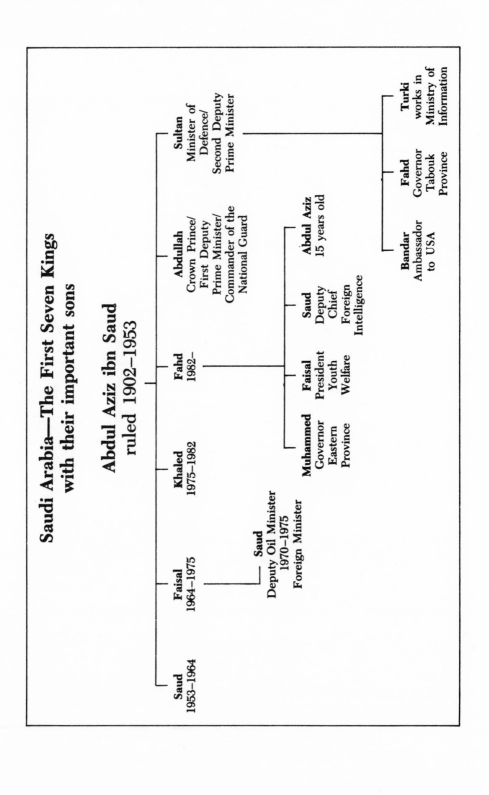

Saudi Arabia—The First Seven Kings with their important sons

Abdul Aziz ibn Saud
ruled 1902–1953

Saud
1953–1964

Faisal
1964–1975

    Saud
Deputy Oil Minister
1970–1975
Foreign Minister

Khaled
1975–1982

Fahd
1982–

Muhammed
Governor
Eastern
Province

Faisal
President
Youth
Welfare

Saud
Deputy
Chief
Foreign
Intelligence

Abdul Aziz
15 years old

Abdullah
Crown Prince/
First Deputy
Prime Minister/
Commander of the
National Guard

Sultan
Minister of
Defence/
Second Deputy
Prime Minister

Bandar
Ambassador
to USA

Fahd
Governor
Tabouk
Province

Turki
works in
Ministry of
Information

Chronology

30 June 1930:	Ahmed Zaki Yamani born in Mecca, Saudi Arabia
1932:	Oil discovered in Saudi Arabia
October 1947:	Yamani attends King Fouad 1st University in Cairo to study law, receiving his degree in May 1951
September 1954:	He arrives in New York to study at NYU
June 1955:	He receives a Masters of Comparative Jurisprudence from NYU and marries Laila Faidhi in Brooklyn, NY
June 1956:	He receives a second Masters degree, this one from Harvard Law School, Cambridge, Mass.
December 1957:	Appointed Legal Adviser to the Council of Ministers under Crown Prince Faisal
December 1959:	Becomes Minister of State Without Portfolio and a member of the Cabinet
September 1960:	Organization of Petroleum Exporting Countries (Opec) formed on the initiative of Saudi Arabia and Venezuela
March 1962:	Yamani is named Minister of Petroleum and Mineral Resources
June 1967:	War breaks out in the Middle East. Some of the Arab states try to use the oil weapon to

pressure America into exacting a peace settlement with the Israelis but the ploy fails

September 1968: Yamani is the main force behind the formation of the Organization of Arab Petroleum Exporting Countries (Oapec). For the first time, at the American University at Beirut, he also makes a public statement differentiating between nationalization and his intentions to participate in Saudi Arabia's oil wealth with Aramco

December 1970: Opec follows Yamani's lead and officially calls for participation with the oil companies on behalf of its members

October 1972: Yamani completes the first stages of the participation accords with the oil companies, known as the Tehran Agreements, on behalf of the Gulf producers

April 1973: Now he travels to the United States, warning the Nixon administration that they must intervene to deter the Israelis as tensions mount in the Middle East and another war looms

6 October 1973: Egypt and Syria attack Israel

16 October 1973: Opec raises oil prices from $3 per barrel to $5.12

17 October 1973: Oapec embargos the United States and Holland while implementing production cutbacks against nations considered unfriendly to the Arab cause

December 1973 The Shah insists Opec raise prices to $20. Yamani's staunch opposition keeps the increased price to $11.65

March 1974: The embargo officially ends

23 March 1975: Yamani completes his marriage contract with Tammam al-Anbar

25 March 1975: King Faisal is murdered as Yamani stands next to him. Khaled becomes king. Fahd is named Crown Prince

Chronology

21 December 1975:	The international terrorist Carlos takes the Opec ministers in Vienna hostage. He holds Yamani four days while promising to murder him. Yamani even writes out his own will, expecting to die
December 1977:	At the Opec meeting in Doha, Yamani and the Shah again clash on oil prices. The Shah now says $100 oil is not overpriced. Yamani fights to keep prices stable
October 1978:	Civil unrest in Iran begins to drive oil prices higher
January 1979:	The Shah is deposed and the oil market comes unglued
February 1979:	Spot market oil reaches $20
May 1979:	Spot market oil prices climb to $34.50
November 1979:	Spot market oil now hits $40
August 1981:	Prices begin to slide back, coming down to $34
June 1982:	King Khaled dies and Fahd assumes the throne
March 1983:	Opec imposes production quotas for the first time in its history and fixes the official oil price at $29
1983–1984:	Yamani fights to keep prices at $28
1985:	The glut takes hold and oil prices begin a steep slide towards $18
1986:	The slide picks up momentum and from $18 prices drop to $9
September 1986:	Yamani speaks at Harvard's 350th anniversary but the speech he wanted to give was not the speech he did give
October 1986:	Opec meets in Geneva for 17 days, the longest session ever, as Yamani clashes with the Iranians over pricing and disobeys King Fahd's instructions. On the 29th, while watching television, he learns of his dismissal

1

Prologue

SINCE DECEMBER 1975 Sheikh Ahmed Zaki Yamani has been constantly surrounded by bodyguards.

At home in Saudi Arabia the government provides a security staff of 15 to protect him and his family.

When he travels, his personal security staff numbers only six. They're British. One of them was once Prince Philip's private detective. Each of them is a former SAS commando or an ex-policeman.

Where local laws permit it, which is most places, they're armed. It's done discreetly but they're armed nevertheless. No matter where they are, and at all times, they carry walkie-talkies to keep each other updated with the position of 'the boss'. They talk incessantly to each other, speaking just loud enough to get their message across . . . the boss is coming to the car . . . the boss is driving past your station . . . the boss is coming up to the flat. They open doors and look all around a room before stepping aside to let him enter. They are the first to walk outside, onto the street, checking to see that the street is clear. They ride with him in his car – he prefers to drive himself – and they stare at every car in front and every car that draws up alongside and every car that follows for too long. They lock and unlock doors and appear silently from out of stairwells in the hallway to check you out, then disappear just as silently, like a doberman pincher.

Of course, if you were standing shoulder to shoulder with King Faisal when he was assassinated at point blank range and if you were kidnapped by the international terrorist Carlos who promised that one day he would murder you . . . if you've had threats made against your life and a couple of times you've only barely escaped . . . well, then, always keeping six large and highly trained men around to make sure that you stay alive is understandable.

They claim he's still in danger.

You ask, From whom?

They answer, 'It's not always easy to know.'

You ask, From elements in the west or the Arab world or some religious fanatics or some political terrorist?

And they nod, 'Something like that'.

If he is in fact still in danger, it's probably less now than before. After December 1975 he often said that he expected to die a violent death. But now, out of government, he hopes and prays that it's a diminishing possibility.

'Some day,' he says, 'I would like to be finished with all of this. I would like to let the boys go and do without them. It's not me to be confined like this. I love to take walks, to stroll along a street and go window shopping. Always being guarded is not me. Someday I hope that I can be free from this.'

Still, whenever anyone knocks at the door he stiffens.

While the danger exists the security staff are forever hovering nearby. And if you hang around him while they hang around the two of you, it's easy to catch a case of paranoia. If you're not used to being protected, when you're with someone who has a professional security staff, you find yourself glancing behind every bush and noticing every car that passes and worrying that someone might suddenly step out from behind a lamp post with a gun. That's when you say to yourself, if someone starts shooting at him what am I supposed to do?

It's an uncomfortable feeling.

And it does not necessarily go away the longer you spend with him. It's sort of like the dentist and his Novocaine. It doesn't hurt. But you know it's there.

It's only when you sit down to talk to him that the security staff fade into the background.

Then you must learn to live with constant interruptions.

People arrive at odd times to pay a courtesy call. It's part of Saudi tradition. People phone to talk business. Other people phone just to say hello. More people stop by to ask his advice.

There is a never-ending stream of people coming to see him, invited in for a chat, offered coffee or juice, and dates or figs from huge baskets spread across the tables in front of the couches. Or, if they're really lucky, they're offered small green logs of pistachio paste sweets that have the same texture as almond paste but are much better than marzipan.

So you sit down to speak with him and in between the interruptions, while the two of you talk, he stares directly into your eyes. He laughs honestly when something strikes him as funny. Or he leans forward to make a point when something is especially serious. There are none of those polite reassuring smiles or yes-I-agree-with-you nods that westerners cast off to pretend they're paying attention.

Not at all.

He sits there and stares at you and fidgets with his worry beads and makes you wonder what he's thinking.

He sits there and looks at you like a poker player, never giving away the hand he's holding.

He speaks slowly, deliberately, the practised habit of a man who knows that his interviews can turn into headlines.

And before too long, he's somehow switched the conversation around to you.

He is forever playing his cards close to his chest.

Even when it seems an odd thing to do.

There are times when he simply won't give away much information that would otherwise seem trivial.

How long will you be in town on this trip? It's difficult to say. Will you be here until Tuesday? Perhaps. Where are you off to next? It depends on many things so I will have to let you know.

He had planned all week to leave the ski resort on Friday for Geneva but he didn't say so until Thursday evening. He had planned all week to leave Geneva on Tuesday for America but he didn't say so until Monday afternoon.

Business? Well, yes. Where in the States are you going? Maybe several places.

Perhaps it has to do with the fact that a security-conscious man never discusses his travel plans. Or perhaps it's just that idle conversation is a western talent, specifically American, and not something Middle Easterners take to easily.

One of Yamani's friends discovered that several years ago while staying with his family in Saudi Arabia. The phone often rang in the middle of the night. Whenever it did, there was hushed conversation for a few minutes and then Yamani would leave. Sometimes he was gone for half an hour. Sometimes he was gone for several hours. It went on like that night after night. Curious, the friend wanted to know, 'What's that all about?' Yamani responded, 'It's nothing. Just some business.' A week later, with the 3 a.m. and 4 a.m. phone-calls as frequent as ever, the friend tried again. But this time the question was disguised in the oblique approach. 'He must be mad to ring you in the middle of the night like that.' And this time Yamani answered straight. 'But you see, the king has the right to call me whenever he likes.'

On the other hand, when he chooses to, Yamani can be totally candid and forthright.

We were sitting on the middle of three large couches that surround the huge coffee table at the end of the 75-foot livingroom that makes up the main part of the plushest hotel suite in Geneva.

It's on the top floor of the Intercontinental Hotel and from 18 storeys high the view of the lake in the distance is magnificent. For years this has been his Geneva office. He's got a 15-room mansion a few miles away on the lake with handsomely manicured lawns, fine antique French furniture, fine antique Persian rugs, an indoor swimming pool, an outdoor swimming pool, and a special room where he can meditate and pray according to his Moslem beliefs. But it was in the big suite at the Intercontinental where he held court during the Opec years and it's there he still feels comfortable, even though those days are now over.

The coffee table was covered in gift baskets of fruit and dates and a silver tray with a cut-glass pitcher and crystal stemware to serve the freshly squeezed pomegranate juice.

The security staff were stationed at the front door of the suite where a closed circuit television camera was aimed down the hallway to show anyone approaching. There was a maid somewhere, hidden in one of the other rooms, and a valet who seemed to be on the other end of one of the two telephones. Yamani would pick it up and say, could you please bring some more juice. Within a few seconds the valet would appear with another tray.

Yamani was dressed in a perfectly cut Savile Row suit.

There were English and Arabic newspapers and American news magazines on the couch between us and the pair of telephones at his right elbow that seemed to ring every few minutes.

And this time he was coming on straight.

I showed him a newspaper clipping that said, in order to get back to his roots, he spent each summer living in a tent in the desert. He gestured to emphasize the setting, then looked at me as if I was crazy. 'Do you see me living in a tent?'

Now I said, 'I've heard a figure of what you're worth.'

He said, 'Tell me.'

I said, 'With your real estate holdings, as much as $500 million.'

He thought about that for a few moments before he decided, 'Less.'

I asked, 'A lot less?'

He said, 'If you take away the real estate, if you don't add that in, yes, much less. Even with the real estate it's still less.'

Then I asked him about his first marriage.

Again he displayed a certain candour. 'My first marriage did not work, perhaps for many reasons, so we separated. Now I am married to a woman I love very much. I waited nine years and was very careful before getting married again. I think of marriage also as an investment for the future. You know, when you get older, maybe in your late 60s or early 70s and you slow down. Then, having someone with you who knows you and loves you . . . having someone there so that you can remember things together – the restaurant where we ate 20 years ago, that time we visited with those friends, that night when we were together in whatever city – yes, an investment for the future.'

Yamani's second wife Tammam is a beautiful dark-haired Saudi woman in French designer clothes who studied biology at the American University in Beirut. They met when someone in the Ministry of Petroleum got married and came to show Yamani the wedding photos. He spotted Tammam standing with the bride and asked who she was. A formal introduction was arranged and after a time, Yamani – in keeping with tradition – asked Tammam's father for her hand.

And if it is true that behind every good man there is a good woman, then the story of Zaki Yamani is also the story of Tammam Yamani.

One of five children, she was brought up in a home where family ties and education were highly stressed. She in turn has made certain that her own children spend as much time as possible with their parents and are comfortable in both eastern and western society. For instance, each of them, from the oldest to the youngest, speaks Arabic, English and French with native ease.

Now in her mid-30s, she is Yamani's constant companion. In Saudi Arabia, where couples are naturally reserved, there are rules of traditional behaviour. But in the west, much like western couples, Zaki and Tammam hold hands and they are forever stealing glances at each other. She'll stand up to leave the room and he'll chide her in English, in deference to their guest, 'Don't eat anything now because we're going to have dinner soon.' She'll grin, 'I'm not going to eat anything.' He'll say, 'Yes, you are.' She'll say, 'No, I've got something important to do.' Then he'll laugh and nod, 'You mean you want to telephone your sister again?' It's one of the games they play to their obvious great amusement.

A man of medium height, Yamani is stockily built with a widish face made to look thinner by his now-greying, but ever-familiar, goatee. His hair is reddish brown, almost auburn. His eyes are dark brown, nearly black. His voice is soft and there's a special look in his eyes. A kind of tenderness mixed together with a supreme self-confidence. It's hard to say exactly what it is but you know it right away when you see it. And you see it best when he laughs. You see it best when his eyes open very wide and his face shows that he is truly amused.

It's something special that women never fail to notice.

And he knows it.

5

Back at the beginning of the 1970s, when he still travelled on commercial airlines, he was booked on a crowded flight from New York to San Francisco. One of the people he'd been meeting with in New York happened to mention that they were also trying to get to California but that all the flights were full. Yamani said, come out to the airport with me and we'll get you on the plane. At JFK, as Yamani checked in, he asked the woman behind the counter to please find another seat on his flight. She apologized that the plane was absolutely full and the standby list was very long. Yamani smiled, reached for the woman's hand, studied her palm for several moments and told her what he could see there. In a very innocent way he rubbed her palm and talked to her and looked at her straight in the eyes.

He walked away from the check-in counter with a pair of boarding passes.

Yamani has two daughters and one son by his first marriage. They're now grown up and have given him five grandchildren. Then he has three sons and two daughters by his second marriage. They're very young and still at home.

Then there is another 'daughter'.

When Yamani was 19, his father returned from a trip to Malaysia with a baby girl. She'd been orphaned and Yamani's father agreed to take her, although the Moslems don't have adoption in the western sense of the word. He gave the baby to Zaki and said, 'Raise her like your daughter.' Even though the girl was brought up by Yamani's mother and is now a grown woman with her own children, Yamani still treats her as if she was his offspring.

'I am totally devoted to my family, my wife, my children and my grandchildren. They are the joys of my life.'

He is frequently surrounded by his family. And friends with their families too.

The winter following Yamani's dismissal, he and his family joined friends in Switzerland to spend a month skiing. The kids raced in the local competitions and, typical of all parents, there were Zaki and Tammam in snowsuits with their Instamatics at the finish line.

Six months later, in Sardinia, Zaki and Tammam led an entourage of friends and children on a day trip to Corsica. He herded 30 adults and a dozen kids on board his 270 foot yacht, which when it was built in 1973 was said to be one of the two most beautiful boats in the world. Arriving in Bonifacio after a three-hour sail, Yamani was informed that there were only three taxis in town – two of which were nowhere to be seen – and no buses. But there was one of those little sightseeing trains with rubber wheels that takes tourists through the streets. So he rented it exclusively for two hours. Much to the glee of the children,

6

everyone piled on for a tour of the village. Later that evening, after taking over a restaurant for dinner, Zaki and Tammam led the group back towards the boat. That's when Zaki spotted a man selling balloons and those green plastic bracelets that glow in the dark. He bought them all. He took the balloons from the seller in one hand and those glowing green things in the other. The children moved in on him, anxiously grabbing for theirs. Just then a French woman and her husband spotted him. She stared at him for a second, clutched at her husband's arm and said, 'Yamani?' She pointed at this man, glowing green and with 15 balloons. 'Impossible. Non, ce n'est pas possible. Yamani?' She kept shaking her head. 'Pas possible!'

Imagine though when her husband convinced her that it was Yamani. Yes, yes, he'd say, it was him. And she'd say with such pity, 'Poor man, all that's left for him now is to sell balloons in Bonifacio.'

He exercises regularly and watches his weight. He walks and swims. He even travels with a portable trampoline. 'Just to jump up and down for 20 minutes every few hours. To keep the blood flowing.' In the winter he spends as much time as he can at a small but comfortable apartment he's owned since the mid-1960s in a Swiss mountain resort known for its excellent cross-country skiing. 'I don't do downhill because that isn't exercise. Cross-country skiing makes you breathe hard and gets your heart pumping. It's very important to do that.' Off season he has a treadmill which he walks on every day, swinging handweights to keep himself in shape.

He is also careful about his diet.

Although Yamani obviously encourages the never-ending stream of people who drop by unannounced throughout the day and well into the evening, often at meal times, he himself doesn't eat much.

The Arabs feel if there's enough food for 15 then there's enough for 20. And it's rare when there are fewer than 10–15 people at the Yamanis' table. Lunch can be as late as 3 p.m. and dinners don't ever start before 10 p.m. Meals are a feast, with at least six to eight different dishes. There is fish and meat and fowl and several platters with rice, potatoes and vegetables. There is melon and fruit and cakes for dessert.

Yet in spite of all the food being served around him, whenever he can he avoids lunch. Even at night he prefers to stick to fish, vegetables, yoghurt, honey, dates, nuts and fruit.

'At dinners in the west people understand when you say no to a second helping, or just take a small portion the first time. They understand when you go lightly. In other parts of the world you sometimes have to eat everything and a lot of it or you'd be insulting your host.'

Once, on a visit to Sri Lanka, President Jayawardene invited him for breakfast. He wore a black suit as a sign of respect and was expecting something like coffee and rolls and maybe some fruit. But he was met by helicopter and taken up to a mountain retreat where the President greeted him in an open white shirt. They then sat down to a very hot curry breakfast.

'He was nice and cool in his whites and I was eating this very spicy food in a black suit with a tie. The perspiration was pouring down my face. Some meals are definitely easier than others.'

In between meals he is particularly fond of pistachio nuts.

As a matter of fact he may be one of the few people on earth who can actually carry on an intelligent discussion about pistachios. 'You like pistachios?' He reaches for the phone and asks whoever answers, 'Where are those pistachios we brought?' Instantly the valet arrives, not with a silver tray covered in nuts but with a huge burlap bag . . . 10 kilos worth . . . ripped open at the top. He puts the bag on the floor between us and reaches in for a handful. 'Turkish pistachios are slightly smaller than the Iranian pistachios but they are much sweeter.' We don't finish the bagful but we put a respectable dent in his supply.

In America, he knows about regional cuisines and can tell you where to find great icecream in Boston.

In England, he prowls the food halls at Harrods, spending most of his time there at the health food counters, looking for whatever might suit his fancy.

At home, he cooks whenever he can, grows his own fruit and vegetables and buys special coffee beans from Yemen which he roasts himself.

Once, just before leaving South America, he drove past a man with a stand full of mangoes. He stopped the car, got out and asked the man how much he wanted for the entire stand. The man, slightly astonished, quoted a price.

Then Yamani spotted a second stand and said, 'That one too?'

The mango seller said no, the price didn't include his second stand.

'That's not what I meant,' Yamani explained. 'How much for that one too?'

He bought the fruit from both stands, which filled his plane, and everyone he met over the course of the next week found themselves laden with fresh South American mangoes.

However, his major failing is oranges.

And when he's really pressed he admits to a secret passion for oranges covered in chocolate.

Every morning for breakfast, when he's home, he has the same special bran cereal. With lunch or dinner at a restaurant, he always brings along a special bran bread that he bakes himself.

As a devout Moslem, he follows the strict dietary laws of Islam. No pork. No meat from animals that eat other animals.

And never any alcohol.

At least not when he can help it.

It sometimes shows up in desserts which he only discovers after he's had a bite. He then politely declines. Once in a while a real drink sneaks up on him totally by mistake. A few summers ago, during lunch with Tammam at a café in Capri, he asked for some fresh squeezed lemon juice to pour over his fish. Whether the waiter didn't understand Yamani's Italian or Yamani simply got it wrong, a yellowish drink finally arrived. At this point he had already eaten his fish so he simply picked it up and knocked it back. To this day he still doesn't know what it was. Perhaps pastis. Perhaps some sort of cognac or brandy. He only discovered it wasn't lemon juice when he swallowed a mouthful, felt the burning in the back of his throat and immediately thought his head was going to explode. Needless to say, he now takes extra care ordering in Italian cafés.

When you dine with him in a restaurant, he and Tammam drink mineral water, but you can order wine for yourself. If you turn down the wine he gives you a baleful look and says, 'Please do not deprive yourself just because we are not drinking.'

'The trick to going out for dinner with Zaki', cautions someone who says he learned the hard way, 'is to make certain he orders first. Otherwise he'll have the waiters bring you everything on the menu and when mounds of food arrive on your plate you'll notice, too late, that he's having one small piece of grilled fish.'

Some years ago, a western friend visiting the Yamanis in Saudi Arabia during the Ramadan period – when daily fasting is in order – was told by his host that lunch would be served in his room. The guest declined. But Yamani was insistent. He reminded his house guest, you are not a Moslem and there is no reason for you to observe the fast so I would like you to take your lunch as you normally would.

Adds a former British Ambassador to Saudi Arabia, 'One of the first things you notice about Zaki is that he's the kind of gentleman a true English gentleman would appreciate.'

He is certainly the kind of man who, if he did drink, would find the collection of great vintage wines a passionate hobby.

Instead he makes his own perfume.

Whenever he goes on a trip, a couple of small gym bags come with him. They're filled with bottles and vials of pure flower essence. He mixes them, taking the time to find the exact scent he wants. Once it's right, he pours it into a pocket-sized, sterling silver, roll-on dispenser which he always carries with him, and several times a day he spreads the perfume over his beard and through his hair.

It is a strong, pungent, exotic, very musky oriental smell.

No one could ever confuse it with Giorgio or Chanel.

He happily shares it with anyone who notices it. The first time he smears this stuff over your hands and your face or puts it in your hair, you smile in a well-bred way and reassure him, 'Yes, it's very . . . ah . . . how can I put it . . . different. It's very . . . interesting.' But you think to yourself, I guess you have to come from that part of the world to appreciate this. Then you discover it won't go away. It won't wash off. Because it's purely oil based, not alcohol based, it seeps into your skin and stays with you.

Yet, by the second or third day, when you can still smell it, you start to say to yourself, actually this is kind of nice. But you don't dare admit that to him because he's so proud of his perfume and likes it so much, he'll gleefully smear a lot more of it on you and then you'll have to wait even longer before it fades into its more subtle state.

* * * *

As one of the most influential diplomats in the world, at least since the oil crisis of 1973, Yamani has hob-nobbed, negotiated, debated and dined with the world's leaders.

He knows a lot of people.

'Imelda Marcos took us once to a palace she and her husband owned in Manilla, which was just for their antique silver collection. It was their private museum.'

And, 'Mike Wallace from American television was interviewing the Shah of Iran and the Shah said, "Yamani is an agent of the imperialists." So Wallace came to ask me what I thought and I told him, "I can't believe his *Imperial* majesty would say such a thing." Even the Shah had to laugh.'

And, 'At Cancun we were invited to a private lunch with Ronald Reagan. It was just the President, King Fahd, Prince Saud, who is the Saudi Arabian Foreign Minister, George Shultz and myself. The President was very charming. But there was only small talk. His people had told us before lunch that this was to be strictly social.' The hint was that Reagan wouldn't be able to talk seriously on any of the issues that might have otherwise come up.

And, on a trip to England in the late 1960s, John Paul Getty invited him to Sutton Place for lunch. Arriving at the home of the richest man in the world, Yamani was shown to a pay telephone and told that any visitors wishing to make a call should use this – although, when Yamani needed to ring someone, Getty quietly assured him, 'It's okay. You can use my personal phone for free.' Before leaving on a tour of Getty's art collection, Yamani was asked if he wanted a coat. Yamani asked, 'Is it outside?' Getty's aide said no. 'I didn't understand the reason for the coat and said, no thank you. But the aide brought it along anyway. I only realized why it was necessary when I discovered that Getty never heated more than a few rooms in his gigantic mansion.' When lunch was served, it turned out to be such a frugal affair . . . 'The three pieces of lamb on my plate were so small I didn't even have to cut them to put them in my mouth' . . . that en route back to London, Yamani stopped at a roadside café for a second lunch.

And, in February 1975, King Faisal sent Yamani on the first official visit by a Saudi minister to India. 'A courtesy call was arranged with Indira Gandhi. Just before escorting me into the Prime Minister's office, the protocol officer asked, she's on a very tight schedule so could you please keep your visit to 10 minutes. As I was really there to see other ministers I said that would be fine.' Yamani and Mrs Gandhi began to chat. After about 10 minutes he said something like, 'I know that you're busy and I must be going.' But she told Yamani to stay and the two kept on talking. After another 10 minutes the protocol officer poked his head into the office to remind Mrs Gandhi that she had other appointments. But she shooed the protocol officer away. As people collected in the outer office waiting to get in to see her, she and Yamani talked for an hour and 45 minutes.

Of course, you'd expect someone of Yamani's stature to know a lot of people. At the same time, as is often the case with men of his prominence, you'd expect a lot of people to claim they know him. I approached more than 150 people to say, I'm writing a book about Sheikh Yamani, and something like 95 per cent of them gave me the exact same initial reaction. 'A book about Sheikh Yamani?' Brief pause. 'You know, Zaki is my friend.'

They didn't say, 'I know him well', or 'I can tell you everything you want to know about him'. They said, 'Zaki is my friend.'

Even if he isn't, even if the truth is that they've only met a couple of times, it is fascinating that so many people think of him as their friend.

It says a lot about the way Yamani relates to people.

Even his household staff think that way. In Saudi Arabia, his valet, his housekeeper and his chef have each been with him for more than 25 years. The junior member of his immediate staff has been with him nearly 15 years.

To put it into one simple straightforward declarative sentence, Zaki

Yamani is a man who makes you think he's as interested in you as you are in him.

Suggests an American who's known him since the 1960s, 'I don't think his personal style has changed much over the years. He's always had that combination of self-confidence and dignity even when I think some of his power had eroded. He's a man with considerable pride and self-esteem. Others may call that arrogant. But there's a problem, particularly amongst the Americans, that when someone is clearly competent, perhaps more competent than thou, instead of saying I can't stand the fellow because he's more competent than I, he's described as arrogant. I think there may be something of that in Yamani's case. But I never found him to be arrogant. Convinced of the correctness of his views, yes. Not one suddenly to say, yes I see your point and I was wrong. He always expresses his views courteously. Firmly but courteously.'

Courteous? To a fault.

Firm? Well, put it this way, he isn't at all shy when it comes to letting you know what he thinks about something once he's decided he wants you to know.

Over the course of two and a half decades, Yamani earned a reputation as, perhaps, the most western-media-wise Arab ever. There are some people who believe he even became the most famous Saudi of the twentieth century and was for many years the most important man in the Middle East. Certainly since the oil embargo of 1973 he's been the Arab world's leading spokesman for oil policy. During much of the past quarter century he was the most visible of all the Opec oil ministers. He was also generally considered to be the oracle for the future of prices in the world's single most important commodity.

Urbane, intelligent perhaps even to the point of brilliance, well educated, handsome, poised, equally at home in front of western television cameras or fielding questions at the often boisterous Opec press conferences of the past 15 years, Yamani easily made friends in the west. But there are those who think he left some of his flanks uncovered at home.

The more famous Yamani became, the more certain factions in Saudi Arabia worried about him.

Especially some members of the royal family.

Some of them began thinking years ago that maybe a commoner had risen too high, that maybe a commoner had too much power.

It was 1974.

The oil flowed and money poured in.

At $3 a barrel the Saudis were rich beyond their wildest dreams.

They could afford just about anything.

But when the price of oil quadrupled in the space of only a few months, they couldn't spend all the money they were making even if they wanted to.

At $12 a barrel the oil ministry was far and away the most important office in the country. The man responsible for it bore the title Sheikh. But he wasn't royal. The title was honorary, a sign of respect for a learned, devout Moslem.

And although the stern-faced King Faisal ruled with an iron hand, skilfully managing to walk through the various minefields that make up day-to-day politics in the Middle East, a secretive group of his younger brothers, who would one day inherit his throne, were extremely concerned.

Government in their part of the world is a family affair.

It is often said that Saudi Arabia is the only family business in the world with a seat in the United Nations.

Modern Saudi Arabia, the nation conceived not 60 years ago by the desert warrior Abdul Aziz ibn Saud, was designed much like a classic corporation. The king rules, passing the monarchy from brother to brother, along the line of all Ibn Saud's sons.

Consider the brothers then to be the board of directors.

Next come the 4,000–5,000 royals with little or no power in the daily workings of the government but who nevertheless, by right of birth, have a say in the overall attitudes of the board of directors.

They are the preferred shareholders.

Non-royal ministers play the role of senior executives. They're the ones who actually make the business work. However, while they possess substantial responsibilities, they are forever commoners. They are not invited to, nor are they expected to take part in, any of the boardroom discussions.

At the bottom are the people.

They hold the company's ordinary shares but their voting power is nil. Yet they represent a large and complex mix of special interests – religious, socio-economic, tribal. So the board of directors dare not totally disregard their wishes. For instance, any radical changes towards modernization and therefore away from fundamental Islamic teachings is always guaranteed to stir up a section of the masses. It's a successful king who knows just how much he can get away with, just how far he can go, before the wrath of the ordinary shareholders crashes violently down upon his head.

The system is unique in the world.

As long as everyone remains in their place, with upward mobility especially difficult, everything seems to work well.

The ordinary shareholders accept that the directors must have their perks. Privilege and royal incomes are passed down to everyone in the family. All of those 4,000–5,000 princes are entitled to a slice of the cake. In the next 20 years that number could easily approach 15,000–20,000. Keeping those preferred shareholders happy – which is synonymous to governing – could some day become as unwieldly task.

But in modern Saudi Arabia something that is not yet broken will never be fixed.

So, while all the directors have their perks, they also make very certain that the company's profits are widely dispersed among the people.

Generosity is an inborn Saudi royal family trait.

So too, it seems, is jealousy.

When someone is bright enough and clever enough and ambitious enough to rise through the Saudi system, from commoner to a position of great power, certain men who were born to power begin to feel uneasy.

For a non-royal, ministerial status is as far as one can go.

By 1974, with oil bringing such fabulous wealth into the kingdom, being Minister of Petroleum was as close as any commoner could ever get to the king.

As you might expect, long before Yamani made it to that point the Central Intelligence Agency had singled him out for watching. They do that sort of thing at the CIA. They keep files on people. They try to look into the future and build dossiers on rising stars. They make notes for future reference.

One of the notes they made in 1974 read, 'Yamani has great respect for and almost blind devotion to King Faisal. Faisal, in turn, likes Yamani and trusts him and confides in him. This solid relationship with Faisal has not made Yamani popular with some members of the royal family. We know for certain that key ministers, [Prince] Fahd of Interior and [Prince] Sultan of Defense, do not like Yamani but they respect him and the power he has due to his relationship with Faisal. Yamani is expected to be finished with government when the king passes on. It is believed he cannot work under Fahd, who is expected to run the country after Faisal.'

It goes without saying that Faisal was an exceptional man.

With brilliant native instinct, he always understood the special place that the oil minister would hold. That's why he decided it should not necessarily be given to a royal. Unlike other members of the Council of Ministers – Defence, Interior, Foreign Minister – he saw a good reason to put a commoner at the top of the petroleum ministry.

Not that a royal couldn't do the job. His own son, Prince Saud, served as Deputy Petroleum Minister before becoming Foreign

Minister. The problem was that removing a royal from any ministry is difficult enough. Removing a royal as head of the petroleum ministry would not only be difficult, it would also be internationally embarrassing.

Removing a commoner was easy.

However Yamani, against the odds, ran his ministry for almost 25 years.

Until 2 July 1985, when Andrei Gromyko was named President of the Soviet Union, the dour-faced Russian who'd served as Foreign Minister for 28 years had been the longest continually serving cabinet minister in the world.

It was Yamani who replaced him at the top of the longevity list.

For more than two dozen years he directed the office which accounted for 95 per cent of Saudi Arabia's exports, more than eight out of every ten rials of the government's revenues and slightly more than 60 per cent of the Saudi GNP.

He was King Faisal's closest adviser and the nation's first non-royal minister to warrant and to live with near-royal status. King Faisal grew so fond of him, had such trust and faith in him, that he sought his advice on every subject. He showered Yamani with gifts and made him fabulously wealthy.

When the king was gunned down he lay dying in Yamani's arms.

Faisal even instructed his brothers to treat Yamani like one of his own sons.

That, however, proved easier said than done.

When Faisal was murdered and King Khaled assumed the throne, there were subtle changes. Khaled was a slow and easy-going man who preferred to live out his days with the tribes in the desert and hunt with falcons. The robust, roundfaced, former playboy Fahd became heir apparent and quickly emerged as the real power in the country. Under Faisal he was Interior Minister. Under Khaled he was Crown Prince and First Deputy Prime Minister. As Khaled's health deteriorated, Fahd's grip on the reins tightened. Long before Khaled was dead, Fahd was king in all but name.

With him arrived the so called Al Fahd faction.

Seven full brothers from a woman named Hossa al-Sudairi.

They moved directly into the line of power and had it in their minds to hold on to that power for a very long time. Seven full brothers now occupied very important seats on the corporation's main board. The Al Fahd, or the Sudairi Seven as they are sometimes known, were systematically taking over Saudi Arabia.

Fahd inherited the throne in June 1982.

But where Faisal was strong and could dictate his wishes, Fahd was inclined to allow his full brothers a heavy hand in the running of the corporation.

Where Faisal spent his youth learning the workings of government, travelling as Foreign Minister and learning to hold his own with statesmen throughout the world, Fahd had been a compulsive gambler who partied his way through Europe.

Where Faisal was self-confident, Fahd was jealous.

It was 1974.

The oil flowed and the money poured in.

Faisal was king and Fahd wanted to be close to the king but his older brother had a favourite.

And that favourite was not a royal.

Fahd even spoke privately to the king about it. Several times. Just the two of them, head to head, behind closed doors. Although he always couched his pettiness and personal jealousies in concern for the kingdom, he argued that certain commoners were assuming too much power. He argued that some of the family were displeased. He argued that oil was the family's business.

In the end the king agreed to create several 'supreme councils' . . . petroleum, education and security, among others . . . and he appointed Fahd to oversee all of them.

That's exactly what Fahd wanted.

Now there would be a royal as the de facto head of the nation's most important source of income. Now the commoner's power would be contained. Now he would be the buffer zone between the king and his oil minister.

At one of the Supreme Petroleum Council's first meetings an important issue was raised and the group voted in favour of Fahd's appraisal of the situation.

Fahd took the council's suggestion to the king.

Faisal listened as his younger brother stated his case. But after a few moments of quiet thought he asked what the vote had been.

Fahd told him, 'Four to one.'

Faisal wanted to know, 'Who was the dissenting one?'

Fahd answered, 'Yamani.'

And Faisal nodded, 'Then we will do it Yamani's way.'

2

Squaring the Circle

Geneva, October 1986.

Oil ministers and their staff and their hangers-on and the Opec staff and the international press corps and a whole bunch of just-curious-on-lookers all descend on the Intercontinental like a swarm of locusts about to ravage a farmer's field.

The driveway is littered with big cars, most of them black, with some chauffeurs in suits and some chauffeurs in Arab robes and all sorts of other men dressed in suits or in Arab robes standing around, waiting.

Guards question everyone coming in through the hotel's front door, demanding to know, who are you? And, are you a guest at the hotel? And, if you're not registered here, what do you want?

Even normal hotel guests are subjected to a security check, just like at the airport.

You walk through a metal detector and if you've got your keys in your pocket the alarm goes off so they frisk you before you're allowed to make your way through the crowded ground floor – where more people stand around in suits or in Arab robes – then up the escalator to the over-busy main lobby.

Men and women, but mostly men, are lingering in the lobby, sitting on couches or milling about next to the potted palms, talking in foreign tongues and drowning out the background Muzak.

The bars are full.

The restaurants are full.

The news kiosk opposite the concierge's desk and the watch shop next to the news kiosk and the store downstairs that rents soft-core video cassettes all do a booming business.

Wherever you look there are white faces and black faces and brown faces. There are men dressed in western clothes, and men dressed in

17

white robes, and every now and then there are a couple of women in French designer clothes who smell of expensive perfume and hurry through the lobby, arm in arm, to disappear quickly in an elevator.

Wherever you look there are security men, carrying walkie-talkies, suspicious of anyone who looks at them.

Zaki Yamani is in town.

For the past dozen years whenever and wherever the Organization of Petroleum Exporting Countries has met, he's been the main attraction.

Never more than now.

In Geneva in October 1986 he's fighting the biggest battle of his life.

And he is losing.

Global oil production is much too high.

Global oil demand is much too low.

Simple high school economics dictate that to get the prices up, or at least to maintain them at a steady level, the only thing the producers have to do is cut back. Once a reduced supply meets the weakened demand, prices will even out. But bending supply and demand curves to make them meet in the middle is never easy. It's all the more difficult now. Too many producers have tasted the wealth that high prices have brought. They've over extended themselves. They've been on a very long shopping spree with thick wads of petrodollars from their never-ending supply of cash.

Then somehow the unthinkable happened.

The never-ending cash came to an end.

Their incomes diminished. Their expenses stayed high.

Some of them reasoned that to keep the money coming in, to off-set lower prices, they merely had to increase production.

Some of them had never been to a high school economics class.

For nearly four years Yamani had tried to warn his fellow oil ministers that a price war was imminent, that if they didn't pay heed to the most basic laws of economics, oil prices could tumble to below 1974 levels.

For nearly four years he'd tried to make the other ministers believe, the good times are over.

But around Opec the other ministers knew of Yamani's talent for theatre and some of them wrote off his scare tactics to just that. They refused to believe him. They shrugged, why should we worry? It's common knowledge that the Saudis are in trouble and if they're in trouble then Yamani is in trouble, so Yamani is just trying to save his own skin.

18

At the same time Yamani was also warning King Fahd that the worst was yet to come.

However, the over-weight, over-slow Fahd could never have understood the complexity of the problem.

Nor was he Yamani's greatest fan.

And the king's personal feelings about his oil minister often clouded his judgement.

In meeting after meeting with his Council of Ministers the thing that most concerned Fahd was finding enough revenue to support the nation's budget, which had years before been heavily committed to bringing Saudi Arabia into the twenty-first century. The way the king saw it, the money he needed could only come from one source.

Oil.

And as long as Yamani was his oil minister, it was Yamani's responsibility to bring in that money.

*   *   *   *

In mid-September 1985 a rumour spread through Wall Street and the City of London that the Saudi oil minister had been assassinated.

Within seconds oil shares took a nose dive and the pound dropped from $1.32 to just under $1.30.

The story was that Yamani had been on holiday at his house in Sardinia when an assassin gunned him down. But when reporters contacted the local police there they were told that Yamani was in fact not on the island. That he'd left a couple· of weeks before. Reporters who knew his private numbers in Saudi Arabia tried to raise him there but were equally unsuccessful. In the meantime, officials at his ministry's offices in Riyadh officially denied the rumour. Yet the ever-sceptical western markets refused to believe the denial. It was only when a reporter spotted Mrs Yamani in Geneva, 'child in arms and smiling', that it was confirmed Yamani was alive and well.

As soon as the assassination rumour was proved false, the markets' losses were reversed.

The story had originated in London. A small brokerage house was caught short speculating on oil shares and they needed to get out quickly.

Normally it takes death rumours of an American president or of a Russian leader to have the same affect.

A week or so later, Yamani hit the markets again. This time he admitted in public what everyone in the oil business knew he was saying in private.

19

With oil prices hovering just under $27, Yamani announced that he was prepared to see prices fall into the $15–$18 range.

As the Saudis had once supplied as much as 25 per cent of the world's internationally traded crude and since that figure had now dropped to just about 10 per cent, he said that rock-bottom pricing was how he aimed to recapture a sizeable chunk of the world market to help meet his country's economic goals.

He said he was going to force Opec and even some of the non-Opec producers to cut back on their production or perish in the blood bath of a price war.

The world according to Yamani in the autumn of 1985 contained only two alternatives.

First: 'For everybody to produce as much as he can and sell at any price dictated by the market and we will see real chaos. We will see a sharp drop in the price of oil, maybe within the range of $15 per barrel. Maybe less. It is very difficult to foresee. And of course we will have an international financial crisis. The banking community in the United States will suffer so much. We will have some political crises in so many countries.'

Second: 'Some sort of coordination between non-Opec producers and the Opec producers and also among the member countries of Opec. That cooperation will see non-Opec producers reducing their level of production a little bit and staying at that level for some time until some Opec producers are able to breathe. And then they can share in the increased consumption of the future.'

But that was all.

The way it looked to him was, only one of the two scenarios could stave off catastrophe.

However, the way it looked to some people, especially within Opec, was, here's Yamani out to protect himself and to protect Saudi Arabia and he doesn't give a damn about us.

And the way it looked to some other people, especially in the United States, was, here's Yamani stuck holding a weak hand and here's Opec on its knees crying let's be friends because we're not as well off as we used to be when we held the world to ransom ten years ago.

Frankly put, the Nigerians couldn't have cared less about Yamani.

Nor could the Iraqis and the Iranians and the Libyans.

Nor could the Reagan administration, which loved every minute of Yamani's discomfort. To hell with Opec. Even if half of Houston, Texas, is about to die broke, that's the price of admission to see the Arabs squirm.

If they won't listen to reason, Yamani decided, it's time Saudi Arabia protected its share of the market and taught them a lesson.

Weary and frustrated, Yamani went to King Fahd to suggest, 'The time has come for us to abandon the policy of carrying the burden alone.'

Yamani wanted to increase Saudi oil production by 50 per cent.

It was a drastic step which, Fahd knew, could have world-wide ramifications.

If Yamani triggered a truly savage price war, how would it affect the Iran-Iraq conflict? Both nations needed oil to keep the war going. If prices fell and one side or the other felt as if its back was firmly to the wall, could that be the catalyst for desperate measures? What would happen to the market if Iran knocked out Iraq's pipelines? Worse still, what would happen if Iran turned against Iraq's ally, Kuwait? And what about the Soviets? If Iraq seriously disrupted Iranian oil flowing into Eastern Europe and if it was up to the Russians to make up the shortfall, how long would they sit by and watch the Gulf War affect their own economy?

There was more at stake than just the price of four star.

Saudi Arabia's credibility as the foremost oil exporter in the free world was also on the line.

So Fahd agreed.

A free-for-all it was to be.

By mid-January 1986 the fall had gained enough momentum to be called an outright tumble.

From $25 prices rushed towards $20.

Yamani predicted $15.

Now the pound slumped. The Bank of England had to step in to support sterling. The Chancellor came up with a bumbling statement about how beneficial lower oil prices would be to the economy. An odd thing to say when it was so obvious that lower oil prices would be devastating to Great Britain.

Within a few days Yamani revised his opinion to, 'Below $15.'

By the end of February, prices had edged under $13.

On 5 March, *Petroleum Times* reported, 'This topsy-turvy, helter skelter, price slide has been slithering downwards since the beginning of December. There is no assurance that the market has in any way bottomed out. Already some traders are talking of $8/$9 per barrel by the end of the month.'

The situation was drastic, and not at all helped, as Yamani saw it, by the dogged refusal of the key North Sea producers – i.e. Great Britain and Norway – to support Opec's efforts to stabilize the market by cutting their own production.

He couldn't hide his feelings. 'The oil glut must be mopped up by the non-Opec producers who are producing at full capacity.'

21

He went to see the Norwegian oil minister, to lobby him on a production cut, and came out of that meeting with a confirmation that the Norwegians would begin to reduce output. Within a few weeks, however, the Norwegians changed their mind.

Nor did the British have any intention of mopping up after Opec. All the Department of Energy could officially think of saying was that the fall in oil prices was 'cause for concern'.

About this time, rumours of Yamani's resignation started to spread. They were quickly denied.

On 16 March, Yamani again struck out against the British.

In an exclusive interview with the *Sunday Telegraph*, he said that Britain was to blame if oil prices were not controlled. 'Disaster lies ahead for which your country will bear the lion's share of the blame.'

He said that, while he respected Britain's leaders and did not wish to comment on domestic politics, he found it hard to fathom their reasoning. 'Just look at the plain mathematics. The British treasury is now losing billions of pounds from reduced oil revenue. Which is better, to have the same income by reduced output at higher prices or by maximum extraction at lower prices? Clearly the former.'

He urged the British to think long term. 'If you go on as you are doing, by the 1990s you will be importing oil yourselves and the 1990s are just around the corner.'

The next day Yamani went to Geneva to address an emergency Opec conference, to lecture his partners that if they could not agree a realistic ceiling in time to help persuade non-Opec producers to cut back, then no one would ever take Opec seriously again.

That's when the Saudi Information Ministry issued a statement retracting some of what Yamani said to the *Sunday Telegraph*. The ministry, it seems, did not wish His Excellency's remarks to appear as if the Saudi government was being critical of Mrs Thatcher's government.

Again, Yamani resignation rumours spread.

And again they were denied.

The emergency meeting in Geneva lasted nine days.

On the final day the Venezuelan minister proclaimed that the members had agreed in principle that 'all necessary efforts would be made gradually to lift the price level back to $28 and then defend it at that level'.

As far as the market was concerned, the Venezuelan might as well have been talking about Disneyland.

One month later Yamani and the other Opec ministers were back in Geneva.

Nine more days at the negotiating table brought about nine more days' worth of confusion.

The Intercontinental was filled.

The public rooms were a mass of activity day and night.

Yamani commuted between his 18th-floor suite and the conference room downstairs. He met with the other ministers in general sessions, then met with some of them on a one-to-one basis for private discussion in his suite. He lobbied them, for hours on end, until the final day.

The question of raising Opec's overall quota was put to a vote.

Hands were raised and the count was ten against three.

Yamani had somehow managed to rally the majority.

Yet the dissenting three – Iran, Libya and Algeria – insisted on severe cutbacks across the board as the only way to get prices up fast. In fact, they even called for a one-month cessation of all Opec output, which they guaranteed – quite rightly – would have an immediate effect on prices.

This is short-term thinking, Yamani argued.

But Gholamreza Agazadeh, Iran's newly appointed oil minister, would have none of that.

A shortish man with close-cropped silver hair and a neatly trimmed silvering beard and moustache, he wore dark suits, high-collared white shirts buttoned at the neck, but never a tie.

Just six months on the job, he'd already earned his place in Opec as Yamani's severest critic. Now he tried to convince the conference, 'Yamani's aim is to force the United States to abandon their own oil business and increase their dependence on foreign oil.'

The meeting ended in total disarray.

Agazadeh's fight with Yamani was just beginning.

Throughout the spring there was talk of the cartel's impending death as oil prices continued to fall.

Agazadeh believed, exactly as the Shah had in the mid–1970s, that the only thing preventing Iran from getting what it wanted at Opec was Yamani.

So Agazadeh began rallying his troops for an assault on the man the world knew as 'Mr Oil'.

Yamani, on the other hand, wanted the over-producers to understand that if they didn't comply with Opec's agreements they'd suffer the consequences. Nigeria, for example, was one of the most drastically hit by the fall in prices. Its oil minister was actually travelling the world to sell his crude anywhere at any price. Obviously, forcing Nigeria's prices down was tantamount to bringing havoc to his country. But that was the cost of stepping out of line. In a real sense, Yamani felt, it was the lesson that Nigeria and the others would simply have to learn for trying to share some of their own economic gloom with the otherwise rich Saudis.

He was also counting on the price fall to force some of the more expensive players completely out of the game. Among them were the British and a whole slew of small independents in the United States. At one point, when he was informed that some Houston-based independents were going broke, he merely shrugged, 'Too bad.'

Then, he had to reassure King Fahd that the end result would be a return to Saudi Arabia's rightful quota of Opec's allotments.

The ace that he held, or at least the ace he thought he held, was that the Saudi Arabian economy was stronger than any of the other Opec states and that, at least for a while, the Saudis could weather any storm.

But this time he'd underestimated the patience of Fahd and his six full brothers.

Not everyone in the royal family, especially the king, was capable of understanding the sophisticated economic realities of Yamani's ploy.

Not everyone in the royal family, especially the king, could think on a truly long-term basis to see how bargain basement prices might eventually, many months down the line, force the rebel Opec members back into the fold so that they could jointly manoeuvre oil up to the $18 mark.

More dangerous still, not everyone in the royal family, especially the king, cared to see Yamani stay in his job.

From outside the game it looked like a bad miscalculation on Yamani's part.

Suddenly he had too many chips on the table.

Suddenly there was more at stake than simply Opec or the Saudi economy.

Condemned internationally by certain Opec members for putting Saudi Arabia's interests above the common interests of the 13 member states, he was also being condemned by certain Saudis for putting Opec's interests above their own.

Zaki Yamani was facing what looked more and more like a classic 'no-win' situation.

When oil dropped below the $12 mark, Saudi Arabia's oil revenues sank like a stone. From $22 billion in 1985, the $12 price brought in less than $16 billion. But $40 billion was already committed to maintaining the government's spending and the completion of massive construction projects.

With economic disaster becoming an ever-greater possibility, a number of important foreign contractors started looking for greener pastures. They packed up and went home. Certain private investors, with assets in Saudi Arabia totalling tens of billions of dollars, began transferring funds elsewhere. One report suggested that the flow of funds out of Saudi Arabia could easily have hit the $1 billion a day mark.

In an unprecedented display, King Fahd made a teary-eyed appearance on national television to announce that the government would not produce a budget for 1986–87. Publicly, he blamed the country's misfortunes on unpredictable oil prices. Privately, he blamed his own personal embarrassment over the incident on Yamani.

The situation had reached crisis proportions.

Saudi Arabia was fast going broke.

As the money dried up, so did the country's regional and international prestige.

'A long, slow decline from the heady days of Faisal and the oil weapon seemed to be culminating in abject paralysis,' wrote the *Guardian*. 'How could anyone take the Saudis seriously about anything at all if they could not stand up for themselves in something of the most urgent national interest?'

That theme was echoed in most newspapers.

Although *New York Times* columnist William Safire thought he'd found a message hidden in between the lines.

In a column entitled 'Thinking Along with Yamani', Safire used the first person to make his point. 'I, Sheikh Yamani, have a much greater challenge than gaining control of Opec production and then raising prices. On the contrary, my strategy is to produce and produce until the low prices bankrupt Iran.'

Contending that Yamani's orders from Fahd were clearly to break Iran, Safire tried to illustrate how the Saudis felt the Persian menace was the single overriding threat to the Arab world. Unless the Ayatollah's fundamentalism was contained, he wrote, not only would Iraq lose the war but Kuwait could fall. If that happened, Saudi Arabia would follow. 'With our very survival at stake we are willing to suffer these falling prices because we know we are starving Iran's war machine. Pouring money into Iraq did not work. Denying oil money to Iran is our last hope.'

Reading the column for the first time nearly a year after it was published, Yamani says that Safire wrote it that way 'because he had political motives'. The suggestion from Yamani is that Safire was exercising a bit of 'journalistic wishful thinking'.

Could be.

It could also be that if Safire needed to find someone to agree with his theory, he wouldn't have had to look any further than Gholamreza Agazadeh.

* * * *

The end of June 1986.

On the northern Adriatic Island of Brioni, off the coast of Yugoslavia.

Yamani arrived for the Opec meeting in his yacht, sporting a freshly starched sailor's suit.

The press loved it.

This was no longer the shy little boy from Mecca.

He tried to sound relaxed and confident.

For a while, the press even believed he was.

It was only inside the closed door session that the tensions of the past several months were plain to see. Iran, Libya and Algeria continued to lobby for sharply reduced production. And Agazadeh warned that, no matter what the allocations turned out to be, Iran would produce two barrels for every one allocated to Iraq.

The meeting broke up with predictions of $10 oil before mid-July.

Yamani looked like a man who was about to win his bet because the weakest links in the chain would have to break soon.

However, it was Opec itself that nearly came unstuck at the next meeting, which began in Geneva on 28 July.

On the second day of that conference, a resolution was put before the 13 that each state would make voluntary cuts in output. Passing such a resolution would mean that Opec's effectiveness as a power had, to all intents and purposes, dissolved.

Again Yamani lobbied the delegates one by one.

This time, though, he managed to convince only six others to join with Saudi Arabia in agreeing to voluntary restraints.

The opposing six sided with Agazadeh.

Desperation ruled.

Opec was sinking fast and it was going to take some of its members down with it.

A breakthrough came at the very last minute and from a most unlikely source.

On Saturday morning, 2 August, Agazadeh asked to meet privately with Yamani in the big top-floor suite at the Intercontinental.

Greeting Agazadeh at the front door, Yamani brought him through the short hallway and into the livingroom.

Yamani wore a suit and tie.

Agazadeh wore a suit and buttoned white shirt without a tie.

Yamani offered tea and juice to drink and dates to eat.

Then he motioned to Agazadeh to please sit down.

But Revolutionary Iranians don't sit on chairs or couches when they can help it. They prefer to sit on the floor.

So Yamani and Agazadeh sat on the floor.

Away from the glare of cameras and reporters, alone without any of the other Opec ministers to hang on their every word, there was no need for forced smiles. There was no need for either man to disguise his mutual dislike. But they both knew what was at stake and so the two put aside their personal feelings to talk for 90 minutes.

Agazadeh reasoned, as long as certain Opec members were unwilling to make long-term promises to limit their oil production, they might try an interim measure. He suggested they come down from 20 million barrels per day temporarily to the group's 1984 quota of 16 mbd. To help accomplish it, in a totally unexpected political concession, Agazadeh abandoned Iran's usual stance of doubling any amount of oil that Iraq produced over their quota. He conceded to Yamani that Iran would limit its production and at the same time allow Iraq to produce whatever it could.

Within a few hours Yamani had convinced the other 11 members that this surprise breakthrough was worthy of their support.

When the deal was announced, prices began to steady in the $12 range.

But the deal wasn't scheduled to go into effect until 1 October. With everything to lose and nothing to gain, the Iranians feared it would be too tempting for member states to overproduce during those two months and in turn ruin the agreement.

So Agazadeh hedged his bet.

Enter here Irangate.

In 1984, according to information obtained from a source involved with a US Senate Subcommittee, the late William Casey, then director of the CIA, met secretly with Fahd on board the king's 495–foot yacht, the *Abdul Aziz*, as it sailed off the coast of Marbella, Spain.

A scenario had been outlined in Washington by Casey which included, among other people, Admiral John Poindexter and Lt Colonel Oliver North, representing the White House and the National Security Council.

It's not clear whether or not the contact with Fahd was made with Ronald Reagan's knowledge . . . although it's now known that the President secretly discussed Saudi contributions to the Nicaraguan Contra rebels when he met privately with King Fahd in 1985.

The point is that nearly one year before the Reagan-Fahd meeting, Casey was already designing a situation where North, acting under Poindexter, could clandestinely sell arms to the Iranians for their war against the Iraqis then launder the money from those arms' sales back to the Contras to be used in their fight in Nicaragua.

The initial success of the scheme hung on somehow getting the Iranians to play along.

Unable, for obvious reasons, to discuss this directly with the Ayatollah, Casey needed a middleman.

Based on Fahd's past experience with other US administrations plus a dyed-in-the-wool hatred of communism – which Casey shared with Fahd – the defiant old CIA boss was counting on the king to be the perfect go-between.

So Casey boarded the *Abdul Aziz* with the express purpose of asking Fahd to open a channel for him to Tehran.

Fahd agreed.

And the moment he did, Irangate was born.

Within a few of months of the Casey-Fahd Mediterranean rendezvous, the Saudi Arabian Ambassador to France, Jameel al-Hojailian, met secretly in Germany with representatives of Iran's Revolutionary government. Shortly thereafter, it was noticed around Riyadh that the once chilly, sometimes even hostile relationship between Fahd and Saudi businessman Adnan Khashoggi had almost magically transformed itself into a warm and friendly one. On at least two occasions Khashoggi was seen at the weekly court dinner holding hands and laughing with the king.

Hardly a coincidence, Khashoggi's return to favour with Fahd was part of Khashoggi's reward for agreeing to negotiate on the CIA's behalf with the Israelis and Iranian arms dealer Albert Hakim.

Using this somewhat unlikely relationship as an entrée to Fahd, Agazadeh now waited until Yamani was out of the country before travelling to Saudi Arabia to establish a direct line of communication between himself and the Saudi monarch.

He was gambling on his own future effectiveness within the Opec cartel by going above Yamani's head.

And Yamani's boss allowed Agazadeh to get away with it because the prospects of an Iranian-Saudi pricing pact, linked to political and military considerations, offered something for both sides.

However, Agazadeh and Fahd both knew that such a deal would not happen as long as Yamani was around to get in the way of it.

Thanks inadvertently to Bill Casey, Yamani was one giant step closer to the end of the line.

On 5 September, with oil prices bordering on $14–$15, Yamani went to Cambridge, Massachusetts, to give the A. J. Meyer Memorial Lecture at the John F. Kennedy School of Government as part of Harvard University's 350th anniversary celebrations.

For a while it was like a homecoming.

He went with his wife Tammam and their five young children and, much like any student on a homecoming weekend, he dragged his family through the streets he'd prowled 30 years before. Daddy, show me your classroom, two of his sons insisted. So daddy pointed out all the sights and even found a classroom window that looked familiar. He showed his family where he had lived and told his children how hard he'd studied.

David Rockefeller was his official host. Old pals like James Schlesinger and Kingman Brewster were there. So were a handful of his former professors.

But this wasn't just a homecoming. And Yamani wasn't just any former student. He was on the bill for a major speech.

Although the speech he gave was not the one he'd originally written.

In the speech he gave, 'I told you so' was the message. But it was couched in a version watered down at the last minute.

'When Opec supplies started to decline sharply in 1981 and 1982, as a result of the fall in demand and the rise in non-Opec supplies, we recognized too late that oil was overpriced, that it had reached an unwarrantably high level, destroying the state of virtual equilibrium between supply and demand that had prevailed for so long. However Saudi Arabia, which in the past had used its production as a tool for restricting the trend towards exorbitant prices, now reversed its position by reducing production in order to support the world price structure.'

To that he added the unscripted aside, 'Unfortunately we were lonely inside Opec at this time.'

Because severe fluctuations in oil prices can cause tremendous instability in the world, he claimed that the recent sharp decline in world oil prices was not good for either producers or consumers.

'Neither part can plan with confidence for long-term energy production, investment and consumption. Nor can they allocate and mix resources in such a way as to achieve economic objectives with optimum efficiency. It is clear, therefore, that what the oil industry badly needs is price stability in the long term.'

In addition, he said, consuming countries were now charging that cheap prices had a negative impact on other sources of energy, such as coal, gas, nuclear or home-grown oil. Low prices limit the incentive for exploration and development of other energy sources and ultimately lead to a decline in domestic production and therefore to a higher degree of dependence on imported oil.

'Hence the call for import restrictions.' And here he cautioned the industrial west,

'Import restrictions, if adopted, might have an adverse effect on friends as well as those whom the advocates of restriction regard as their adversaries. They must know full well that discrimination in world trade provokes retaliatory measures, can lead to trade wars and spells the end of free trade practices. Such a vociferous demand for the imposition of trade restrictions on account of low prices, as is currently prevalent, could constitute an invitation to producers to raise prices again, to restore them to their former levels . . .'

In another aside he finished that sentence with 'no matter what the sacrifice might be'.

The speech was followed by a question and answer period in which Yamani made two outstandingly frank remarks.

The first was his answer to the question, 'How would you achieve cohesion and stability among the Opec countries?'

He said, 'It won't be easy because so many members of Opec will be angry over what I've said here today.'

The hint was that certain countries, for instance Iran, had no interest at all in price stability. All they wanted was to assure an increased flow of oil revenues to support the war.

The second was his answer to the question, 'Can you describe the process by which oil policy is made inside Saudi Arabia?'

He replied, 'We play it by ear.'

A few knowledgeable people in the audience wondered among themselves if Yamani would have come up with the same answer had Fahd not been king.

What no one at Harvard knew was that there'd been a stronger version of his speech.

The speech he wanted to give said, it's a crime what you Americans were doing. You do not want to become dependent on the Persian Gulf. I assure you it is not the part of the world you want to be dependent upon.

But he didn't say that because he thought to himself, why the hell should I explain to the Americans what their interests ought to be?

The speech he wanted to give not only lashed out at the non-Opec producers but also took some of his Opec partners to task. The speech he wanted to give did not hide his feelings about the Gulf War. The speech he wanted to give would have put men like Agazadeh in their place.

The speech he wanted to give would not have pleased his hosts.

'I wanted to say that the United States worked hard to bring chaos into the world oil market. I wanted to say that President Reagan was obviously very proud of himself in January 1986 when he bragged that it was his policies which brought Opec to its knees. America put pressure on US producers to keep stocking oil and on Britain and Norway to overproduce and frankly I wanted to give America credit for having done it so well. But it was short-term thinking and that's dangerous. If America ever manages to break Opec, which they will keep trying to do, leaving the price of oil solely to market forces, well, then America will have to accept all of the consequences.'

That's what he wanted to say.

'But I couldn't. I was still an official of my government. It wouldn't have been proper for me while on a visit like that to accuse the United States of crimes against Saudi Arabia. That's what I wanted to say but I felt it wasn't prudent of me to do that. Anyway, I knew, history will make those points for me.'

Another thing that no one at Harvard realized that weekend was how Fahd and his brothers were becoming less and less tolerant of Yamani's openly receptive attitude towards the industrialized west.

The last thing he wanted to do now was make a speech that sounded as if he was the best friend the west ever had.

Fahd and his brothers would never have stood for it.

Although, with hindsight, maybe he could have got away with the stronger version of the speech after all.

With hindsight, by the time Yamani got to Harvard it was probably already too late.

The free-for-all of the first half of 1986 had cost the Opec members $100 million a day.

When the cartel met in Geneva in October, for the fifth time that year, none of the ministers could have guessed just how extraordinary this particular meeting would be.

None of them knew it would be Yamani's final meeting.

As they sat down to talk, Yamani said that he was still hopeful the 13 could come up with a new agreement and that he was determined to help achieve it.

But when the majority of members proposed to extend their production-sharing pact until the end of the year, Yamani and his Kuwaiti counterpart strongly opposed it.

Yamani explained, 'We favour a new agreement on quotas, to reach something constructive. Not a rollover.' He warned that a firm decision had to be made this time or the world oil market would no longer take Opec seriously. 'They will then drive the prices down.'

He then told his fellow oil ministers in their secret session that, if an agreement wasn't found, Saudi Arabia – with Kuwait alongside – would refuse to continue limiting oil production simply to support the poorer Opec nations.

He said he was sick and tired of abiding by Opec's rules while other member countries, such as Venezuela, Ecuador, Gabon and the United Arab Emirates, paid no heed to their assigned quotas.

And he didn't win a lot of new friends when he reminded the meeting that, should Saudi Arabia open the taps and let the oil flow, only his country and possibly Kuwait could survive.

But this battle with his fellow Opec members was only one of the fronts he'd opened in Geneva.

The other was with Fahd.

The king wanted production increased and prices raised. He told Yamani several times that the Saudi quota had to be upped and that oil had to be sold for $18.

Fahd was, in effect, asking Yamani to square a circle.

Yamani dared to explain to the king that the world didn't work that way.

On Monday, 20 October, the cartel came close to the type of agreement that Yamani could live with.

But the militant three – Iran, Algeria and Libya – balked.

Increased production and $18 a barrel, Fahd had said.

There was no way Yamani could make that work.

For a while there was talk of extending the oil output levels which were due to expire on the 31st. A compromise deal would see those levels taken to the end of the year with a radical new formula introduced from 1 January.

But Yamani's instructions were clear.

Increased production and $18 a barrel.

Fahd's voice was beginning to haunt him.

On the 22nd, after 16 days, the Opec ministers finally agreed to a small increase in their production quotas, which was supposed to last until they met again in December.

Increased production and $18 a barrel.

There was no way Yamani could make Fahd believe that supply and demand curves don't work like that.

Seven nights later, at a friend's home in Riyadh, while playing the French card game belote in front of the television, Yamani heard on the evening news that he'd been fired.

Just like that it was over.

Increased production and $18 a barrel.

The next day he was told he couldn't leave Saudi Arabia.

Most people believed then and still believe now that Yamani was fired by Fahd because he couldn't square the circle.

The truth is that was merely the straw that broke the camel's back.

Squaring the Circle

The real story has to do with a deadly power struggle, jealousy, corruption, billions of dollars, the richest teenaged boy on earth, religious fanatics, the stability of the Middle East, and possibly even World War III.

3

The Early Years

HE CAME to America for the very first time in the autumn of 1954.

The war in Korea was history. The New York Giants had just won the World Series. There was a car in every garage. There was a chicken in every pot. Eisenhower was in the White House. And all was well with the world.

Fresh out of the Middle East on a government scholarship, the 24-year-old Yamani was starting a one-year course at New York University, eager to earn himself a Masters of Comparative Jurisprudence.

Before he left home an Armenian friend gave him a very stern warning.

He said that America was filled with homosexuals. He cautioned Yamani, you are young and they will try to make you do unnatural things. He admonished, 'Zaki, you must be careful.'

Greatly concerned, Yamani wanted to know how he could recognize such people.

The friend assured him, you will always be able to tell a homosexual in America because they wear red neckties.

The flight to the States took 17 hours from Cairo via Scotland. Yamani arrived totally exhausted but thrilled to be in New York. He was so anxious to see everything that, as soon as he got to his hotel, he rushed upstairs to his room, took a fast shower and jumped into clean clothes. He couldn't wait to get back to the lobby to begin sorting through the pile of tourist brochures he had spotted at the front desk.

He didn't know where he wanted to go first.

From across the lobby a man with a red necktie stared at him.

Yamani turned away.

The man in the red necktie kept looking at him.

Uneasy, Yamani pretended to concentrate on his tourist guides.

34

Now the man in the red necktie began walking in his direction.
Keeping his face buried in the brochures, Yamani moved away.
The man with the red necktie came closer.

Not sure what to do or how best to handle such a situation, Yamani
finally decided on the direct approach. He reassured himself, I'll simply
confront him and tell him point blank that whatever he has in mind,
I'm not interested . . .

'Excuse me,' the man in the red necktie said.

Yamani drew in his breath and summoned up his courage. 'Listen
you . . .'

'Excuse me, sir,' the man in the red necktie said again. 'But your
flies are open.'

* * * *

The birth of modern Saudi Arabia happened at about the same time
that a group of geologists from California realized the Arabian deserts
were floating on oil.

That was coincidence.

The rise of modern Saudi Arabia as a force to reckon with in the
western world began that very same day.

That was anything but a coincidence.

Abdul Aziz bin Abdel Rahman al-Saud – the man who came to be
known throughout the world as Ibn Saud – was born in the Nejd, the
region surrounding Riyadh, sometime between 1876 and 1880.

For more than a century and a half, the House of Saud had been
struggling to dominate and somehow unite the desert's collection of
feudal sultanates and sheikhdoms, each independent of the other. At
various times they had stretched their influence across the peninsula
from the east coast to the holy cities of Mecca and Medina. But maintaining control by force over such a huge expanse of sand . . . and over
such varied and often fanatical groups . . . was not easy. By the time
Ibn Saud came into the world, his family's hold on the peninsula was
well on the way to disintegrating.

In 1891 an attack on the Al Saud by the House of Rashid, leaders
of the Shammar tribe, forced them to give up their rights as rulers of
the Nejd. Ibn Saud spent the next two years literally slung over the
side of a camel, travelling in a saddle bag, living the nomadic life of
desert rulers in exile. The family eventually made their way to Kuwait
where in 1897 word reached them that Muhammad bin Rashid, the
Shammar's chieftain, was dead. Within a couple of years the now
teenaged Ibn Saud was leading small raiding parties into the desert
against the Al Rashid, building for himself the reputation of a brave

young warrior, dreaming of the day he would take the Al Saud back to the Nejd.

He finally managed it with a daring, if not totally foolhardy, stunt.

Having set off from Kuwait several months before with 40 followers – 40 is the number the Bedouin use in their legends when they don't know exactly how many there were but are certain that the group was not very large – he arrived at the adobe walls of Riyadh one night somewhere between mid-January and early February 1902.

Supposedly with as few as nine men, he scaled the walls and hid within the city until dawn, waiting for the Governor of Riyadh to walk by. When he did, Ibn Saud murdered him. Within 20 minutes, on the basis of the sheer bravado of that assassination, Riyadh was reclaimed for the Al Saud.

A large and imposing man – 6'4" he must have literally towered over most of his followers – Ibn Saud spent the next ten years consolidating his power in the area around the Nejd, all the time trying to superimpose a disciplined central government on the area by uniting the various fanatical clans of the central desert. When he defeated the Ottoman Turks in 1913, he extended his rule eastward to the Persian Gulf. Eight years later, when he had finally beaten the last of the Al Rashid, he took his reign as far north as the border with Iraq and Transjordan. Then he sent his son Faisal to the southwest, to command the troops which finally occupied the region of the Asir, between the Hijaz and Yemen. Finally he turned his attention westward, to the Hijaz and the holy cities of Mecca and Medina. He captured Mecca in 1924 and the following year assumed complete rule of the region, including the trading port of Jeddah. In 1926 he proclaimed himself King of the Nejd and Sultan of the Hijaz.

In all it had taken him nearly 25 years to tie together the particular customs, traditions and interests of the people from four distinct and different regions. Some of it was won by the sword. Some of it was won by marriage. Ibn Saud married several hundred times . . . many of those marriages being politically astute unions designed solely to bring together various clans.

By 1932 he had fathered 24 of his 43 sons and a countless number of daughters.

He'd formally named his kingdom, Saudi Arabia.

Yet all Ibn Saud could claim as his own was a £60,000 a year pension from the British for his help during the First World War in their fight against the Turks and a kingdom filled with sand whose only real source of income was the Haj – the annual pilgrimage to Mecca by the faithful from throughout Islam.

By 1932 Ibn Saud could have put the entire kingdom's wealth into his camel's saddle bags.

Then oil was discovered in Bahrain.

If it was there, geologists reasoned, the whole peninsula could be sitting on oil. A pair of Americans working for Standard Oil of California (Socal) came to Saudi Arabia and for £50,000 worth of gold they received permission from Ibn Saud to prospect the Eastern Province. The first exploratory well was sunk in 1935. It was dry. So they tried again, six more times, each time going deeper beneath the sand, before they brought in Dammam Number 7.

The moment they struck oil, Saudi Arabia was patched into the world economy. An ancient society was hurled onto a collision course with twentieth century western materialism.

Pilgrimage traffic ground to a halt because of the Second World War, but as soon as it ended, the king turned to the oil companies to keep Saudi Arabia's books in the black. He demanded $6 million from Socal and their partner Texaco as an advance against future royalties. Unwilling, or possibly even unable, to come up with that much, they invited another pair of oil companies into the venture: Standard Oil of New Jersey (then called Esso and now called Exxon) bought 30 per cent; the Socony-Vacuum Oil Company (soon to be called Mobil) bought 10 per cent.

The four united under the name Aramco – the Arabian American Oil Company.

Nearly 10,000 miles away, a young lawyer named Juan Pablo Perez Alfonzo, a member of Venezuela's newly installed government, believed the time had come to increase the nation's oil revenue by taxing the American companies that exported Venezuelan crude. But instead of allowing the Americans to pay a flat royalty per ton, the Venezuelans issued a decree retroactively taking a 50 per cent cut of the companies' profits.

Then the Iranians renegotiated their agreements with the British.

Now there was no question but that Aramco would have to give more to the Saudis.

So Ibn Saud passed a tax law similar to the one in Venezuela.

By the time the old king died in 1953, Aramco employed more than 24,000 people, had stretched pipelines across the desert all the way to the Mediterranean, and was pumping enough Saudi oil even with the 50/50 cut on profits to make a lot of Americans very rich.

Unfortunately for Aramco, by 1953 a few young Saudis were starting to wonder about that arrangement.

Ibn Saud's oldest living son, Saud, became King.

The next son, Faisal, became Crown Prince.

However, Saud lacked his father's political savvy and was a far-distant second to Faisal's native intelligence. State revenues in 1937 had totalled approximately $24 million. Now, in 1953, thanks to oil royalties and taxes paid to the government by Aramco, Saudi Arabia could count on $200 million coming into the treasury. The Saudis were rich beyond their own wildest dreams. Not surprisingly, financial chaos reigned. With such a fortune his merely for the taking, King Saud figured he might as well spend it.

Ostentatious is too weak a word.

Saud built himself a fabulous palace and lived in some sort of psychotic no-man's land between mind-boggling extravagance and total debauchery. The amount of money squandered through graft and corruption, not only at the highest level but at all levels of government, must have been ludicrous, even by Arab standards.

The situation wasn't helped by the Americans who fuelled the fires by tempting the puritanical Saudis with new means of communications, new forms of transport, American sports, foreign films, gadgets, strange food and rock 'n' roll.

Having gone too far morally, socially and even politically – it was Saud's dream to challenge Egypt's Nasser in his role as self-appointed leader of the Arab world – a group of royal princes, tribal sheikhs and religious leaders set about pushing Saud aside in favour of Faisal, who would rule as Prime Minister.

It worked. But not for very long. Too many tribal leaders yearned for their handouts. Austerity, as practised by Faisal, was not to their liking. A group then known as the 'Free Princes' made a deal with Saud, promising to return him to power in exchange for some sort of constitutional monarchy. He agreed and in 1960 Faisal resigned. Saud came back to power. But he reneged on his promises to these so-called 'modernists'. He even rewarded some of them for their support with imprisonment. The idea of a constitutional monarchy was not one he cared to entertain.

In 1962, a coup d'état in Yemen posed a direct threat to the Saudis.

If the monarchy could be overthrown there, the Saudi princes wondered just how secure their own future was.

The new Yemeni regime advocated socialism.

The naturally conservative, strongly anti-communist Saudi royal family quickly came to the decision that King Saud might not be strong enough to stem a similar groundswell. Not only was his political base shaky, he was also in failing health. So, the Yemeni revolution was just the excuse they needed to bring Faisal to the throne.

It took them a couple of years, as the Saudis are, by nature, reluctant to make changes no matter what kinds of changes have to be made.

Maybe it has to do with life in the desert. Maybe it has to do with their roots as nomads. It's a trait that plays an important role in all aspects of Saudi life, from the way they raise their children to the way foreign policy is practised. They simply believe, if you do nothing the problem will go away.

When the Yemen problem hadn't gone away by November 1964, family consensus removed Saud from the throne. He left Saudi Arabia for exile in Beirut, then Cairo and finally Athens.

Faisal was elevated to King.

The mark he was about to make on Saudi Arabia – and especially on his country's history – would be indelible.

He would also change the course of Zaki Yamani's life.

* * * *

Yamani was born in Mecca, Saudi Arabia, on 30 June 1930.

In those days Mecca was a city with camels in unpaved streets and almost no electricity. It wasn't until 1939 or 1940 that the Yamani family connected an electric generator to their house. Before that, the young Zaki either read by oil lamp or went to the nearby Grand Mosque where electric lights were still very much a local novelty.

His father was a *qadi*, a chief justice of the supreme court in the Hijaz.

But he didn't really get to know his father until he was nearly eight years old. Not long after Zaki was born, Yamani Senior left for Indonesia where he spent eight years as a *grand mufti* of the Shafei school of Islamic thought. He returned for a year, then left again for Malaysia where as *grand mufti* he was the nation's premier interpreter of Moslem law.

Yamani's grandfather was also a *grand mufti* of the Shafei school, but under the Turkish regime.

The youngest of three children – Yamani has a brother and a sister – it was his mother who strongly influenced his formative years, insisting that he get a formal education. Although here he adds that his grandfather helped to raise him and there were always uncles around too.

'The Yamani clan is a large, well-known one in Saudi Arabia. There are so many cousins, aunts and uncles. Each year during Ramadan we have an open house for the Yamani side of the family and some years as many 300–400 people come for dinner.'

The Yamani clan is also one where longevity counts. 'My mother is now in her 90s. My father died at the age of 86. My grandfather passed away only four months short of his 100th birthday. And I can assure you I had an aunt who lived to be 112.'

The name Yamani originally derives from Yemen and he notes that he's traced his ancestors back more than 40 generations, one of his great-great-grandfathers having gone there from Mecca. He is a Hashimite Moslem, which is a branch of the Koraish tribe from which the Prophet Muhammad came.

Raised in a very religious home, Yamani remains strictly observant. On nights when he simply can't sleep, he's been known to drive to Mecca to pray at the Grand Mosque.

He does the Haj whenever he can, but celebrates Ramadan each year without fail.

'It is the holiest time of the year for Moslems. It's a special time, with fasting during the day and large suppers at night to break the fast. But every year, during the last 10 days of Ramadan I go on retreat to Mecca.'

Tens of millions of the faithful pray at the Grand Mosque during the month-long feast of atonement. Day and night, as one great seething mass of humanity, they file through the prayer hall to the Ka'ba, the sacred black rock, the most revered place in all of Islam.

Yamani prays there too.

But he's fortunate enough to have a private room on the second floor of the Grand Mosque.

It's a small, simple, now air-conditioned, 6' x 18' bare-walled cell, given to him as a special privilege for being the grandson of a man of great scholarship and devotion.

There are two windows that look out at the Ka'ba and a lot of cushions to sit on and a small refrigerator in the corner for cold water and copies of the Koran piled neatly on a cushion waiting to be studied.

'I spend from afternoon till sunrise meditating and praying in my room and at the Ka'ba. When Ramadan is over I am physically exhausted. But it is a special type of exhaustion. I think it would be difficult for someone who is not devoutly religious to understand how very cleansed it makes you feel.'

Another childhood passion is his love of music.

He adores opera, especially Wagner, although his first love is the ancient music of Mecca.

'The society in Mecca is one that is so naturally concerned with music. I have always collected recordings of ancient Meccan folksongs. And although I don't play any musical instruments, I know all the various melodies.'

During the mid-1950s, when he was living in New York, Yamani discovered a small club where a young black singer sat at a piano and played it like it was. Yamani found himself going there almost weekly. As a regular he got to know the singer and after a while, every time

Yamani walked into the place, Nat King Cole would do his rendition of 'Haji Baba'.

Schooled in Mecca, Yamani says he was always top of his class and actually skipped three years. At one point when the king came to visit, he was the one selected to shake Ibn Saud's hand. 'I still remember how big he was and how big his hands were.' At the ceremony where Yamani graduated first in his class, Prince Faisal presented him with a small gift. 'Years later I reminded Faisal of that. I remembered it very well' But now he pauses, shrugs and grins. 'I'm sorry to say that he didn't.'

Encouraged to continue his education, Yamani was sent at the age of 17 to the University of Cairo to study law.

'I was always fascinated by my grandfather. He was a very famous scholar and when I was growing up I wanted to be like him. I always imagined that I would become an academic. By the time I was in university, my father had come home and we began spending a great deal of time together. I remember that he had students. They would come to our house in Mecca. Many of them were famous jurists and they would discuss the law with my father and argue cases. I started to join them and often after they left, my father and I would stay up for hours and he would teach me and he would criticize my arguments.'

Cairo was Yamani's first trip abroad. He'd travelled a little bit inside the country when he was a boy scout, riding on a donkey up in the mountains. But he didn't see anything of the outside world until he left for Egypt.

A fellow student there was Yassir Arafat.

'I must have seen him at Cairo but I didn't know him there. He was an engineering student, just the other side of the fence. He used to go on strikes. I wasn't involved in any of that. But I did get to know him many years later. He was introduced to me through an Egyptian friend who happened to have been a professor at Cairo. I then introduced him to King Faisal in 1968. The first sum of money given to Al Fatah was done through me. It was 100,000 Saudi rials. [@ $33,000].'

Having completed his law degree at the age of 20, Yamani returned to Saudi Arabia to take a job in the head office of the Ministry of Finance in Mecca.

'I always intended to teach but I was convinced that taking this job was a good idea. So I made a compromise. I taught Islamic law courses mornings and evenings without payment, and went to the office during the day.'

Again singled out as being exceptionally bright, within a few years the government offered Yamani the opportunity to attend New York University's Comparative Law Institute for non-American lawyers. The curriculum consisted of the essentials of the common law approach and of American law.

It was Yamani's first trip to the States.

It was also his first opportunity to live outside the Middle East.

'I was very excited about it. And I don't think I suffered much from culture shock. You know, by nature I'm very adaptable to any new environment.'

He took a studio apartment up town on 73rd Street. It was a long way from NYU in Greenwich Village, where all of the other students were housed on campus. The way the programme was designed, each of the foreign students was assigned an American roommate. But he preferred to live alone.

Yamani says simply, 'It was better for me that way.'

One of his NYU law professors, Bernard Schwartz, explains why. 'Zaki was very shy. I think he was overwhelmed by New York. Overwhelmed by everything. Then again, it was understandably difficult for him. His English was fine and he gave me the impression of being very bright and very serious. But I don't recall that he socialized very much. If I remember correctly, he was slightly isolated. However he got along very well, all things considered. He was slow in the beginning and it might have taken him a little time to adjust but he caught on quickly and became one of the programme's better students. In the second semester he even got very good grades.'

NYU classmate, New York attorney Don Fox, also remembers Yamani well. 'Zaki was considerably less worldly then. And he had a strong religious orientation. He kept his faith and prayed whenever he was required to. I remember he did most of his own cooking. You know, to keep to the dietary laws of Islam. He always had a number of friends because he was a very likeable guy. But he was not a hail-fellow-well-met type. I don't think anybody could say that he was a social gadabout.'

While at NYU, Yamani met a young Iraqi girl named Laila, the daughter of Sulaiman Faidhi, a well-known author and lawyer. She was there to get her PhD in education.

Both a long way from home, they were naturally drawn together and at the end of the school year they were married, in Brooklyn, in the home of a Moroccan who had converted part of his living room into a mosque.

Now with a Masters of Comparative Jurisprudence in his pocket and with the helpful intervention of a favourite NYU professor, Yamani moved to Cambridge, Massachusetts, for a year at Harvard Law School where he studied the problems of capital investment and international disputes.

Dr Erwin Griswald, dean at the law school in those days, recalls that Yamani was a very impressive young man. 'He was the only Saudi student enrolled at the time and I can still see him sitting in my office. Apparently he was a little nervous or apprehensive about being in the dean's office. He was never called there or summoned there, because he was a good student. But I can remember him coming in to see me about something or other and sitting there fingering his worry beads. He was forever fidgeting with them between his fingers and frankly I had some trouble to keep from saying, put them in your pocket they annoy me.'

Later, when he was world famous, Yamani would use the worry beads as a prop when he did after-dinner speeches or spoke at seminars in the States. He'd hold them up, explain briefly what they are, and then joke that each bead represented one of his wives.

'I still get Christmas cards from him,' Griswald goes on. 'He's the kind of person who stays in touch. It's interesting because he sends very Christian cards. They're pictures of Mary and Joseph carrying the infant Jesus on a donkey's back. Things like that. But that never really surprised me because he's very thoughtful that way. You could see that he adjusted very well to the west early on. He always seemed to me to be in full control of the situation at all times. Frankly, I never got the impression that anything was difficult for Zaki.'

Someone else who knew him at Harvard was Kingman Brewster.

'It's a long time ago but I seem to think he was in the course I taught on the legal problems of doing business abroad. I do remember that once when I was Ambassador to the Court of St James's and he was the star of Opec I reminded him, everything you know about cartels you learned from me. And he gave me that enigmatic smile of his and said, but I don't know anything about cartels because I learned it from you.'

According to Ambassador Brewster, and in spite of Dean Griswald's story about the worry beads, Yamani was pretty well Americanized by the time he left Harvard. 'He was never a typical Saudi. He's the kind of fellow who makes an intuitive decision about trust. You know, once a friend, always a friend. He's always been very aware of personal relationships and he's maintained them. That's important, particularly when you're dealing with a society built on distrust. When they accept you it's a tremendous advantage. And I always thought we were lucky to have Saudi Arabia's oil might in his hands. He was never one to upset the applecart.'

Then, too, Dr Brewster thinks that one of Yamani's great strengths is that he probably never panics. 'It might not bear any relation to what he felt, but he would stay calm. And that is very special.'

Returning to Saudi Arabia in 1956, now with a Master's of Law from Harvard to add to his NYU degree, he joined the newly formed Department of Zakah (religious tax) and Income Tax under the Ministry of Finance.

He soon divided his job between that office and the Office of Petroleum and Minerals under Abdullah Tariki where he was entrusted to write such highly technical and complicated contracts as the Japanese Off Shore Concession agreements in late 1957.

A friend of his father's offered Yamani a good salary to work three hours every morning as the manager of a Coca Cola bottling plant. Ever ambitious, Yamani accepted. But after eight months of coming to work at 5 a.m. he finally had to admit that he'd taken on too much and his soda pop career ended.

That's about the time he took a leave of absence from the government to establish his own law practice in Jeddah.

As it happened, it was the first real law office in Saudi Arabia.

'Before that we didn't have lawyers in the western sense. We had people who would help represent you in court. We had advocates. But we didn't have law firms where you could go to someone who'd write a contract for you or give you legal advice. I knew there were many banks and foreign companies being started and that there was a need for these services. There had been a lot of new statutes passed but no one was around who could interpret them for foreign companies.'

His first office comprised three people. A secretary. A typist. And himself.

'I admit that I wasn't very busy in the beginning.'

But he set his mind to finding clients and before too long he signed up a few foreign banks and foreign companies on a retainer basis. These days – employing a very large staff in several offices, including women attorneys, which is still just about unheard of in Saudi Arabia – Yamani's law firm is considered the most successful in the country.

By 1957 he and Laila had started a family. Their first daughter Mai was born. Their second daughter Maha was born in 1959. Their son Hani was born in 1961.

As his client list built up he pleaded regularly in the Shariah Court, earning a reputation as an expert in Islamic law.

In those early days, he was also a part-time journalist.

At the end of his normal working day he'd write and edit stories until bedtime.

'I was writing for several newspapers in Saudi Arabia. One in particular was a weekly tabloid called *Arafat*. Well, Crown Prince Faisal had just introduced a new law for the Council of Ministers which gave the Prime Minister and the cabinet a real status vis-à-vis the king. So

I wrote a bunch of articles trying to explain the various legal points and interpret this new law. I must have written three different series of articles in all. I didn't know it then but Faisal was reading my articles very carefully. I later discovered that he used to read everything I wrote.'

4

The Birth of Opec and the Rise of Yamani

SAUDI ARABIA is a huge expanse of sand, where villages and towns dot the map like tiny, isolated islands in the sea.

It is a largely unpopulated, treeless land where there are said to be 150 species of butterflies.

It is the birthplace of Islam.

It is the traditional home of Islam.

And the laws of Saudi Arabia are the laws of Islam.

No one is quite sure just how many people live in Saudi Arabia. A census is accomplished with aerial photos. The census taker multiplies the number of roofs he sees by the average number of people he reckons live beneath each roof. When it comes to nomads, some get counted once. Some get counted two or three times. Some never get counted at all. There have been times when the government has claimed as many as 8.4 million people in the country. But other estimates have put the population as low as 5 million.

The point is that Saudi Arabia's real strength in the Gulf and its place in the world are dictated not by population but rather by the land it occupies and the fact that under much of it lies an unfathomable reserve of crude oil.

Ibn Saud often said that the man who controls the oil beneath the sands of Saudi Arabia has the power to control war and peace in the region.

It was his son Faisal who was first fully to understand that.

As a child, Faisal was not offered any formal education. He was taught to ride a horse like a Bedouin, to recite the Koran by heart, to shoot a rifle and to wield a sword. But his father sent him abroad on official visits while still a teenager and he mingled with the statesmen of the day. At the age of 24 he was named Foreign Minister, a post he continued to hold through Ibn Saud's reign.

An austere man, with a sombre, almost mourning-like expression and questionable health – in addition to a blood disease that required regular transfusions, he also suffered from stomach ulcers which kept him from a regular night's sleep – Faisal was a devout Moslem. Unlike his father and brothers, he was basically monogamous, living most of his life with his third wife.

Yamani describes Faisal as a gentle man, who never shouted, who never said anything nasty. 'If he didn't like someone or something he'd simply turn his face away and you could tell that he'd reached his limit.'

Despite Faisal's always-stern public demeanour, Yamani claims the king actually had a sense of humour. 'In his private rooms, sometimes he'd have lunch or dinner with intimate friends and then you would see his humour. He could be very funny. But in public he was always very regal.'

Although Faisal didn't speak English, Yamani says he understood it well enough so that anytime an interpreter mistranslated something, Faisal would correct him. 'He read all the time and he was curious about everything. You could discuss anything with him. He travelled in the west but I don't think he ever felt at home in the west. In many ways I found him to be extremely brilliant. When it came to dealing with other people, I used to think he had the ability to read minds. He was that perceptive. Of course as a human being he had his faults. But as I said, he had that special quality of being regal. He was very unique.'

A great traditionalist, Faisal was at the same time modern enough to establish television in the kingdom, despite condemnation by the religious leaders. He created schools for girls, also against religious advice, and believed so strongly in the formal education he never had that he sent his own sons to the west for degrees from Princeton, Harvard, Oxford and Cambridge.

It was Faisal who 'invented' Yamani.

At the end of 1957 he summoned the young lawyer to his home in the mountain village of Taif.

As Yamani recalls, 'It came totally out of the blue. At the time I didn't even realize he knew who I was.'

Yamani was escorted into the Crown Prince's small office.

Faisal shook hands with him.

Then there was a long pause.

Faisal looked at Yamani and waited.

Not knowing what else to do, Yamani sat down.

Faisal just kept staring.

So now Yamani stood up.

'I want you to work for me as a legal adviser,' Faisal said. 'Have you got any conditions?'

Yamani thought fast. 'I don't think that anyone who could have the opportunity of working for you would have any conditions.'

Faisal liked that.

And Yamani was hired on the spot.

* * * *

By the mid-1950s, Faisal had come to understand that Saudi Arabia's fledgling oil economy required a different sort of bureaucrat to help solve the myriad of newly created problems in banking, currency and budgeting. As part of his plan to clean up the nations's rampant administrative disorder, the Crown Prince merged the Ministries of Finance and Economy, created the Office of Petroleum and Minerals and appointed a brash young western-educated technocrat named Abdullah Tariki to be Director General.

Over the next five years Saudi oil revenues climbed towards the $300 million mark.

And Aramco became the single most powerful entity in the Kingdom.

Notes a former Aramco executive, 'What we did for Saudi Arabia is a story that's never been told. We brought them into the world. We buried them. Oil was almost just a sideline. I've never seen anything so paternal. We helped eradicate malaria. We set up hospitals. We set up camel troughs for the Bedouins. We started a farm to take care of the table for the royal family. Something like 40 per cent of our work force were Shi'a from the Eastern Province and they loved Aramco because the government wasn't doing a damn thing for them. The government used to refer to them as "the dogs". It was Aramco who went out to the oasis and cleaned it up and gave them home loans. People used to say, we wish that Aramco could run the government. When King Fahd was Minister of Interior he got very upset with us. He said, "Aramco is getting too much credit." Those were his words. Can you believe that? He was upset because too many people knew what Aramco was doing.'

Fahd and a lot of other Saudis were upset because the more Aramco accomplished, the more arrogant they grew about their accomplishments.

It was also widely known throughout the Middle East that many of Aramco's senior executives had direct links to the CIA.

In fact, until the international construction company Bechtel came along, Aramco was America's main listening post in that part of the Gulf.

It's no coincidence then that, as Aramco grew in stature, Tariki became more and more militant, modelling much of his thinking on Perez Alfonzo's experiences with the oil companies in Venezuela.

He explains, 'The discovery of oil in the middle of the desert gave us a great opportunity to build a better life. When the Americans came to Saudi Arabia, King Abdul Aziz treated them as friends. The idea that a company would always be out for what they could get and that they would look at the government as something to be exploited whenever possible, this never occurred to him. It didn't occur to King Saud either. So the oil companies went right on exploiting him. It only stopped when they realized that a small character like me could make the king agree to what I wanted.'

First he wanted Aramco to become an integrated company, one that would handle petroleum from the well all the way to the petrol station. Then he wanted more Saudi control over Aramco and participation in the company's profits.

'The oil industry in my country was not controlled by my country. It was controlled by foreigners. They didn't take Saudi Arabian oil to the markets as a Saudi Arabian company. I wanted Aramco to be run from Saudi Arabia.'

As support for Tariki's ideas gained ground in the royal court, Aramco made minor efforts to appease him. They opened a headquarters in Saudi Arabia. But the seat of the company's power remained in the United States because that's where the four owners were.

By the late 1950s, Tariki vocally shared Perez Alfonzo's spirit of nationalism. Drawn together as patriots, they both believed that their countries' natural resources belonged to the people and not, by divine right, to the foreign companies that originally found the oil.

However, the concept of nationalization, while very much on Tariki's mind, was not yet a viable one. He knew it. And so did the Americans. The softer term he chose to use was 'integration'.

'We couldn't have nationalized the oil companies then even if we had tried. We had to cooperate with the west because that's where our markets were. But it was time to begin making changes.'

That's when Perez Alfonzo sold Tariki on the idea of creating an organization of petroleum exporting countries.

Says George Ballou, a retired Socal executive, 'Perez Alfonzo put the bug in Tariki's ear. The Venezuelans were very anxious to organize the Middle East so that the Arabs would not become serious competition for them. Perez Alfonzo had an advanced degree in sophistication where oil matters were concerned. He helped to bring the Saudis up to speed.'

At Tariki's insistence, the Arab League Economic Council convened its first 'Arab Oil Congress' in Cairo. Two non-Arab delegations were invited to attend. One was Iran. The other was Venezuela.

The whole thing probably would have wound up a non-event had Shell and British Petroleum not played their cards so clumsily. Without consulting the producing nations, they sparked off a round of severe price cuts, blaming the situation on market forces.

It was too much for the fiery likes of Perez Alfonzo and Tariki.

A bond of open defiance was soldered between the two.

The congress called for 50/50 participation agreements with the oil companies. Of course the Arabs lacked both the technical know-how and the financial resources to press the issue. But unofficially, and surrounded in secrecy, Perez Alfonzo and Tariki steered the meeting into what was known as 'The Gentlemen's Agreement'. Saudi Arabia, Venezuela, Iraq, Kuwait and the UAR established the Oil Consultative Commission, intending to meet at least once a year and discuss problems of mutual interest.

High on their list of priorities was the very structure of the industry. It's a business with huge fixed costs and negligible variable costs. Put another way, the greatest expense is getting the first barrel out of the ground. The production of an additional barrel costs next to nothing. Perez Alfonzo and Tariki both knew it was therefore in the interests of the oil companies to grant discounts on the posted price so they could sell this additional barrel instead of leaving it underground. But such discounts were entirely at the expense of the producing countries.

The two men spent much of late 1959 and early 1960 crying foul. Unable to change the system from within, they rallied the call for a cartel which could somehow force a showdown with the oil companies.

Until Tariki arrived on the scene, the major ministries in Saudi Arabia were Finance, Defence and Commerce. Yet by 1960, he'd transformed the oil directorate into a full-fledged ministry and became such a power that he could make the nationalization of Aramco a cause célèbre and help turn the Organization of Petroleum Exporting Countries into a reality.

As founding fathers, Tariki and Perez Alfonzo were determined to see Opec unify the oil policies of member countries and lay down the best means for safeguarding its members' individual and collective interests. . . . although no one in 1960 imagined Opec would one day become a force which could raise prices by creating artificial shortages. In 1960 Opec was thought of by the member states merely as a defensive instrument.

'The oil companies took us seriously,' Tariki insists. 'They had to. Believe me, everybody was afraid of Opec.'

Good try. But not quite.

It's a fact that the major oil companies resented Opec. And, yes, it's also a fact that a handful of the more far-sighted oil executives in the west prophesied that such a grouping could in fact one day become more than the toothless tiger it was then.

But that's where Opec-phobia ended.

The truth is, not a lot of people cared.

Even if Tariki and Perez Alfonzo considered it a major step, Opec's birth announcement was missed by just about everyone else in the world in 1960. Especially in the United States and Western Europe . . . where front pages were filled with the American presidential race between John Kennedy and Richard Nixon as it entered the home stretch . . . Opec's arrival looked like yet another unimportant collective of basically powerless interest groups.

Shortly after the formation of Opec, Faisal resigned and Saud returned to full power. Among Saud's supporters were the politically motivated 'Free Princes' led by a younger brother, Prince Talal. Tariki found himself attracted to their spirit of nationalism, Saud put up with them only until he felt strong enough to govern without them. Then he dumped them. Tariki was the only so-called 'liberal' who remained on the Council of Ministers.

According to Yamani, Tariki was invited to stay simply because Saud couldn't find anyone else for the job. 'I'd been a Minister of State in the Council while Faisal was Crown Prince and Prime Minister. When he left, I did too. I returned to my law practice and taught an introductory course of law at the University of Riyadh. The conflict between Saud and Faisal which had been created by the Free Princes continued for some time. It came to a head when Prince Talal and the others quit and went to live in Egypt. No one knew it then, but King Saud had wanted to get rid of Tariki and offered the job to me. I apologized and did not accept.'

Six months later, after that next cabinet resigned, a new coalition was formed.

Saud was King and Prime Minister.

Faisal was Crown Prince and Deputy Prime Minister.

And this time Tariki was shown the door.

He'd placed all his eggs in the wrong basket.

He'd alienated too many people.

He quickly removed himself from Saudi Arabia.

An interesting thing about the Saudi royal family is that, even after

Tariki left the country to live in exile, he still continued to receive his monthly pension as a former government minister.

An interesting thing about Faisal was his unswerving conviction that the best person to follow Tariki's rabble-rousing act had to be the soft-spoken young lawyer from Mecca named Ahmed Zaki Yamani.

* * * *

Yamani's relationship with Faisal evolved step by step over the years.

It started out as a working relationship.

It ended as a deep and warm friendship.

It was the single most important male friendship in Yamani's life.

It was also a friendship that changed the course of history, at least in the Middle East.

'The confidence we shared was built slowly. He was the boss. I worked for him. But he came to treat me like a son. And to a great extent I thought of him as a father. I loved and respected him very much.'

Even Abdullah Tariki is these days willing to admit, 'Faisal was very impressed with Yamani and grew to trust him more than maybe anybody else in the Kingdom. Yamani was very bright. There is no doubt about that. Perhaps later on Yamani became arrogant. But he wasn't arrogant as a young man. At least he wasn't arrogant towards me. But then I was much bigger than him.'

Some Americans who knew Yamani in the late 1950s claim he had a nickname.

Although Yamani himself doesn't remember this, they swear that he was referred to as 'Camille'. Perhaps no one called him that to his face. It appears to be a reference, albeit fairly obscure, to a French actor. And according to those Americans, the reason they used the term was because in many ways they thought of him as an actor. In many ways, they claim, he was always acting.

Such a remark comes as a genuine surprise to Yamani. 'This is the first time I've ever heard this. Camille?' He shrugs and shakes his head. 'Maybe it was said behind my back. But I'm surprised because by nature I'm very quiet.'

That quiet nature was just one of many major changes in style that took place in March 1962 when Faisal appointed Yamani to take over at the Ministry of Petroleum.

'Yamani had just become minister,' says George Ballou. 'I met him in San Francisco when he attended his first board meeting of Aramco. No one knew who he was. Come to think of it, no one knew much about Saudi Arabia in those days either. Their role in the world oil

52

scene wasn't anything like what it eventually became. So Zaki arrived in San Francisco and none of us really knew what to expect. But he wasn't anything like Abdullah Tariki. He was very quiet and very personable. The first or second night he was there someone in Aramco wondered if anybody had arranged dinner plans for Zaki. We discovered that no one had. Well, we were having a family birthday party at home but I figured I couldn't just leave Zaki on his own like that because it would have been rude. So I invited him to the party. He enjoyed himself so much he came back to the party several years in a row.'

In 1962, Ballou points out, Yamani wasn't being lionized. He was also less sophisticated in those days. But in other ways he hasn't changed all that much.

'He's still basically a very nice man. He had lived in New York City and in Boston so he's been tuned into the west for a long time. He was, even then, the epitome of charm.'

It seems as if everybody who's ever met him has a favourite Yamani story.

One friend who's known him for years recounts, 'Yamani was in the States and heard that an old friend was in a California hospital, so he took a day to fly out to see him. Now, this guy happened to be wealthy enough that he didn't have to worry about money. But, rich or not, like most people who find themselves in an expensive private clinic, complaining about the prices is a common pastime. Yamani listened while the fellow told him how ridiculously expensive it was to be a patient there. That same day, without saying anything to anybody, Yamani paid the man's bill '

While John Bruton, as Energy Minister for the Republic of Ireland, met Yamani only once. 'I went to Saudi Arabia to cancel some long-term contracts. I arrived in Jeddah to find Yamani's private Gulfstream jet waiting to bring me to Riyadh. Then in Riyadh, I found Yamani waiting at the airport to greet me. Being the Minister of Energy of a small country I was in awe of this world figure. But he was informal, casual and urbane. There was some sort of Opec meeting going on with ministers shuffling in and out of Riyadh. His business with them was important while he was only seeing me out of courtesy. Still, he met me at the plane, talked at length with me and then saw me off at the airport. He spent three hours with me. That's what really struck me. The trouble he went to for me.'

Mike Ameen, a former Aramco executive, is one of the many people who agrees that Yamani's open, relaxed personality was a significant change when he became minister.

'Tariki was way ahead of his time because he wanted to go all the way downstream. But the Saudis weren't ready to get into that. The real problem was that Tariki was also very political and had a terrible temper. Instead of just talking, Zaki was quiet and got things done. He was diplomatic and soft-spoken. He thought about other people. He's always been the sort of person who knew how to go about getting something done without upsetting everyone in his way.'

Comments about 'legendary charm' are met with an embarrassed smile. However, Yamani isn't quite so shy when it comes to discussing his views on the change of ministerial styles from the Tariki years.

'We might have had the same objectives, but Abdullah Tariki and I were two different people. The first thing I needed to change was the way he treated Aramco. He either used to look down on them or ignore them completely.'

To put a barrier between himself and Aramco, Tariki had dictated that the company's executives could not address the minister directly because they were not on the same level. When they had business with him they had to write to the Director General in Dammam who would send all the mail to Riyadh where an answer would be prepared. That answer would be then returned to the Director General who'd sign the correspondence before sending it to Aramco.

That was the first thing Yamani changed.

Mail was now to come directly to him.

Another Tariki rule was that when the chairman of Aramco wanted to meet the minister, he'd first have to request an appointment, then wait several days before a meeting would be arranged. More often than not, when the chairman showed up, Tariki would keep him waiting.

That was the next thing Yamani changed.

'When the Aramco chairman wanted to see me, he was granted an appointment immediately and never kept waiting. I remember that when I said this is how we were going to operate, the secretaries were amazed. They told me, this is not the way these people should be treated. But I told them this was the way I would treat them.'

As he grew more confident in his job, Yamani also began to find his own identity in the fledgling Opec cartel.

'Opec was an organization that no one had ever heard of in 1962. When it was created, the oil companies fought the whole idea of it violently. They refused to recognize the word Opec. They refused to talk to Opec. They even refused to send correspondence to anything called Opec.'

It was obvious that, if Opec was going to survive much longer, it had to be taken seriously by the world's major oil companies. So Yamani decided, if the mountain won't come to Muhammad, Opec had somehow to impose its presence on the oil companies.

He wasn't quite sure how to go about it until a situation arose at the end of 1962 that seemed tailor-made.

A group of oil producers were due to negotiate certain royalties with a group of oil companies. Yamani, representing Saudi Arabia, was basically concerned only with Aramco. He knew that if he told the four Aramco partners that they were going to face ministers representing Opec, they'd instantly say, we have nothing to do with Opec. So he got the other producers to agree to let Saudi Arabia negotiate with all of the oil companies on their behalf.

'I called the companies in to talk to Saudi Arabia. Because it was Saudi Arabia they were meeting with they had to come. Then I got some Opec members to sit next to me as Saudis. I told the oil companies who they'd be dealing with, but always under the banner of Saudi Arabia. Frankly, there was nothing much they could do about it. They were talking to Saudi Arabia but they were finally seeing Opec.'

Yamani had opened the door.

Registered in accordance with a United Nations charter, the Organization of Petroleum Exporting Countries was originally based in Geneva. But the Swiss would not grant them ambassadorial status. So Yamani proposed Opec move to Vienna. He now admits there were two good reasons for the suggestion. Not only would the Austrians give Opec the diplomatic recognition Yamani felt the organization should have, but this way he'd be just down the block from the best opera in the world.

* * * *

On 4 June 1967, with tension mounting between Israel and Egypt, the Syrians, the Iraqis and the Egyptians demanded that, should war break out, all Arab oil fields be shut down.

The very next day Israel attacked Egypt.

That Syria, Iraq and Egypt should have made such a proposal only one day before the Six Day War was hardly the coincidence it then appeared to be. Yamani notes, 'The Israeli attack on Egypt was expected. But no one knew when or where. President Nasser had been warned ahead of time by the Americans. He was the one who told us that Israel would start a war.'

Nor was their call to use oil as a political weapon an original idea.

Oil was already on centre stage in Iran when the Mossadeq regime was overthrown in 1953, the Shah was returned to the Peacock Throne and the Iranian oil operations were turned over to an international consortium. In 1956, when Abdel Nasser nationalized the Suez Canal, oil was again a political theme. The Egyptians blocked the Canal, the

Syrians blew up the Iraqi pipeline to the Mediterranean and the US had to 'oil lift' energy to Europe.

However, in the eleven years between Suez and the June War, European dependence on Arab oil had nearly tripled. Syria, Iraq and Egypt now believed that the west needed Arab oil more than the Arabs needed to sell their oil to the west. At a meeting of Arab oil producers in Baghdad, they called for a boycott.

Yamani was less than enthusiastic. 'A complete shutdown is impossible,' Yamani tried to make his Arab colleagues understand, 'and a partial shutdown is useless.'

The Syrians were furious that Yamani should say such things. And one of their senior delegates shouted at him, 'You will be eliminated.'

It was the first of many serious death threats that Yamani would receive over the years.

Yamani knew the Syrians would do whatever they felt they had to in order to save face. He also knew that he would lose face unless he stood up to them. So he deliberately eyed the man who'd made the threat and answered as calmly as he could, 'I will make it easy for you. I will tell you exactly when the best time to do it is. I will be coming back to my hotel from a club just after midnight. I will be alone. That is the best time for you.'

The others at the table were shocked.

The Syrians stormed out of the meeting.

Yamani's friends in the group begged him to leave right away for Saudi Arabia.

But Yamani felt he had to prove his point.

He went to the club as scheduled, and left just after midnight as promised.

True to his word he walked back to his hotel alone.

Obviously the Syrians didn't make good on their threat.

However, Yamani doesn't believe for a minute it was his own bravado that saved him. Instead he thinks it was the prevailing climate of humiliation in the Arab world. 'Their superiors figured it just wasn't the time to do such a thing.'

Now Yamani tried to caution his colleagues. 'If we do not use the oil weapon properly we are behaving like someone who fires a bullet into the air, missing the enemy and allowing it to rebound on himself.'

And that's exactly what happened.

The Arab militants shot themselves in the foot.

They had badly misread the world situation.

To begin with, the Saudis weren't all that interested in the embargo. Diplomatic relations between Saudi Arabia and Egypt were at an all-time low because of the war in Yemen. At the same time they couldn't really afford to turn off their oil because they needed the associated gas that comes with oil production. If they stopped pumping, they'd have no natural gas to run their electricity generators. Neighbouring Kuwait would suffer a similar fate, and they'd also be without water because without electricity the desalination plants would have to shut down.

Anyway, the United States, as prime target of the boycott, was then immune to such things. In those days America's oil requirements could be totally filled by western hemisphere oil.

Venezuela saw no reason whatsoever to join the Arabs. Nor did Iran. The two of them promptly made a fortune filling the rest of the world's needs.

Before too long even Libya turned its back on its Arab brothers by increasing exports to West Germany.

No quota ceilings had been imposed on the Arab producers.

They did not speak coherently with one voice.

They did not create any sort of oil shortage.

The oil weapon was a total and abject failure.

However, the Arabs learned some vital lessons from their mistake.

One of them was that the Arab producers themselves could never count on non-Arab producers to stand by them.

And that gave credence to the existence of the Organization of Arab Petroleum Exporting Countries.

It was Yamani's idea.

'I felt that such an organization could serve two purposes. One was a political objective. Until this point, Arab oil had always been considered within the framework of the Arab League. That didn't seem right to me because so many countries who did not have any oil were influential in decisions passed by the Arab League. When they met in Baghdad in June 1967 and then again in August 1967 to discuss the possibility of using oil as a weapon, the few oil producers there were subjected to serious pressure from Egypt and Syria. This is where we first discussed the embargo and this is when the idea of an Arab oil organization came to my mind. I mentioned it to the Kuwaiti oil minister and told him that we had to think seriously about establishing an organization where Arab oil producers could talk about oil alone, without anyone else interfering.'

The Kuwaiti liked the idea so Yamani went to discuss it with Faisal.

'I didn't take the idea to the Iraqi government at that time because they were very radical. I didn't even want them to know about this yet. First King Faisal had to approve the idea. Then I wrote the by-laws. I gave a draft to the Kuwaitis who accepted it. And I gave a draft to the Libyans who also accepted it. It wasn't until 1968 that we sent the draft to the Iraqis, who then rejected most of the items in the by-laws and categorically refused to join with us.'

Before too long they realized that Yamani had structured the organization in such a way that they could not possibly accept.

Admits Yamani, 'We didn't want them to join in the beginning. Our idea was to establish Oapec as a commercial entity and not the political one that the Iraqis envisioned.'

Algeria, Abu Dhabi, Bahrain, Dubai and Qatar were admitted in 1970.

Iraq joined a year later.

By the time the Yom Kippur War broke out in October 1973, Oapec had its act together.

That's when Yamani convinced the others, oil as a political weapon is finally a viable option.

5

Taking on Aramco

HOME FOR Yamani throughout the 1960s changed with the government, as the king moved back and forth between Riyadh, Jeddah and
Taif.

But by 1964 his first marriage was breaking up.

'I left my family house in Riyadh and decided to live in a hotel
because it was easier for me. My marriage was not succeeding and we
separated.'

There were only a few hotels in Riyadh in those days. The Hyatt,
the Marriott, the Intercontinental and all the other large, modern,
western-style hotels that you see now on the way into town from the
airport didn't happen until the oil boom of the mid-1970s.

The best of the paltry few in the mid-1960s was the Al-Yamama, a
tired-looking place decorated with strange glass tiles on the outer walls.
But it was convenient, being only half a mile down the block from
Yamani's office.

He took a long lease on a ground-floor suite which he then altered
so that he'd have his own tree-shaded private entrance at the back. It
was a one-bedroom flat, hardly opulent by anyone's standards. Some
years later he added a couple of rooms and closed off the terrace so
that he could use it as a library and sitting room.

He lived at the Yamama for over 15 years.

'It was very grand for those days,' he says. 'It was home. I furnished
it. I decorated it. I suppose I considered it to be a long-term
arrangement.'

Not long after he moved into the hotel, Yamani began to sense that
a showdown over participation with the four Aramco partners was in
the offing. To remind them that he meant business, he swung a barter
deal with the Romanians, trading oil for goods. It was his way of letting

59

the Americans know that Saudi Arabia could market oil if the need arose.

But certain religious factions in the country objected. They didn't want Saudi Arabia to have any dealings whatsoever with the communist bloc. And now they put pressure on Yamani to resign.

That, coupled with the effects of a crumbling marriage, gave him reason to reconsider his future.

'I told King Faisal that I wanted to leave government, that I wanted to return to my law practice. But he answered, "I won't allow you to do this, any more than I would allow my son to leave my house." So I stayed.'

The longer he stayed, the more he came to certain inevitable conclusions about the fate of his country's oil policy.

He saw quite clearly that Aramco would have to become a Saudi company.

According to at least one Aramco executive, Yamani confided in him shortly after he returned from the Baghdad meeting where he'd been threatened, 'As long as Aramco remains in the hands of the Americans we're going to continue having this kind of trouble.'

Today Yamani doesn't remember saying this to anyone. 'Certainly not to anyone at Aramco.'

But he does admit that the thought was very much on his mind.

'I was thinking from the beginning that eventually Saudi Arabia would have to own and control its own natural resources. From the first day I walked into the ministry I believed that. Yes, I spoke of participation. But you should understand that participation was always intended to be just one step in that direction. Maybe in the beginning I didn't say it like that. Perhaps you're right to think that in the beginning I didn't make the point too clearly. Yet I soon made it quite clear that if we started with 25 per cent our share must eventually increase to 51 per cent or whatever the agreed percentage would be.'

What he most definitely did not say at the time was that he was translating 'whatever the agreed percentage would be' to one day mean 100 per cent.

'No, I didn't explain it that way. Not in the beginning. I spoke about that later on. I called it "complete participation". That was the term I used. I meant by that we would have technological and marketing assistance, plus access downstream from the other party. That's the type of participation I always felt we had to have. As far as I was concerned, I never varied my position. I always moved towards the point where we would own the assets and we would control the oil in the ground.'

But that's not the song he was singing at the American University in Beirut (AUB) in 1968.

In what is now considered a turning point in Saudi relations with the four Aramco partners, and perhaps just as important a landmark in commercial relations between the west and all the oil-producing nations, Yamani publicly dealt with the question of nationalization versus participation.

The analogy he used to describe the bond he wanted with the oil companies was 'indissoluble, like a Catholic marriage'.

He suggested that participation would provide the oil companies with an enduring link to the producing countries. Although he acknowledged that the oil companies themselves might not look upon participation quite the same way.

Some of them, he said, were 'obsessed with the empire they have built. It is so vast and it took them so many decades to achieve. And now they see these newcomers, these national oil companies in the producing countries, wanting to come and take a piece of their cake, which is the last thing they want to happen.'

These days he willingly concedes, 'When I took over the ministry I was looking for participation within ten years. But I was very young and, well, maybe I wanted it a bit too soon. As I got a little older I was willing to wait a little longer. However, we were preparing the ground for that plan through the legal concept called "changes of circumstance". We spoke about that from time to time in other contexts with Aramco and they accepted it. We were preparing the ground for participation at least four years before I started calling for it.'

Yamani explained at AUB that the first aim of the Arabs in their quest for participation was to support the major oil companies, directly or indirectly, in maintaining price levels. Their second aim was to make it possible for the national oil companies to strengthen their position in the downstream operations 'without harming ourselves or anybody else in the process.'

What he proposed was a package deal. In exchange for participation, the Arabs would agree to gradual integration on a commercially sound basis.

'I was talking in general terms. But I left no room for any misunderstanding when I said that I wanted Saudi Arabia to control its natural resources. Here I had a common objective with Tariki. But he wanted to control our natural resources by political force. I knew this would be impossible. So one of the first things I did when I became a minister was to establish a national oil company and a petroleum university.'

He was convinced that Saudi Arabia wouldn't be able to cope with participation until its own university was producing home-grown engineers, scientists and managers to suit the needs of its own national oil company.

By the mid-1960s the University of Petroleum and Minerals at Dhahran was in full swing, and so was Petromin, the national oil company.

These days Yamani looks at the university as one of his most notable achievements. It was the first school of its kind in the oil-producing world and is today the largest of its kind in the Middle East. The curriculum was designed by a group of professors from MIT, Princeton and AUB with all classes taught in English. The first year's student body numbered 100. Today there are nearly 3,000 seeking degrees in engineering, applied engineering, science and industrial management. There is also an important research centre attached to the university.

Interestingly enough, immediately after Yamani was dismissed from his ministry, the university had its name changed. For whatever reason, today is it officially known as King Fahd University of Petroleum and Mineral Resources.

Yamani continues. 'Right from the start Aramco fought me on the formation of the university because they saw what was coming. They knew I wanted to get inside the oil business and have a share of what was going on. Once I got inside, the next step was getting into the market. Of course I wanted participation from the first day. But I didn't talk about it until the time was right. That was in Beirut in 1968.'

The reaction of the oil companies to the AUB speech was just as clear as Yamani's message to them.

They were angry and showed every intention of digging in for a fight. After all, he was saying that he was going to try to take away from them what they always considered to be theirs to keep.

'Their hostility surprised me a little. It was not so much that there was a lot of money involved. It was the idea of a change in status that bothered them. They would lose their full control. Aramco would be different. Now we could know what was going on. This was not what they wanted.'

Obviously not.

Bob Brougham, then president of Aramco, saw Yamani's eventual target was 100 per cent and argued with him that such a goal would be harmful to the United States. 'If you take everything away from the Americans they'll lose interest.'

Yamani answered, 'We aren't taking everything away. Instead we're giving you a secure source of supply.'

Brougham assured Yamani, 'That isn't enough.'

'It will have to be,' Yamani proclaimed, absolutely convinced that participation was a concept whose time had come.

Aramco wasn't going to give up without a fight. Although certain executives were mumbling among themselves that it might be best if they negotiated a quick peace settlement with the Saudis. Brougham and Mike Ameen even went on record in favour of participation, their argument being that giving up a little now would be considerably cheaper in the long run than giving up a lot later on. But the four parent companies back in the States ruled it out. No one in New York or San Francisco seemed to understand that Yamani was in truth saying, you can either give it to us or we can take it.

Put that way, Yamani sounded like Tariki

Although, here again, George Ballou points out there were marked differences between them. 'At the end of his days as minister, Tariki was sounding more and more like a politician. After the first Arab Oil Congress he even took a public speaking course to learn how to handle himself like an Arab politician. That's what got him into trouble. He got too political. Yamani was always very low key. He always sounded like a reasonable man. Except of course, he never left any cards on the table.'

* * * *

Since the end of the Second World War the price of oil had been determined in two very different ways.

Through the 1950s and into the 1960s, prices were determined by the oil companies, which usually offset prices with production according to market forces – when demand rose, they increased production, when demand fell, they decreased production. Their aim was to keep prices stable.

That changed radically in the late 1960s.

Global demand for oil was just beginning to overtake the world's supply. When the Suez Canal was shut in June 1967, and stayed shut, the Mediterranean producers – Libya, Algeria and Iraq – discovered an increased market for their crude. By 1969, coinciding with the coup masterminded by a 27-year-old army lieutenant named Muammar Qaddafi, the Libyans were providing more than a quarter of Europe's oil requirements.

Now the world was divided into two distinct camps.

There were oil sellers.

And there were oil buyers.

More than a few historians feel it was Zaki Yamani who forever split the world into these two factions as a result of his negotiations with Aramco.

'No.' Yamani strongly disagrees with that. 'The trend was evident for many years. In the 1950s and the 1960s, oil companies were the only group determining the price of oil. They did that with the full cooperation of the major western consuming countries. They had a margin to play with. They paid us our share based on a posted price of oil. It the 1950s, they used to play with the posted price anyway they wanted to, reducing it from time to time and in so doing reducing our income. The last time they reduced the price was August 1960. The creation of Opec was in itself a deterrent to the oil companies.'

Between 1968 and 1971, he says, the oil companies came to see that they could no longer treat the producing countries with the same attitude they had before the June 1967 war.

In May 1970 a strange incident occurred. The Tapline, an oil pipeline running from Saudi Arabia to the Mediterranean port of Sidon, was damaged well within Syrian territory. For their own reasons, the Syrians refused to allow Tapline to be repaired. And oil did not flow through the pipe again for eight months. The shortage of less than half a million barrels a day to Europe was felt immediately. For the first time in oil history prices went up sharply.

Over a brief period they rose as much as 50 cents a barrel.

Seeing a golden opportunity to drive a wedge between the various Gulf producers, the Americans now tried to make a deal directly with the Shah, offering him an increase in exchange for a guaranteed steady supply. But there has always been a natural friction between the Saudis and the Iranians and when Yamani heard that the Shah was considering a deal for himself, Saudi Arabia balked.

'We told the Shah that we would not stand by and allow him to make his own deals outside Opec. This annoyed him very much. He was hoping to make all sorts of additional profits for his country out of this separate deal.'

To appease the Saudis, the Americans offered them a small increase in one type of crude. Yamani refused, still spoiling the deal for the Shah.

The world's biggest stakes poker game had begun.

Qaddafi saw that demand for his oil was way up so he ordered a cutback in production. He announced he was conserving oil. But then he 'invited' the oil companies to renegotiate their concessions. Dealing with them on a one-to-one basis, an obvious divide and conquer technique, he pressed for price increases. Within six months Libya's revenues were up nearly 30 cents a barrel.

Now all the producers looked for price increases.

A few of them managed tax rate rises to 55 per cent.

In December 1970, Opec passed a resolution calling for immediate negotiations to determine additional increased payments to all its member nations. The cartel even set 55 per cent as the minimum rate of tax and demanded the establishment of a general uniform oil price increase.

The basis of Opec's resolution was, if these negotiations failed, the cartel would be forced to introduce measures to achieve its own objectives.

The talks were set to begin in Tehran on 12 January.

One week before the meeting, Venezuela increased its tax rate from 50 per cent to 58 per cent.

Then Qaddafi issued an ultimatum. The non-negotiable terms for oil companies based in Libya would include higher taxes, monthly rather than quarterly payments, and mandatory increased investment in both oil and non-oil areas. Non-compliance meant nationalization.

A panic gathering took place in Washington, bringing together representatives of the US, Great Britain, France and Holland. The four governments agreed it was best to act as a unified force in support of Exxon, Chevron, BP, Gulf, Mobil and Texaco.

However, when they got to Tehran the discussions quickly dissolved in disarray. The companies wanted to negotiate with all the producers at one table. The producers' representatives – Yamani, Iranian Finance Minister Jamshid Amouzegar and the Iraqi Oil Minister Saadoun Hamadi – wanted separate negotiations, one for the Gulf states, another for the Mediterranean producers.

President Nixon rushed a special envoy to Tehran. Under-Secretary of State John Irwin II, later to become US Ambassador to France, called on the Shah, King Faisal and the Emir of Kuwait, pressing home the message that America did not want to see the negotiations split in half. The US wanted to avoid the obvious problem of leapfrogging. But the Libyans refused to negotiate concurrently with the Gulf producers and in the end the companies had no choice.

Talking only to the Gulf producers, the oil companies initially offered a 15 cent per barrel increase.

Yamani, Amouzegar and Hamadi held out for 54 cents.

The compromise settlement worked out to 35 cents immediately with an annual upward adjustment of 2.5 per cent plus a further 5 cents annually over the five-year term of the agreement.

When the scene shifted to Tripoli, the Libyans demanded a $12 per barrel increase. In the end they settled for 90 cents as well as other concessions, giving them a much better deal than the Gulf producers managed.

'If the oil companies were as surprised by these developments as they sometimes pretended to be,' says Yamani, 'it was their own fault. They should have known that the increase in consumption would one day lead to a shortage in the supply of oil and that would lead to a sharp increase in the price. You don't have to be intelligent to understand that. You just have to do your calculations. It had to happen. There was no way to avoid it. But they didn't do anything about it until the day came.'

The Tehran/Tripoli agreements did not last the agreed five-year term.

World events threw a *sabot* into the works and all bets were called off.

However, once the issue of price increases was out of the way, Opec demanded participation.

In July 1971 the cartel adopted a resolution urging its members to take immediate steps in that direction.

Then Qaddafi nationalized BP.

That got the other oil companies off the mark and, on 15 January 1972, participation talks between six Opec countries and the oil companies got under way in Geneva. Opec set a deadline for participation by the end of the year.

Within a month, the talks bogged down.

The chairman of Exxon, on behalf of the Aramco four, contacted President Nixon to see if he'd intervene with King Faisal on their behalf. Nixon's message to Faisal was, 'Yamani is taking an unreasonable position which will ultimately hurt the interests of Saudi Arabia.'

As soon as the message was received, Faisal called for Yamani. He was angry. 'Nixon says you are too harsh. No, I am the one who is too harsh!'

Together they drafted a two-sentence response to the oil companies which was then broadcast on Saudi radio. Faisal told the oil companies, we will do our best to reach an agreement on participation. However, if you fail to cooperate we will have to take action to implement our objectives.

Nixon's intervention had backfired.

On 3 March 1972 the oil companies attempted to cut the other oil states out of the game by offering a fast, cheap settlement directly with the Saudis. But that was immediately rejected by Yamani, who showed his own displeasure with Aramco by letting them know, 'Your attitude so far has convinced us that we must prepare for battle.'

They knew he meant what he said, so one week later the four partners agreed to an immediate 20 per cent Saudi participation. Before the month was out, Iraq announced it had gained 25 per cent, while Abu Dhabi, Qatar and Kuwait claimed 20 per cent, of their resident companies.

The Venezuelans and the Indonesians kept the ball rolling by demanding 51 per cent of Shell's interests there, only to be told by Shell that 51 per cent was intolerable and that 100 per cent state ownership, with long-term contracts, would be preferable.

In June, Iraq nationalized IPC.

Four weeks later Iran dropped out of the participation talks by announcing a separate deal with the consortium based there.

Throughout the summer of 1972 the negotiations continued and confusion reigned.

Opec kept threatening nationalization if participation failed.

So did King Faisal.

In September, Yamani addressed the North Sea Symposium in London, repeating there much the same theme of his AUB speech which had sparked this issue four years previously.

With the world media listening, he explained 'participation is our substitute for nationalization'.

The message could not have been more clear.

With few real options, the four Aramco partners agreed to 25 per cent participation rising to 51 per cent in gradual stages by 1982. Also included were payments for equity shares based on updated book value payable to the companies over three years.

Throughout the course of the negotiations, each of the American companies had a representative on the team to face Yamani. Exxon sent their senior vice-president, and a veteran of the Tehran/Tripoli talks, George Piercy.

'The talks at Tehran were very different from the participation negotiations. Yamani himself was different. At Tehran he wasn't alone. There was Amouzegar and Hamadi. And at various times these negotiations came close to breaking faith. For a Saudi to be implicated in something like that, going back on his word, was unheard of. We even wondered if Yamani was speaking his own words or just being a good servant. At times we believed there was pressure put on him from somewhere outside the kingdom. It was a progressive thing. Towards the end he became much more recalcitrant and in a way more arrogant. Of course he's always been arrogant in his dealings with the other oil ministers. He didn't always show a lot of charity for their views. Amouzegar was the exception. Amouzegar was Yamani's intellectual equal. But Yamani definitely rode rough-shod over the others.'

Yamani strongly disagrees. 'I have always gone out of my way to be respectful to the other ministers. Even those ministers with whom I have been at odds. I don't think I've ever been arrogant with them at all.'

One of the Opec ministers sides with Yamani. 'Did you know he used to send us all birthday cards? And there were always baskets of dates and figs in our hotel suites before each Opec meeting. Remember when he came to Brioni on a yacht? What no one knew at the time was that he'd been sailing on his big yacht but insisted on leaving that a few hours down the coast and coming to the meeting on a much smaller boat because he didn't want to show off in front of the other ministers. Maybe he was arrogant with the oil company executives during those negotiations, but never with us.'

Be that as it may, where the Tehran/Tripoli talks were formal, the participation talks were relatively relaxed.

They began at Yamani's house in the Lebanon.

He'd bought the place some years before. It was on the top of a hill with sweeping views, in a settlement behind Beirut. Part of it had been built on catacombs where he found spectacular mosaics which were then used to decorate the swimming pool.

The four American oil men met with Yamani there every morning, usually sitting outside by the pool, having lunch together like old friends, each of them hoping to find an amicable solution.

'It wasn't as if the Saudis were holding a gun to our heads,' Piercy continues, 'because there was merit on both sides. The companies were absolutely necessary to run the operations at that time. We recognized that they wanted control of their natural resources and, yes, they could have just nationalized them. But at that time I think Saudi Arabia was very concerned about its image in the world.'

The meetings with Yamani were cordial, Piercy adds, but Yamani was always tough and always in control. 'He sometimes discussed points with each company separately because in negotiations when you reach a hard spot it's often easier one on one. Although he never tried to play one company off the other. He wouldn't do that. But make no mistake about him. He's a very skilled negotiator.'

Unlike fishermen who talk about the one that got away, negotiators obviously prefer stories about the one they landed. Piercy notes that a point had been raised at an afternoon meeting in the Lebanon to which he told Yamani, no. The meeting broke up then and there. The next morning the four Americans gathered, as usual, next to the pool. They were sipping juice when Yamani arrived. He said hello, sat down and turned directly to Piercy. He asked about the demand he'd raised the day before. Piercy repeated his answer. 'No.'

Yamani shrugged and announced, 'In that case, there's no reason to continue the meeting.'

Piercy's response was just to sit there and stare at Yamani. He didn't say a thing.

And for the longest time Yamani just sat there and stared at Piercy. He didn't say a thing.

Piercy remembers that the silence lasted several minutes.

Then, without any mention of the deadlock, without any further threats to abandon the meeting, Yamani simply raised another issue.

And the morning meeting began.

Not long into their stay near Beirut, the local authorities advised Yamani that the political situation was getting very shaky. It was suggested that the four Americans might be a lot safer in another country. So the negotiations were moved to Yamani's office in Riyadh.

Of course, as long as they'd been in the Lebanon, the Americans had Yamani's undivided attention. Back in Saudi Arabia, Piercy says, they had stiff competition.

'In spite of all the pressures on Yamani, he was always close to his children. You'd go to visit him and it would be like open house. More damn people would come to call on him. His own kids were in and out of the house all the time.'

Ironing out the final deal took the better part of a month. 'We hammered at that thing for a long while. Looking back, I think the Saudis were definitely on a very moderate course. They wanted partial ownership so that they could get all the help they needed and they paid us for what they were doing, which made them look honourable in the world. Need I point out that in lots of other places it didn't happen like that.'

Piercy doesn't believe that Yamani sincerely thought it could ever be in the Saudis best interests to nationalize. 'But let's face, he was holding the cards. If you want to know what cards we were holding I'd have to say, not many. Western technology, western management and Saudi honour. We thought we could negotiate on the value they'd pay for the resources, which they undertook to do. But they always talked about resources above ground. We never got any payment for the reserves, which had a terrific value. The thing we gained was payment for above-ground resources which, in the world as it was then, was quite an accomplishment.'

If the negotiations concluded in a gentlemanly fashion, Piercy says, it was because the four Aramco partners knew whom they were talking to. 'Yamani is cordial and courteous with an almost European flair. In those days there was never any doubt that he was a most sincere person. Later on it was a little hard to know what he was doing or why he was doing it. You see, Yamani always understood Americans very well. And while King Faisal was alive he wasn't under the political pressure at home that later developed. I don't think Yamani and Faisal could have been any closer even if Yamani had been his son. Faisal depended on him. But after Faisal died there were times when you had to wonder, is Yamani doing what he wants to do or is he doing what he's told. I think a lot of it was the latter.'

That's not quite true.

After Faisal, Yamani didn't always do what he was told to.

In fact, that's one of the reasons he became an irritant to Fahd.

In 1979, for example, the then US Secretary of Commerce, Dr Juanita Kreps, visited Saudi Arabia and was granted an audience with Fahd, then Crown Prince. According to an ex-official at the US Embassy, Fahd made some wild promises to Kreps regarding Saudi oil policy towards the four Aramco companies. He then drafted a formal letter which he sent to Yamani, ordering his oil minister to make good on those promises. Copies of that letter were widely circulated at the time around the Embassy and in Washington. But Fahd's pipe dreams were never put into effect. Yamani refused.

Participation meant more money coming into the producing countries. It also meant compensation had to be paid out. To cover that, in January 1973, oil prices went up. The Saudis put another 15 cents per barrel on their crude. Abu Dhabi added 30 cents. Then the Iranians upped their prices, and before long Kuwait and Qatar raised their prices too.

Throughout 1973 confusion was still the order of the day. The Libyans took 51 per cent shares in certain oil companies and nationalized others. The Nigerians got 35 per cent of their Shell-BP concessions. And Iraq nationalized the Exxon, Mobil and Royal Dutch shares in the Basrah Petroleum Company. Before the year ended, Kuwait moved towards 51 per cent participation . . . a full nine years before the promised 1982 deadline. In light of that, Opec announced that 51 per cent participation under the present schedule was insufficient and unsatisfactory.

'At the beginning of the 1970s,' Yamani explains, 'the producers stepped in to be partners with the oil companies in determining the price of oil. We had the Tehran Agreement and then we had the Tripoli Agreement and then we raised the price of oil together with the companies. But it was only for a brief period because so many things changed. We felt the time had come for us to renegotiate.'

New talks were opened in Geneva and were due to be continued in Vienna.

That's when the October War broke out.

'The oil companies believed they could not work as a buffer element between the producers and the consumers. The political events and the supply and demand picture made the producers much stronger than before. Now they could dictate prices. If the oil companies accepted to raise prices with the producers to a level higher than what the consumers would accept, then they'd be in trouble. So the oil companies decided to withdraw. They would not cooperate. That merely encouraged the producers to decide on the price of oil themselves. I am convinced that the price increases would have happened even without the war. It was only a matter of time. The war simply accelerated the event. But there was no doubt that a new era had begun.'

6

The First Oil Crisis

THE YEAR kicked off well, with the signing of the Vietnam Cease Fire Agreement and the first American POWs coming home from North Vietnam.

But on 7 May 1973, in a bold-faced lie to the American people, Richard Nixon categorically denied all knowledge of the 'second-rate' burglary at the Watergate.

Three months later – to the day – a Federal investigation was opened on allegations, with possible criminal overtones, that Vice-President Spiro Agnew had taken a $10,000 bribe.

On 2 September, presidential adviser Henry Kissinger completed the successful mini-coup which sent Secretary of State William Rogers into retirement and moved Kissinger from the White House to the big office at State.

On 6 October, Egyptian troops stormed across the Suez Canal and Syrian troops invaded the Golan Heights.

Four days later Agnew resigned in disgrace.

Six days after that, as Israeli tanks crossed the Suez and the British called for a ban on all arms sales to the Middle East, the Nixon administration announced a $2.2 billion arms sale to the Israelis.

Within 24 hours, Arab producers cut oil supplies to the rest of the world, claiming the embargo would last until Israel withdrew from the occupied territories.

On 22 October, a United Nations proposal for a ceasefire was agreed by Israel, Egypt and Jordan, although it was marred by frequent violations on all sides.

On 6 December, Gerald Ford was appointed Vice-President of the United States and would, within a matter of months, become America's only never-on-an-election-ballot President.

One week later, in a bid to help conserve fuel, British Prime Minister Edward Heath called for the three-day work week.

And ten days after that, on 23 December, Iran announced that the price of Persian Gulf oil was being doubled.

1973 was one helluva year.

*   *   *   *

As far as Zaki Yamani is concerned, oil and politics have always gone hand in hand.

It was that way for the Arabs under colonial rule.

It was that way once they achieved their political independence.

But until October 1973 none of the Arab states had ever really managed to convince anyone else of that.

Now the world was different.

In the six years since the June War there had been both an overwhelming change in the structure of the oil industry plus a growing dependence of the world's economies on Middle Eastern oil. The Arab–Israeli conflict sharply focused the world's attention on the Middle East. The Arabs found themselves uncharacteristically united in cause. And on 17 October 1973, when the Arab oil ministers finally reached for the oil weapon, this time it worked.

Although these days Yamani objects to the use of the word 'weapon'.

'Why do you refer to it as the oil weapon? Why don't you think of it the way we did, as a political instrument? A weapon is used to hurt people. A political instrument is used to make a political point and hopefully effect political change. We did not believe in the use of oil as a weapon because we knew that this was not the best way for true cooperation with the west, notably the United States. But King Faisal saw American policies in the Middle East as being so very one-sided. He said to the west on several occasions that he wanted the United States to negotiate on Israel's behalf to find a solution to the Palestine situation and the Israeli occupation of Arab territories seized in the June War six years previous. Oil as a political instrument was saved as a last resort measure only to make that happen.'

In September 1972, in a speech to the Middle East Institute in Georgetown, Yamani suggested that by 1980 his country could be pumping 20 million barrels per day and that it would be more than enough to satisfy even the thirstiest American requirements. His point was, Saudi Arabia might be willing to assure a steady supply of oil to the States if in return he could obtain from the United States an exemption from oil import levies, a privileged status for Saudi investments and access to oil activities downstream.

It was heralded by the oil press as a unique proposal worth considering.

However, as Ian Seymour of the *Middle East Economic Digest* explains, 'This never to be repeated offer met with a surprisingly luke-warm reception in Washington, where officials made it clear that such a deal would be politically unacceptable in the form proposed and the matter was never followed up.'

Still, that oblique reference to the economic might of a nation which could produce 20 mbd was supposed to serve as an early hint that Saudi Arabia understood how to mix oil and politics.

A couple of months later, when Yamani was interviewed by *Newsweek*, he reinforced the idea that it was due time the United States realized his country held a special position in western economic affairs. 'Don't forget that Saudi Arabia has the jewel in its hand'.

His spoken message was, with its enormous oil reserves and production capabilities, Saudi Arabia could, if it wanted to, guarantee stability in the market.

Left unsaid was, Saudi Arabia could just as easily destabilize the market if it had due cause.

In that interview, Yamani was asked straightforwardly about the potential threat of the oil weapon. His answer carried a between-the-lines warning. 'We do not believe in using oil as a political weapon in a negative manner. We think that the best way for the Arabs to use their oil is as a foundation for real cooperation with the west, mainly the US. We think of using Arab oil positively rather than negatively.'

Alongside that interview, *Newsweek* published a general feature on Saudi Arabia, noting that the kingdom was 'now ready to assume first-class citizenship in the Arab world'.

To which they added, 'and the man responsible for that is Sheikh Yamani'.

On the same day the *Newsweek* interview appeared, the highly informed and well-respected *Petroleum Intelligence Weekly* published an interview with Yamani's Deputy Petroleum Minister, Prince Saud ibn Faisal – the king's son.

A handsome man with a black goatee, a black moustache and his father's piercing eyes, Prince Saud was born in the kingdom in 1941. Western educated, he earned an economics degree from Princeton. When he returned with his diploma in the mid–1960s, the king called Yamani into his office and said that he wanted Saud to work for him.

'But,' the king added, 'no favours'.

So Yamani gave Prince Saud a job in the outer office, as one of several assistants in the ministry's secretariat.

Some months later, at a Petromin board meeting, with the junior assistants sitting at the far end of the room, a sensitive matter came up which Yamani decided was not for the ears of his secretariat. He asked them all to leave. Without any hesitation, the king's son joined the others and left the room.

'That's the way Faisal raised his children,' comments one of the men who was there that day. 'Prince Saud did not eventually become Deputy Petroleum Minister simply because he was royal. Faisal insisted first that he learn how to do the job. And the old king knew that the best place in the world to learn everything about the oil business was under Yamani's wing.'

Today Prince Saud is Saudi Arabia's Foreign Minister and clearly the most influential of Ibn Saud's grandsons. He is often considered to be the brightest, most competent man in the government. Articulate, western-wise, shrewd and charming, he inherited much of his father's bearing and manner.

During those years under Yamani's wing, he also inherited his master's touch for dealing with the press.

Saud told *Petroleum Intelligence Weekly*, 'You always hear that you can't separate oil from politics. I simply do not see why not.'

Taken as a whole, and with the benefit of hindsight, their public statements seemed to be casting the die.

And the Saudis were not alone.

On 6 January 1973, the Kuwait National Assembly unanimously passed a recommendation that oil be used as a political weapon against Israel. The parliament called on other Arab countries 'to freeze all existing oil agreements with western companies the moment the armed struggle against the Zionist enemy is relaunched'.

Somewhere towards the middle of the month, the White House appeared to take some notice. John Ehrlichman, Nixon's chief domestic aide – soon to emerge as a major conspirator in the Watergate scandal – scheduled a trip to the Gulf. Evidently someone in the White House was hoping that Ehrlichman could somehow mollify the Saudis and all this oil weapon talk would go away.

James Akins, then on loan to the White House from his job at the State Department as Director of the Office of Fuels and Energy, contacted Aramco's Mike Ameen, asking him in confidence to hand deliver a message to Yamani. Ehrlichman's trip was to be kept top secret. The State Department would not be advised of it. As long as Kissinger was directing the nation's foreign policy from his White House office anyway, his people saw no reason at all to play by the State Department's rules. At least, not until Kissinger actually got the Secretary's title to match his already assumed responsibilities. Akins wanted to be certain that Yamani arranged audiences for Ehrlichman with Faisal and the Saudi Minister of Finance. Akins wanted Ameen to tell Yamani it was very important that he take Ehrlichman under his wing and see to it that Ehrlichman was given the message, 'We Saudis love you people but your American policy is hurting us.'

At the same time, John O'Connell, a senior vice president with Bechtel – where Treasury Secretary George Shultz had been his boss – approached Socal to see if Aramco would brief him on the Middle East situation as the oil companies perceived it. Because Bechtel has long had heavyweight financial commitments throughout the area, O'Connell was keen to be sure that his interests there were protected. Aramco chairman Frank Jungers cabled Socal's Middle East director Jones McQuinn in San Francisco with all the information anyone would want to know.

Oddly enough, Jungers prefaced the information with the sentence, 'Briefing material, which follows, should be typed on plain paper with no attribution or Aramco identification.'

In the cable, Jungers made reference to Anwar Sadat's mid–1972 expulsion of Soviet advisers from Egypt. Labelling it an attempt to bring about a peaceful resolution to the dispute with Israel, Jungers observed, 'USA, paralyzed by excesses of presidential campaign, was unable (or unwilling) to take advantage of what was probably most promising opportunity for resolution of this problem since the establishment of state of Israel 24 years earlier.'

Then he outlined current events. 'Syria is escalating its press attacks on USA. In Baghdad recently, President Bakr addressed a seminar on use of oil as weapon and said, "We can now use Arab oil in all our battles against our imperialist enemies." International conference of Arab trade unions in December called for complete economic boycott of USA and urged Arab governments to begin destroying and striking at American interests throughout Arab world. Economic Council of Arab League met in Cairo last month to discuss use of Arab oil as weapon against USA and an Egyptian newspaper called for Arab people to adopt attitude of "positive hostility" toward US interests and US individuals throughout Arab world.'

Acknowledging that similar situations had in the past been largely ineffectual, Jungers felt that pressures for Saudi Arabia to change its pro-US policy were strong and growing even stronger. 'Last September, Petroleum Minister Yamani made a bold and imaginative proposal for what would amount to a special economic relationship between Saudi Arabia and USA. It took considerable political courage for Yamani to make such a proposal and although he has been severely criticized for it in other Arab states, he has repeated it and clarified it several times.'

However, Jungers felt the Saudis could resist whatever pressures the Arab world levied against them unless there should be a renewal of the Arab-Israeli war or if an over-reaction by the Israelis was followed by some blatantly pro-Israel response by the United States.

'If either of these things should happen, it is possible that Saudi Arabia might be forced to decide to cut off oil exports to USA and Western Europe. With financial reserves amounting to three or four years' annual income, Saudi Arabia is quite capable of doing so and surviving, if driven to it by us and Israeli actions.'

According to a very reliable source, O'Connell passed that message on to Shultz, who then circulated it to 'the proper authorities'. One assumes that means the White House – perhaps to Richard Nixon or more likely to Henry Kissinger – or at the very least to William Rogers at the State Department.

No action was taken.

In March, the Emir of Kuwait called a press conference and publicly restated his country's policy. 'When the hour comes, we will use our oil as a weapon against Israel. That is our irrevocable position.'

His warning was published in the United States.

No action was taken.

In April, Faisal dispatched Yamani and Saud to Washington to convey a very specific message. The king wanted the top American officials to know, 'We would like to cooperate with you. We are friends. But you must do something for the Arab-Israeli conflict. You must make a move. Do not allow it to stay like this. The status quo is not acceptable to us. You must do something to resolve the conflict, otherwise we will be forced to withdraw our cooperation with you and use oil in this dispute.'

The status quo as both Yamani and Faisal perceived it was the Nixon administration's continued indifference to the Middle East conflict.

Yamani and Saud met separately with George Shultz, William Rogers and Henry Kissinger. They very carefully explained the situation to each of them. They relayed the king's message and were well received by Shultz and Rogers.

Kissinger's reaction, however, struck Yamani as being most odd.

'He was only concerned to know if I'd talked about this with any other officials. I said yes, Shultz and Rogers. He wanted to know what I said to them. I answered, exactly what I'm telling you. Then he asked me not to discuss it with anyone again. It was obvious that he didn't want anyone to know about my talks with them. I left the White House with the impression that the message I had conveyed to Kissinger would not reach Nixon. He seemed more concerned with hiding my talks and watering down my message than with what I had to say.'

Just before Yamani left Saudi Arabia, King Faisal specifically asked him not to have any contact with the American press. But the meeting with Kissinger worried Yamani so much that he took a decision against Faisal's wishes. 'I leaked the reason for my visit and the message I had come to deliver to the *Washington Post*.'

The following day, Yamani flew to London on board a Mobil Oil Company private jet.

As soon as they landed, a confidential memorandum from Aramco senior vice president, J. J. Johnston, who accompanied Yamani, was dispatched to the chief executives of the four Aramco parent companies.

It illustrated Yamani's concern for Saudi-American relations.

Johnston wrote, 'He [Yamani] said that he saw Kissinger and Shultz. He told us that his principal point to all of the officials that he talked to was the terrible danger in US policy . . . He said that there were many officials in Saudi Arabia already who were very much opposed to increases in production and for various reasons many of them were in favor of limiting production, some because they felt it was a wasting of the national asset, others because they felt it merely enabled the US to continue its present policy of support to an unfriendly State and just for this reason he was meeting a good bit of criticism . . . He had therefore said to all the officials he talked to that in the face of continued US policy the government might well, despite its desire to maintain good relations with the companies and with the United States, find it absolutely essential to limit production.'

By any other name, 'absolutely essential to limit production' sounded like the oil weapon.

That same day, the *Washington Post* printed the story that Yamani had come to town with a specific warning from King Faisal.

'The leaked story raised some interest,' Yamani says. 'Other journalists contacted the State Department to check on it. But when they were asked about my visit, the State Department spokesman replied, "Yamani doesn't represent the king's view or his country's view." The State Department said I was there representing my own personal view.'

In June, two journalists – one from the *Christian Science Monitor* and one from the *Washington Post* – came to Saudi Arabia. Yamani arranged a brief audience for them with the king.

Faisal repeated to them the same thing Yamani had said to Kissinger, Rogers and Shultz. 'We are friends and we want to cooperate with the United States, but unless you change your attitude and make it more even-handed regarding the Middle East, unless you start doing something to solve this problem, we're afraid we cannot continue our current policy of cooperation.'

Yamani claims that after the interview, over lunch with him, both journalists asked that he confirm what they'd heard through the

78

interpreter. He assured them the king's message was correctly translated.

Almost as soon as their stories were published, a State Department spokesman announced that the views expressed in those stories did not represent official policy in Saudi Arabia. Again they said these were Yamani's views.

A few evenings later Yamani was alone with Faisal in his office. It seems that the king enjoyed listening to the news from the BBC and the Voice of America. When he heard the State Department's disclaimer, he smiled and said, 'If I don't represent the official view of Saudi Arabia, who does?'

Some weeks later a CBS Television crew requested an interview with Faisal. Yamani encouraged him to accept the invitation in order once more to explain to the American public the official policy of Saudi Arabia.

The king did just that.

Says Yamani, 'It was only after CBS interviewed Faisal on camera and showed him saying those words that the State Department was forced to admit these were not merely the petroleum minister's personal views.'

Still the Nixon administration refused to believe that an embargo was a real possibility.

At least they didn't act as if they believed it.

James Akins, who eventually left the Office of Fuels and Energy at the State Department to become Ambassador to Saudi Arabia, claims to have been the only voice in the administration wilderness who saw that Faisal meant business.

'They weren't taking it seriously. They assumed that he was bluffing. I'd known Faisal a long time and I knew he didn't make idle statements. He'd made these statements from the very beginning of 1973. The first messages were sent through Yamani who made this point very explicitly to the American administration. It's not that Faisal was forced to do it. It was something he felt he had to do. He was an Arab leader and he felt that Arab issues were at stake.'

According to a former CIA executive, 'No one took James Akins' view of the situation seriously because none of it checked out. When reports came into the intelligence service they were verified with the Israelis who were supposedly more knowledgeable about the Middle East than any of us were. Our analysts got the usual assurances from the contacts that the CIA maintains. The Israelis assured us there was nothing to worry about.'

There are those who believe that Nixon didn't concern himself with the political ramifications of oil and the Middle East because all of this landed on him smack in the middle of the Watergate crisis and the President's brain was overloaded with his own survival.

Yamani is one who thinks that played a significant role. 'I saw the effect of Watergate on Nixon. Yes, I think his mind was elsewhere. I think he was too far gone into Watergate to care about anything else. At one point Prince Fahd, who was then Deputy Prime Minister, and I came to Washington together to try to reason with the Americans. We met with Nixon but he was very tense. Neither of us felt that we could deal with him. We both got the distinct impression that serious discussions with Nixon at that point would have been too difficult.'

Another school of thought has it that the administration's ambivalence derived from the miscalculated assumption that oil simply wasn't very important.

James Akins is among those enrolled here. 'Kissinger at that time wasn't very interested in oil. Neither Nixon nor Kissinger. For the whole administration it was too novel an idea. You couldn't get people to focus on it. We'd never done anything like that before. Furthermore, there were no problems. Everyone thought the price of oil was going down forever. Everyone thought there was a permanent glut of oil in the world.'

A third theory is that Americans have always had a tendency to believe that Saudi Arabia has no place else to go but west . . . that the Saudis couldn't and wouldn't ever turn to the Russians . . . that they have to depend on the Americans for defence and commerce. The conclusion therefore becomes, in the end there's no need to worry about them.

That idea comes from several sources, including Sir James Craig, a former British Ambassador to Saudi Arabia. 'The reason the Nixon administration did not heed Faisal's warning was because the Americans always took the attitude that Saudi Arabia was a staunchly anti-communist state and that, by definition, made it pro-American. The Americans believed that Saudi Arabia was safe.'

Akins agrees. 'That's frequently said about many countries. That's certainly true of Saudi Arabia. It's true of Jordan. It's true of Switzerland. It's true of Ireland. It's true of a lot of other countries.'

But James Schlesinger, a former US Secretary of Defense, Energy and head of the CIA, isn't convinced that's quite the case.

'That we don't have to worry about the Saudis because they have no place to go is a conviction that was surely not universal. It tended to be said by those who were pro-Israel for reasons of protecting Israel. Jim [Akins] puts it too forcefully, I think. He makes things that are ambiguous and grey seem clearly black and white. There was that sentiment around. But it was a partial sentiment. It was not, by and large, the universal sentiment. I don't think for a moment that Kissinger was guided by such a sentiment. I know full well that he wasn't. Kissinger's understanding was clearer than that. There was deep concern that the Saudis could go elsewhere.'

In fact, Schlesinger feels, the Saudis can, and to some extent have, gone elsewhere. 'They've distanced themselves from the Americans. More important than that, they cannot be seen to be associated with the Americans because it undermines their position in the Arab world and undermines the position of the royal family within the country. It's a very complex thing. To say they have no place else to go is clear overstatement because these things are shades of positions. By contrast, to say that they have a clear alternative to go to deal with the Russians is wrong, clearly wrong, too. It's a question of how they posture themselves and how willing they are to support us and collaborate with us and trust us. That's where they have to go.'

Yamani happens to believe that the 'can't go anywhere else' attitude did indeed play a role. 'Yes, I think it was one of a complex series of factors that led the Americans to take Saudi Arabia for granted up to October 1973. But after October 1973 they had to deal with us on another basis.'

If it is accepted that the Americans took the Saudis for granted, the question then is, was it Nixon? Or Kissinger? Or both?

Now Akins answers, 'It wasn't Nixon so much. Nixon's position was quite different from that of Kissinger. The point I made in my review of Kissinger's book, the second volume, is that Kissinger tells how Nixon wanted to move on peace in the Middle East, how he wanted to put pressure on Israel to withdraw, and how Kissinger very cleverly subverted Nixon. He was able to do this because of Watergate. This is an extremely revealing book. In fact, my conclusion in the review was that the real tragedy of Watergate is that we lost an opportunity for peace in the Middle East. It comes through very clearly how Nixon wanted to go in one direction and how Kissinger was able to frustrate Nixon. He was able to get away with it. Nixon had a very good understanding of the Saudis and a very good relationship with Faisal. I showed this review, by the way, to Nixon and asked him if this was essentially correct and he said, "Don't change a single word".'

* * * *

Running directly parallel to the Arabs' threatened use of the oil weapon was Opec's concern that oil prices were too low and that the Tehran/Tripoli Agreements should be abandoned.

Throughout the first few months of 1973 the market was hardening.

Prices were pushing against their imposed barriers towards an increase. A devaluation of the dollar in February adversely affected producers' incomes and by March they were demanding compensation from the oil companies for their exchange rate losses. The companies stalled as long as they could. But in the rising tide of Arab militancy they were forced to make a deal. In June an agreement was reached which redefined the formula Opec used to establish prices and oil was suddenly 12 per cent more expensive than it had been.

By September, with prices still edging up, Opec called for a renegotiation of the Tehran/Tripoli Agreements. The radical three – Algeria, Iraq and Libya – had been asking for just such a renegotiation since the dollar's devaluation. But Saudi Arabia and Iran would not agree.

Now, with world-wide inflation at 7–8 per cent, plus a huge increase in oil company profit margins far above those outlined in the original deal, Saudi Arabia decided something had to be done.

Iran held out.

So Yamani went to Tehran to convince the Shah and Dr Amouzegar that the time had come for new talks with the oil companies.

'By that point,' Yamani says, 'the Tehran Agreements were either dying or already dead. The world situation had changed in the two years since we had negotiated those agreements and they had to be extensively revised.'

The Shah and Dr Amouzegar were sympathetic to the idea, so the talks were reopened.

On 8 October, with the war two days old, the oil ministers of Saudi Arabia, Iran, Iraq, Kuwait, Qatar and Abu Dhabi met in Vienna to face a team of five men representing the oil companies. It was headed by Exxon's George Piercy and the Frenchman André Benard from Shell.

The oil ministers wanted to take the price from around $3 a barrel to twice as much.

Piercy and Benard tried to hold out for a 15 per cent increase.

Yamani came down to around $5.

Piercy and Benard went up to 25 per cent.

And there they sat, $1.25 apart.

'It was a very delicate moment,' Yamani says. 'Two very separate issues were at stake. One had political implications. That was the war and the question of oil as a political instrument. The other was the price of oil. The problem was that these two issues could be easily confused as being the same. I did not want to alienate the companies. I needed to keep them with us. I did not want to mix politics and oil prices.'

But that was easier said than done.

Piercy and Benard dug in to make a stand. They claimed that the market simply did not justify such severe price hikes.

The oil ministers found themselves entrenched on the other side. They claimed that the current prices were much too low and that, because the game had changed, the rules needed to be changed too.

Having seemingly reached an impasse the meeting ground to a halt.

Yamani stayed on another two days, urging the oil companies to improve their offer.

Dozens of telexes from Piercy and Benard were fired off to London and New York.

But just after midnight on October 12, when no further instructions were forthcoming, the two men went to Yamani's suite at the Intercontinental to ask for a postponement. They told him they could do nothing more at this point.

By dawn Yamani was gone.

When Opec met four days later in Kuwait, the six Gulf oil ministers took it upon themselves unilaterally to raise the price of oil by a staggering 70 per cent, to $5.12.

Not quite a dozen years into Yamani's ministry, the oil producers had permanently reversed the trend.

'I realized the political and economic impact of the date as soon as it happened,' says Yamani. 'For the first time the producers faced the consumers of the major industrialized countries without anyone in the middle. October 16 was the demarcation. It was the day that Opec seized power. The real power.'

7

The Embargo

WHEN WAR broke out, Yamani was in Geneva.

'In the beginning we didn't know who took the initiative. We were concerned. When we discovered that the Egyptians and the Syrians started this, we were enthusiastic. We all wanted to know the outcome.'

That's when Yamani put two and two together and decided that Faisal knew all along about the Egyptian plans for the war.

Sadat visited Saudi Arabia in August 1973 and had a very long and private audience with the king.

After such meetings in the past it was not uncommon for Faisal casually to mention to Yamani what topics were discussed. Often he'd ask Yamani's advice. At other times it was just a question of having someone to talk to.

This time Faisal appeared to be a man with a serious concern.

And this time Faisal said nothing.

According to Saudi protocol, Sadat was accompanied during his stay in the country by Hisham Nazer, who was then the Minister of Planning. When Sadat left the king's office to return to his guest palace, he turned to Nazer and confided, 'After a meeting with King Faisal, you feel as if someone has taken part of the burden off your shoulders.'

A couple of weeks later Yamani went to tell the king that he was leaving the next day for a conference in San Francisco.

Faisal kept silent. He stared at Yamani as if he were debating whether or not to tell him something.

Yamani reminded him, 'I have to leave tomorrow.'

The king asked, 'When do you come back?'

Yamani said, 'Immediately after the end of the conference.'

Again Faisal kept silent.

Realizing that something must be bothering the king, Yamani asked, 'Shall I go or not?'

Faisal thought about it for the longest time before he said, 'All right go. But come back quickly.'

In all their years of friendship, Faisal had never acted like that before.

The day after Yamani left for the States, the king called for his son, Saud. He wanted to know, 'When is Zaki coming back?'

Saud said, 'I don't know. Do you want me to cable him or call him and ask when he's coming back?'

Faisal thought again for a long time, then said, 'No, don't do that.'

In all their years of friendship, Faisal had never done that either.

As soon as Yamani returned, Saud told him about his father's concern. Yamani immediately went to see the king. He asked, 'Did you want me for anything?'

But Faisal said, 'No. Not now. Maybe later.'

Within a few days of his return from San Francisco, Yamani was scheduled to go to Vienna to chair the Opec ministerial committee meeting where the renegotiation of the Tehran/Tripoli Agreements was to be discussed.

As was his custom, he went to see the king to say that he was going to the meeting.

Now Faisal answered, 'Send somebody else.'

Yamani tried to explain that he couldn't send someone else because only a minister can preside over this committee. He reminded the king, 'If I don't appear it might seem as if Saudi Arabia wasn't anxious to see the agreements revised and that would be very serious for the negotiations.'

Faisal understood and nodded, 'All right, go.'

But it was very clear to Yamani that he didn't want him to go. 'He wanted me to stay at home. He knew something was about to happen.'

As it turns out, Faisal did know about the plans for war. Sadat made the trip in August specifically to tell Faisal where and how . . . although he did not say when.

Dr Ashraf Marwan, President Nasser's son-in-law and now a London-based businessmen, was head of Egyptian Intelligence and the only other person in that meeting with Sadat and Faisal. 'It was important that King Faisal be kept informed because he was the most respected, most important ruler in the Gulf. My own father-in-law fought a war with King Faisal in the Yemen and the two men were enemies. But President Nasser never ceased to respect King Faisal. So it was only natural that President Sadat confer with Faisal to tell him what was planned. But we did not tell the Saudi Arabians when the war would start. It wasn't that we feared the Saudis would inform the Americans and that word would get back to the Israelis. No. There just wasn't any reason to reveal anything more than that the war was planned. President Sadat told King Faisal it would happen soon, very soon, but he did not say when.'

As Arab jubilation dissolved into a second humiliation, Yamani came to realize the time was fast approaching when Saudi Arabia would have to act.

'The Arabs, especially the Palestinians, have always talked about using oil as a political weapon, as a means of punishing the west. I knew that the Arab oil producers would meet to discuss what they wanted to do. You know, how they wanted to use oil as a weapon or a political instrument or whatever it was to be. I knew I had to be prepared. I had to engineer something.'

In Vienna he met separately and secretly with two of his colleagues. One of them is still in the Ministry of Petroleum. The other is an Egyptian working for the Kuwaitis. He gave them both his view that, if the Arabs were going to use oil as an instrument to drive their points home to the west, the best way was jointly to reduce their level of production right away. Then every month, they could reduce it again by 5 per cent. His idea was to create a climate for world public opinion to give the world time to think about this dispute between the Arabs and the Israelis.

'I spoke with the two of them in confidence and I am positive that neither of them ever revealed anything. You can imagine how amazed I was then to read in the International Herald Tribune, two days before we met in Kuwait, exactly what I had said in my Vienna hotel room. It meant that my room was bugged.'

He's asked, by whom?

He answers, 'I don't know.'

He's asked, whom do you suspect?

And he shrugs, 'Does it matter?'

If he sounds a bit blasé about such things, it's probably because over the years there's been a lot of surveillance activity aimed at him. In fact, since the late 1970s his personal security staff includes a debugging expert.

Without saying that electronic eavesdropping is more likely to happen in the west than it is in the Middle East, he insists it takes place in the west more consistently than most people realize. And he can't deny that he has always expected to be bugged while in the United States.

Hotels are where most of it happens because it's so easy to arrange. His security staff have found microphones and transmitters hidden in everything from dressers to huge bouquets of flowers sent to Yamani with the manager's compliments. The most annoying occurrence was the night someone in a nearby building beamed a laser listening device on him. Something wasn't working correctly and the windows in Yamani's suite rattled and buzzed all night, keeping him awake. In a hotel, which he refuses to name, he notes the bugs are actually built into the wall. And because hotel switchboards are easily tapped, he uses a portable scrambler whenever he wants to discuss really sensitive information over the phone.

He's convinced the best weapon he's got against any type of surveillance is the knowledge that it's happening. 'I have to be philosophical about it. When you're in public life these things happen. You have to accept that and learn to live with it.'

Being bugged doesn't necessarily matter to him now and didn't particularly matter to him then. But where the oil weapon was concerned, the behaviour of the more radical Arabs has always mattered a great deal.

'I knew that the radicals, Iraq, Libya, Algeria and Syria, were about to call for something very destructive. So I went to Faisal with my proposal. Immediate joint reductions of 10 per cent and then 5 per cent per month. I told him it would lead to a specific reaction in the west but that it wouldn't harm the west. I told him it would only be enough to create a new climate. And he immediately accepted it. I remember it didn't take him one minute to say yes.'

As ruler of a nation that considers itself leader of the Moslem world, Faisal never left any doubt about his anti-Zionist feelings or his obligation to Islam. As protector of the holy cities of Mecca and Medina, he was also protector of the third most holy spot in Islam – Al Aqsa, the Dome of the Rock mosque in Jerusalem.

Now that was in the hands of the Israelis.

Because of the war, Arabs were united in spirit. But they also found themselves joined together by oil in a sellers' market. Using oil as a weapon seemed a more viable proposition now than at any other time in the past.

Of course Faisal and Yamani both knew that if, for whatever reason, the oil weapon didn't work or wouldn't work, face would be lost. So the game was not without its risks.

Faisal also feared that American indifference to the Arab cause might be enough of a catalyst to drive certain Arab extremist leaders into the hands of the Russians. And the one thing he dreaded more than an American stand for Israel's rights was a communist foothold in the Middle East.

All of those factors came into play, in varying degrees, during a meeting with the Aramco chairman on 3 May 1973. Frank Jungers was paying a courtesy call on the king when Faisal lectured him about American policy in the Middle East.

According to Jungers' classified notes, 'He [Faisal] went to great lengths to explain his predicament in Middle East as staunch friend of U.S.A. and how it was absolutely mandatory USG [the United States Government] do something to change the direction that events were taking us in the Middle East today . . . He emphasized he was not able to stand alone much longer. He barely touched on the usual conspiracy idea but emphasized that Zionism and along with it the Communists were on verge of having American interests thrown out of the area . . . (and that) a simple disavowal of Israeli policies and actions by the USG would go a long way toward overcoming the current anti-American feeling.'

Jungers concluded, 'The tone of this meeting, as contrasted with other discussions with him on this subject, was not of belaboring the Israel/Zionist/Communist problem but rather a well-reasoned and clearly stated one of extreme urgency that something be done to change the course of events. He kept emphasizing that it was up to us as American business and as American friends to make our thoughts and actions felt quickly.'

It's obvious now that Faisal was making the same mistake that all the Arabs frequently made before October 1973.

As any number of historians have since pointed out, up to then the Saudis were convinced that America could solve the Israeli problem with just one sentence.

All it would take, the Saudis decided, was for the United States to say, 'No more money for Israel.'

They honestly believed this 'one-sentence-solution' was a viable possibility.

That, in turn, made America's refusal to utter the one sentence look as if America was not only siding with the Israelis against the Arabs, but at the same time saying to the Arabs, we will not help you.

October 1973 was when that began to change.

By the time the oil crisis had run its course, the Saudis at least had come to understand that the question of Israel, of Arab lands and of Palestine was not merely an international issue for America, it was a domestic one as well.

'Faisal was understandably disturbed about the American attitude,' Yamani explains. 'He kept saying this to me several times after he sent me on that mission to Washington. About one month later, I remember, I was meeting in Geneva with the Middle East directors of the American oil companies that made up Aramco. Faisal was on his way back to Saudi Arabia from Paris and stopped in Geneva. So I arranged a meeting for the Americans. He told them precisely, inform your government that if they don't move, if they don't become active in trying to find a Middle East settlement, their interests will be harmed.'

In other words, Faisal was now threatening nationalization.

Yamani denies it. 'No. I don't think he was doing that at all. He was simply telling them, don't take us for granted. He was very friendly. He said, please convey to your government in Washington DC that we are friends and want to be friends forever. But the situation in the Middle East is becoming very critical. Washington has to move so that we can continue our oil policy on a friendly basis. Otherwise, don't blame us. These were his words.'

Well, sort of.

The meeting took place on 23 May 1973.

Among the Americans present were Jungers of Aramco, Al DeCrane of Texaco, C. J. Hedlund from Exxon, H. C. Moses from Mobil and Jones McQuinn from Socal. Among the Saudis present was Prince Sultan, who frequently travelled with the king.

Confidential notes transcribed after the session reveal that Faisal said, 'Time is running out with respect to US interest in Middle East, as well as Saudi position in the Arab world. Saudi Arabia is in danger of being isolated among its Arab friends because of the failure of the US Government to give Saudi Arabia positive support, and that HM is not going to let this happen. "You will lose everything".'

So the oil concessions were clearly at risk.

Or at least the Americans believed they were, because as a group they decided, 'Things we must do (1) inform U.S. public of their true interests in the area (they now being misled by controlled news media) and (2) inform Government leaders.'

With their commercial interests on the line, the four Aramco partners did what most people do when the heat is turned up.

They started to sweat.

One week later, Messrs DeCrane, Hedlund, McQuinn, Moses and Johnston made the rounds of the White House, the State Department and the Department of Defense. They were in Washington to sing Faisal's song.

While their reception was described as 'attentiveness to the message and an acknowledgement by all that a problem did exist', the official Aramco report of those meetings revealed that there was also 'a large degree of disbelief that any drastic action was imminent or that any measures other than those already underway were needed to prevent such from happening'.

To begin with, they never got to the really heavy guns. They didn't see Kissinger or the President. At each stop they were farmed out to senior underlings.

The State Department's man in charge of Middle Eastern Affairs assured them that his information contradicted theirs.

A White House military adviser explained that Saudi Arabia had faced much greater pressures from Nasser than they apparently faced now and had handled them successfully then and should be equally successful now.

The Acting Secretary of Defense – an interim appointee awaiting James Schlesinger's arrival – assured them that Faisal needed America and their fears were unfounded.

A CIA official told them, 'Faisal is bluffing.'

The Aramco conclusion was, 'Some believe His Majesty is calling wolf when no wolf exists except in his imagination. Also, there is little or nothing the US Government can do or will do on an urgent basis to affect the Arab/Israel issue.'

In June, the Bunker Hunt Oil Company was nationalized by the Libyans and Anwar Sadat called it 'the beginning of the battle against American interests in the Middle East'.

Then the governor of the Emirate of Abu Dhabi announced, 'We will not hesitate to use oil in the fateful battle.'

Then the Vice-President of the Command Council of the Iraqi revolution announced, 'An armed conflict would set oil ablaze.'

And then the US State Department announced, 'The Saudi threats do not worry the United States.'

To drive Faisal's points home – or if nothing else, to appease the Saudis – Mobil bought a large ad in the *New York Times*. The gist of it was that America depended on Saudi Arabian oil but that US–Saudi relations were deteriorating and would continue to do so unless the US really pushed for a settlement in the Middle East. If not, the ad warned, 'Political considerations may become the critical element in Saudi Arabia's decisions.'

Taking a lower-profile approach, Exxon sent Howard Page, the senior executive they considered to be their Middle East expert, to deliver a speech to the Alumni Association of the American University in Beirut.

While Socal mailed a letter to all their shareholders, stressing the point, 'There now is a growing feeling in much of the Arab world that the United States has turned its back on the Arab people.'

On 27 August, an Aramco executive called on Yamani in Dhahran to discuss recent media coverage and King Faisal's continuing interest in changing US policy. The confidential memorandum of that meeting pointed out, 'His Majesty's answers to questions posed by *Newsweek* were written by Yamani.'

Furthermore, the memorandum stipulated, 'The king feels a personal obligation to do something and knows that oil is now an effective weapon. He is additionally under constant pressure from Arab public opinion and Arab leaders, particularly Sadat. He is losing patience and "often nervous".'

To indicate Faisal's preoccupation with the problem, the Aramco official wrote that the king had been asking Yamani to give him detailed and periodic reports on Aramco's production, expansion plans and the expected impact of curtailed production on consumers in the US.

'He has asked for example, "what would be the effect if Aramco's current production were reduced by two million barrels a day?" "This is a completely new phenomenon," said Yamani, "the king never bothered with such details." '

The Aramco official also reported that there were elements in Saudi Arabia which, 'for their own reasons', were trying to tell the United States that Saudi Arabia would not follow up on its threats. 'Reference here to Fahd's group.' There were also elements in the US which were misleading Nixon as to the seriousness of Saudi Arabia's intention. 'Yamani mentioned Kissinger. For that reason, the king has been giving interviews and making public statements designed to eliminate any doubt that might exist.'

On 2 September, NBC television interviewed Faisal.

The king told the American network, 'It is a serious worry to us that the United States is not changing its policy in the Middle East and continues to side with Israel. Such a situation affects our relations with our American friends because it puts us in an untenable position within the Arab world.'

When NBC asked if Saudi Arabia was planning to limit oil exports to the US, Faisal answered very plainly, 'America's complete support for Zionism and against the Arab world makes it extremely difficult for us to continue to supply the United States with oil.'

Three days later, in a press conference, President Nixon responded to Faisal, saying it was inappropriate to link US foreign policy towards Israel with Arab oil. 'We are not pro-Israel and not pro-Arab. We are not more pro-Arab than pro-Israel just because the Arabs have oil and Israel does not.'

On 6 October, the day war broke out, Faisal sent a message to Nixon asking the President to pressure Israel into a withdrawal from the occupied territories. Nixon instead resupplied the Israelis with whatever equipment had been lost in the first three days of fighting.

On 12 October, Faisal sent a second message to Nixon, this time warning him that Saudi Arabia could not stand on the sidelines if America continued to contribute to the hostilities against the Arabs.

The next day Nixon ordered an airlift to begin, further resupplying Israel.

On 15 October, Faisal tried one last time. He ordered his Foreign Minister to deliver a third message to Nixon, saying that if the Americans made some sort of gesture to limit the damage already done, it was not too late to save the Saudi position in the Middle East.

The Foreign Minister's appointment was scheduled for the 16th.

But reports were being received inside the White House that the Soviets were engaged in a massive operation of shipping arms to the Arabs. Afraid that a Russian stronghold in the area would endanger the balance of power in the area and oil imports to the US, Nixon and Kissinger decided that America's first priority was to restore equilibrium on the battlefield. Once the Israelis were up to strength again and able to hold off the Arab advances, then the United States would step in to arbitrate an end to the hostilities. Then and only then would the United States try to find a post-war solution to the problem.

The White House deliberately postponed the meeting with the Saudi Foreign Minister until the 17th.

Faisal took that as a personal insult.

Still he held out hope.

He gave his Foreign Minister permission to hold a press conference in Washington. He needed to be certain that the President understood the Saudi position.

However, these were difficult times in the United States. The mood of the American people was turning against the Arabs and their Russian silent-partners. True or not, it was all too easy to group them together. With even the slightest possibility of Soviet intervention, the concept of moderate Arabs and extremist Arabs flew out of the window. The mood of the American people was echoed by one journalist at the press conference who confronted the Foreign Minister by saying, 'We do not need your oil. You can drink it.'

The Saudi Foreign Minister answered, 'All right. We will.'

Faisal told Yamani, 'Go ahead.'

First there was the Opec meeting to deal with.

They gathered on 16 October at the Kuwait Sheraton.

The session lasted only a few hours.

With the renegotiation of the Tehran Agreements a dead issue, Yamani and Amouzegar voted with the rest of the cartel to raise the price of oil to $5.12.

That same afternoon the non-Arab delegates checked out of the hotel, leaving Oapec to have its turn.

The Embargo

On the morning of 17 October, the Iraqis demanded total nationalization of all American assets in the Middle East.

Now there were three separate issues. The price hike was one. A production cutback by Oapec members was another. The embargo was a third.

Concerned that the world would never believe these three issues were separate, Yamani was more determined than ever to see that the radical factions, especially the Iraqis, understood why they couldn't just nationalize all of the American assets in the Arab world.

We had to make them understand why the best thing was what we proposed. As you can imagine, it was very violent in that meeting.'

Voices were raised and tempers were lost.

'As usual,' Yamani sighs, although he insists that he never loses his temper. 'Unfortunately.'

'Why "unfortunately"?'

'Because sometimes if you lose your temper it helps. Not always. But sometimes it can clear the air.'

That morning the radicals held their ground, insisting that the group shut off America's supply.

Yamani held his ground too.

It was clear to everyone around the table that without Saudi Arabia there could be no effective action.

But then it was just as clear to Yamani that without Saudi Arabia the anger of the Arab states would be nothing but a joke in the west.

And he wasn't about to let that happen.

He spent the end of the morning lobbying the Kuwaitis and the other Gulf countries to assure himself that they were on his side. Then he turned his attention to the weakest link in the radical chain, the Algerians.

He spent that afternoon with them, alone, face to face. And before the day was finished he'd managed to convince them that the proposal to keep cutting back on production was a practical one.

That broke the ice.

Once Algeria agreed, the Syrians came along.

At the end of the day only the Iraqis were still holding out.

Pressured by the rest of the group, they withdrew.

The Iraqi delegation walked out and dissociated themselves from the meeting.

Act Two now began.

A decision was written to reduce oil production immediately by 10 per cent and then 5 per cent on a monthly basis thereafter, with the added clause that they would not reduce exports to friendly countries.

'We divided the world into friendly countries, neutral countries and hostile countries,' Yamani explains. 'But then, although we recommended an embargo, we left the actual decision for that up to each government.'

Yamani returned to Riyadh for the third and final act of the drama.

King Faisal would have to decide whether or not to go ahead with the embargo. And, at least according to Yamani, it was not necessarily a foregone conclusion.

'He was never anxious to impose an embargo against the United States. But Nixon didn't leave him any choice.'

Jim Akins, on the other hand, feels the embargo was always inevitable. 'He [Faisal] was not happy he had to do it but there was never any question about it. It was never debated. In fact, Faisal told me at one time that if he hadn't imposed the embargo the Saudi people would have strongly objected. Faisal made several statements about this. He said, we are producing more oil than we need. We cannot rationally absorb the income we have from this oil production. We're only doing this because you've asked us to. And we will not continue unless there is some progress in restoring Arab lands. He made that point over and over again. They were sorry to have had to impose the embargo but we were sending arms to Israel during the war. We were flying planes from Germany straight into the occupied Sinai with military equipment. This was considered a hostile act against the Arabs. Then Congress voted for a massive increase of aid to Israel and that was the last straw. It made the embargo inevitable.'

King Faisal announced the embargo by saying, 'In view of the increase of American military aid to Israel, the Kingdom of Saudi Arabia has decided to halt all oil exports to the United States of America.'

Both at the State Department and at the White House, Faisal's announcement was greeted with some surprise.

It seems that up to this point certain assurances were still being given to the US Embassy in Saudi Arabia by an 'inside and highly reliable' source close to the king.

Word was forthcoming that, while Faisal would of course have to make a verbal stand to satisfy his fellow Arabs, he would never do anything to harm the Saudi relationship with the United States.

Unfortunately for the United States, the information turned out to be unreliable. The source of it, according to an Embassy staff officer who was there at the time, turns out to have been the Minister of Interior, Prince Fahd.

By 22 October, all the other Oapec members had joined with Saudi Arabia in an embargo of oil to the United States. Holland was also added to the list because the Dutch steadfastly refused to condemn

Israel for the war and volunteers from the Netherlands were being openly recruited to fight for Israel.

Holland said, we will not pay blackmail.

Their stand won praise and respect from the Americans.

But not from Yamani. 'Rotterdam is a major market, filled with refineries. It's obvious that if they couldn't get any oil they'd be hurt. Business would stop. They knew that when they made their decision to act the way they did. But I don't necessarily respect them for their decision because I don't consider what happened to be blackmail.'

He calls it a legitimate political action and says, as a matter of fact, that Saudi Arabia learned how to implement an embargo from the United States. 'We watched America and learned how they use one's economic power to meet political objectives. We studied this carefully.'

Anyway, he goes on, 'The Dutch relationship with Israel was different from the rest of the European community's? So it wasn't even a question of their standing up against blackmail. There was inside political pressure at work. There was a group of politicians in Holland who, as we heard later, were emotionally affected by what happened in the Netherlands during the Nazi period. They were reacting to that. Frankly, I don't see how you can accept injustice inflicted by a person just because that same person was once subjected to the same thing. It does not justify what the Israelis were doing.'

The price rise, the production cutbacks and the embargo all happened at the same time, sending a shock through the industrialized world. The west needed to point a finger at someone and say, this is the villain. But, to accuse Opec was inaccurate. And to accuse Oapec got the less than satisfying response, 'It's not us, it's the Arab oil ministers acting independently.' So the world went looking for an Arab oil minister. And the cameras turned towards the most familiar face.

As the news magazines put it, this was suddenly the age of 'Yamani or Your Life'.

'Our mutual inclinations are western,' he kept repeating, trying to make some sense of it for the western media. 'Your interests and ours lie in working together for the betterment of all. We live together in the same world. We tried to make you see that you will have to meet us, the Arabs, half way. We tried to make you understand that perhaps if you do, we will all discover interesting things about one another and it will be a better world.'

But the media, especially as queues for petrol formed in the United States, weren't buying it.

As one columnist observed, 'Not since the Trojan war and the atomic bomb had a new war weapon been devised that was as devastatingly effective as the Arabs' use of their newly acquired oil power.'

Even now, Yamani feels the need to explain. 'You must understand that the production cutbacks and the embargo of oil to the United States were separate issues. The embargo was another type of political statement. It did not really imply that we could reduce imports of oil to the United States. You see, if oil from Saudi Arabia and all other Arab countries were to go everywhere except the United States, then someone else would compensate the United States for it. The world is really just one market. So the embargo was more symbolic than anything else.'

Totally symbolic, if you listen to Mahdi al-Tajir, the Bahrain-born, former United Arab Emirate Ambassador to the United Kingdom and today a leading Arab businessman in Europe and the United States.

'In 1973 there was a lot written and said about the Arabs trying to use the oil weapon to influence the United States and the rest of the free world. But you don't believe that, do you? Tell me where? Was there really an embargo? There was no embargo. There were no actual shortages. That was all said for local consumption. It was a lie we wanted you to believe.'

As far as Tajir is concerned, the only way oil could actually be used as a weapon is if the fields themselves were shut.

'You want to use oil as a weapon? You shut the fields. That's the only way. But that did not happen in 1973. How could you say there is an embargo when you deliver oil to the port knowing that you have no control over where it then goes? When you speak of an embargo without shutting the oilfields, then that is not a true embargo. It is nothing but a symbolic gesture.'

Perhaps, he says, the Arabs merely wished they could have used oil as a weapon. And maybe some day they will. 'I cannot find any reason why it might not happen one day. It will affect the producing countries more than the consumers because we don't have any other source of income to live. But it all depends on who is running the Arab countries in the future. Today you have the Iran–Iraq war. You don't believe for a moment, do you, that this war is going to come to an end and things will return to normal? Not in that region. We'd all be fooling ourselves to think, when the war ends, life there will be the way it used to be.'

8

Yamani's Shuttle Diplomacy

THE EMBARGO itself changed nothing.

Saudi oil originally destined for the United States and shipped elsewhere was merely replaced with oil rerouted from other destinations.

What hurt were the production cutbacks.

The lifestyle of every major industrial power was directly affected. Fissures came to light in the Atlantic Alliance. And the world's currency markets were thrown into a tailspin.

The Common Market, led by France, was the first to genuflect to the Arabs.

In November, the EEC adopted a joint policy 'strongly' urging both sides in the Middle East conflict to return immediately to the positions they occupied on 22 October. In other words, Israel should withdraw. They also proclaimed their mutual agreement that the peace settlement should be based on such points as the end to Israeli occupation of the territories seized in 1967, recognition of the sovereignty, territorial integrity and independence of every state in the area, plus the acceptance of the legitimate rights of the Palestinians.

Nor did the Japanese hesitate to kiss the ring.

Publicly acknowledging that Japan did not wish to offend the Arab states with its proclaimed neutrality – while privately in a desperate panic over the possibility of Arab oil supplies to the oil-dependent island being turned off – the Japanese appealed to Israel to withdraw, along the lines of the Common Market proclamation.

On 4 November, with the oil crisis having had no real effect on the American position towards Israel or the Israeli occupation of the seized territories, the Arab oil ministers tried again. They expanded the production cutback to 25 per cent. Only Iraq refused to abide by

97

the decision, still favouring nationalization of US and also of Dutch interests.

At the Saudi's insistence, however, the Arab oil ministers did not tar everyone with the same brush. Yamani wanted 'friendly' nations to receive the same amount of oil they'd been getting before the action. That would include Spain, India, Brazil, all the Arab states of the Middle East and North Africa, plus the Moslem states of Turkey, Pakistan and Malaysia.

Cut off would be the United States and Holland.

The rest of the world would be given a chance to prove themselves.

Because, as Yamani claims, the embargo coupled with the production cutbacks were first and foremost designed to be a force to sway public opinion, the Arab oil ministers figured that in order to sell their political motives they'd send a spokesman on the road. Now that they had the sinners' attention, they'd start preaching their sermon.

The natural choice for evangelist was Yamani.

The other ministers then decided that the Oapec president, Belaid Abdesselam should go along.

It was a good choice. As oil minister for Algeria, Abdesselam was in the radical camp, and so his presence helped to reinforce Yamani's views as the moderate course.

The tour kicked off in Paris and London.

In the French capital, where he and Abdesselam were welcomed warmly by President Georges Pompidou, Yamani made it clear that the chief purpose of his tour was to get the European countries to bring their full weight to force Israel to withdraw from the territories occupied since the Six Day War.

In the British capital, where he and Abdesselam were welcomed warmly by Prime Minister Edward Heath, Yamani wanted to drive home the point that oil was being used as an instrument for political purposes and not as a weapon to hurt anyone.

But he'd just spent the weekend in Geneva.

His two daughters and his son were going to school there. Whenever time permitted, he'd go to Switzerland to spend weekends with his children. They'd go shopping. They'd go to the movies. They'd go out for meals.

On that particular weekend, as an economy measure to save fuel, the Swiss had banned Sunday traffic.

He and his children had gone for a walk. With Christmas just around the corner they'd expected to find some seasonal joy on the streets. Instead they'd found downtown Geneva empty and still.

There were no cars on the streets.

The city was depressing and lifeless.

And it saddened him that this was one of the effects of the oil crisis.

So the next day, when he and Abdesselam arrived in London, Yamani said that he honestly hoped all of this would soon be finished. He said he wished Britain a happy Christmas and that he was sorry for the inconvenience the British were experiencing. 'I assure you that I was sincere in saying that.'

He said he hoped that the Israelis would soon realize the high price they were making the world pay for the illegal occupation of Arab lands.

He said, the Arabs merely wanted to do something to attract the attention of ordinary people and never wanted to go to the extreme.

However, for the British this could have easily been confused for the extreme.

In December 1973 all hell had broken loose at the same time.

The secondary banking crisis crashed down on the City, taking everyone by surprise. In one stroke it literally wiped out the UK real estate market. At the same time there was a miners' strike which cut off coal supplies to the country and soon forced Heath to declare the three-day work week. Throughout Britain electricity got turned off at odd times.

Sales of storm lanterns and candles boomed. Garbage piled up on the streets. Business ground to a halt. There was talk of fuel rationing. The government was about to topple.

Even though the oil crisis was a separate issue, the problems in Britain were so severe that Yamani saw a gesture was needed.

As a show of good faith he made an exception of the UK and promised that Saudi Arabia would restore the oil supply to Great Britain to the same level it had been before the embargo.

With the French playing up the Arab cause and the British sounding grateful, the tour was off to a promising start.

He and Abdesselam were grabbing all the front pages that Yamani had counted on.

Moving through the rest of Europe, like Hansel and Gretel dropping breadcrumbs to find their way home, they doled out exemptions to the cutbacks whenever a government acknowledged the Arab cause.

Belgium was reprieved because it issued a declaration in Parliament condemning Israel. It had a pipeline from Rotterdam to one of its inland refineries, so Yamani allowed oil to be shipped to that pipeline.

Next came the nine-nation Common Market.

Yamani and Abdesselam went to West Germany to meet with Willy Brandt.

Over a long discussion in the Chancellor's office in Bonn, Yamani found Brandt to be very pro-Israel. The West German leader, who had not yet won the Nobel Peace Prize, argued that the Jewish state had a right to exist. Yamani argued that the Palestinians also had a right to live like human beings.

Then Brandt compared the Palestinians to the Red Indians of North America. He said, 'There is nothing like a Red Indian nation. No one even talks about the Red Indians.'

Yamani answered, 'Maybe that's because the Red Indians are not lucky enough to be surrounded by a large group of nations that are of the same race and who want to help them. It might be different today for the Red Indians if they were.'

Brandt didn't agree with Yamani. 'I remember that discussion in Bonn having been an almost cordial exchange of views, even if I objected to the oil embargo being used as political leverage. The mentioning of the American Indians must have resulted in a misunderstanding. It was one of my general observations that the world has lived with highly disputable solutions on issues of borderlines and indigenous populations.'

Brandt did however use his considerable influence to appeal for complete European solidarity in dealing with the energy crisis. The EEC confirmed support for the United Nations resolution condemning Israel and calling for its immediate withdrawal from the occupied Arab territories.

Insists Brandt, 'My government wanted to be in accordance with United Nations' resolutions.'

West Germany's reward was one of those exemptions.

While this was going on the American attitude hardened.

Henry Kissinger and William Simon, the newly appointed Energy Czar, both went public with the sentiment, 'There is blackmail in the air.'

To counter that blackmail, Kissinger called for the industrialized nations to meet in Washington DC at the earliest possible moment. He wanted the oil-consuming west to make a united stand against the Arabs.

Although these days, just as he did then, Yamani insists blackmail was not the case. 'I don't believe this was blackmail. I'm not sure that Kissinger and Simon believed it either. But they're politicians and that was the word that suited them to use.'

Kissinger, now firmly entrenched at the State Department, scheduled the Washington Oil Summit for February.

While this was happening, James Schlesinger, as Secretary of Defense, turned his attention to the Saudi oilfields and the possibility of military intervention.

Not as surprising a concept as it may have seemed at the time, the

United Sates had contingency plans for that, just as they always have contingency plans for a variety of situations.

'The Arabs were pretty pissed at me,' Schlesinger points out, 'but if you go back and read my press conferences at the time you'll see that someone asked, if the President orders you to do so, can you seize the oilfields? To such a question I would answer, yes. Kissinger then got onto this business of "strangulation", if you recall. It was one of his geo-political observations. Something like, a great power cannot allow strangulation to occur by a lesser power without being prepared to take action. He told me to climb in behind him and the President and I was prepared to do so under those circumstances. But I don't think anyone else was serious about this.'

Yamani says he was told about the US Rapid Deployment Force and their plans to capture the Saudi oilfields either at the end of 1973 or the very beginning of 1974. 'I was very disturbed when I first heard about this because I knew it would be a disaster. Not only for Saudi Arabia but for the whole world.'

It seriously worried him that anyone could even suggest it. All the more so because he knew that desperate people sometimes do desperate things.

What he didn't know at the time was that the American military was crawling with soldiers who not only thought America could manage it, but were anxious to give it a try.

As one former high-ranking Defense Department official observes, 'The Naval War College was filled with Marine colonels walking around saying, we're going to put those Goddamned rag heads back on their camels. The oil crisis made the average American very angry, particularly the ones who had to stand on the gasoline lines. It increased the appreciation of the Arab role and raised their profile, yes. But it did not increase the regard for the Arabs in the United States. There were plenty of American GIs who were saying, this isn't Israel's fight, this is ours.'

In spite of that, Yamani is still persuaded that a campaign to take the Saudi oilfields would have been doomed to failure long before it began.

'An invasion of the oilfields would have been suicide. From a practical viewpoint it was impossible. It still is. If you know where the oilfields are, you know why. They are scattered in the desert with so many installations that you'd need a few hundred thousand troups to take them. Then if you wanted to operate the fields you'd need many thousands more. No, it could not have been done. It cannot be done now.'

What's more, he says, if anyone destroyed the fields instead of trying to run them, they'd be destroying themselves at the same time. 'It would be like a wife cutting off her nose to displease her husband. You couldn't afford to destroy the fields and you could never take the fields and run them.'

Naturally as soon as he heard about the plan, Yamani went to consult with Faisal.

He says he found his king just as convinced as he was that it could not be done.

'He said to me right away, if they try it they will fail. He knew they could not accomplish it. Frankly, I don't think the plan was taken too seriously by us because we knew the Americans also knew they couldn't do it. Frankly, I think it was just talk. You know, bravado.'

But Schlesinger disagrees. 'Bravado? No. I was prepared to seize Abu Dhabi. Something small. But nothing big. Militarily we could have seized one of the Arab states. And the plan did indeed scare them and anger them. No, it wasn't just bravado. It was clearly intended as a warning. I think the Arabs were quite worried about it after '73. Then the whole thing receded and all that was left was a kind of residual anger. I never detected any seriousness on the part of anybody. I was more willing to contemplate it than others were but it was never serious. Anyway, Zaki wouldn't have taken it seriously.'

As it turns out, according to a source in the Middle East, Faisal took it more seriously than Yamani suggests. Not only had he learned about the Pentagon's plans, he'd heard that the Israelis also had a contingency plan to take the oilfields. So he instituted top-secret precautionary measures, instructing the National Guard that in the case of an invasion they were to destroy specific sensitive targets. Once these sites were put out of commission, Saudi oil production would have dropped to the very bare minimum. It would then have taken an occupying power at least one year and perhaps as much as $5 billion to get the fields working again.

Having played Europe to packed houses, Yamani and Abdesselam brought their roadshow to the United States.

Abdesselam's role was by now very much reduced to being second banana.

Yamani was top of the bill.

Yamani was the man everyone wanted to meet.

He was already emerging as perhaps the most western-media-savvy Arab ever. He was a man with a message. He was also a man with enough natural talent and highly tuned skills to make certain that his message was widely heard.

They flew into New York and the press was waiting for him.

He refused to talk to anyone.

They went straight away to Washington where a TV interview had been set up. As far as he was concerned, Washington was where his mission was. That would be his first American interview.

Playing hard to get only made him more in demand.

Facing the cameras, smartly dressed in a dark suit, relaxed and confident, there was an awkward moment for him at the very beginning of the interview when he decided that the questions were specifically intended to antagonize him.

'I could see that they wanted to get me angry.'

But he kept his poise and stayed calm.

'I explained the situation as a friend. I even apologized for any inconvenience the crisis had brought. And you know what? The television people were very disappointed. I could see it on their faces. I later discovered that the interview was not televised. I can only imagine that they were trying to show the American public a specific type of Arab. You know, the backward Bedouins of the desert. I'm afraid they didn't get what they wanted.'

On the other hand, *Newsweek* did get what they wanted – a frank and open confrontation – for their Christmas 1973 issue. In a straight question-and-answer format interview, Yamani kept referring to the 'oil weapon', instead of using the softer, more palatable term he chooses today, 'political instrument.'

With that exception, he kept close to the script he had been using all year. He insisted that Saudi Arabia was very anxious to continue its cooperation with the United States but they now needed the United States to cooperate in solving the Middle East problem and bringing peace to the Arabs.

Newsweek: 'Isn't there a danger that nations suffering from your oil policies may be compelled to take some sort of desperate action?'

Yamani: 'This may be true if you think the Arabs intend to carry the oil weapon to the point where your economy will collapse. But short of this I don't think you would take such action. Because you know that we have a really strong weapon in our hands which we have not used and which we do not intend to use.'

Newsweek: 'If then you don't intend to do real damage upon the American or Japanese or the European economies, how can you expect the oil weapon to work?'

Yamani: 'Since the oil weapon is not intended to damage the others, only to draw their attention to our problems, I think we will use it in that context.'

Accompanying the interview was an in-depth feature on Yamani with the enticing headline 'Merely a simple Bedouin'.

The title came from Yamani's own description of himself.

In the piece, *Newsweek* explained that adjectives like brilliant, tough and awesome were frequently bestowed upon Yamani whose answer to such accolades was by now becoming something of a trademark. 'Flashing a Mona Lisa-like smile, his arms spread wide in mock supplication, he protests mildly, "But I am merely a simple Bedouin",'

The next paragraph began, 'Well, not quite.'

Not quite, indeed.

Newsweek found him 'The complete international sophisticate right down to his neat Cardin suits and his mod black boots. But anyone who got the impression that he is some sort of playboy of the Arab world is in for a rude shock. Yamani is a slick oil expert who knows his business cold.'

As far as *Newsweek* was concerned, he'd become 'the man of the moment'.

As far as the rest of the press was concerned, especially the Washington press corps, he was hounded and followed and trailed and photographed and quoted like a rock star.

His stay in the capital became a series of breakfasts, lunches, dinners and an endless round of cocktail parties. He met with the newly installed Vice President, Gerry Ford. He met with Henry Kissinger. He met with cabinet officers, Senators, Congressmen, diplomats, bankers and businessmen.

The printer's ink flowed.

High on his US success, in spite of the fact that he didn't convince the Nixon administration to denounce Israel, Yamani took his act to Japan.

By early 1973 the Japanese had heard the warnings that Washington seemed willing to disregard. They realized that by cutting off the oil supply the Arabs could effectively grind Japanese business to a halt.

Hoping to head the crisis off at the pass, the then Industry Minister Yasuhiro Nakasone visited the Middle East and paid his dues by kissing the various rings. When he returned home he announced for all the world to hear, 'I have become strongly aware of the need to approach Middle East oil not simply as a tradable merchandise but something more deeply politically involved.'

Oil, he didn't have to remind anyone, was then – and still is – a very critical resource for Japan. That's why, he said, the nation's oil policy could never be left to the whims of Japanese industry. It required the full involvement of the government. He even labelled the government's approach as 'petroleum diplomacy'.

Defining his nation's views, Nakasone said, 'The international oil situation is in a period of transition with producing nations seeking partners among consuming nations for long range oil contracts.

Establishment of a co-operative relationship between a group of the world's largest oil-producing nations and Japan, as one of the world's largest consuming nations, will have an important influence over the international oil scene.'

That, he obviously hoped, would placate the Arabs and ensure the oil did not get turned off.

But then the war broke out.

Suddenly the Arabs cast a foreboding eye on Japan's stated neutrality towards the Arab-Israel fight.

Believing that an embargo would ruin the economy and topple the government, the Japanese came up with a face-saving measure. Unable for whatever reasons, including all of the obvious ones, to get down on their knees and beg their Arab suppliers for mercy, they conceded that fence sitting would be an affront to the Arabs. So the Japanese cabinet took a fresh look at their stated neutrality where Israel was concerned.

They had oil reserves which would last 59 days but no one knew if that would be enough to get them through the crisis.

It seemed they had only two options.

They could listen to the United States and remain neutral, as America wished them to. But that would not assure them of any oil after their reserves ran out either.

Or, they could woo the Arabs, at the risk of American disfavour.

They made the easy choice.

They appealed to Israel to withdraw from the Arab lands.

When Yamani arrived in Tokyo he was greeted with full honours and received by the Emperor in a way usually reserved for a head of state.

He was given full coverage in the Japanese press. Some newspapers even produced special supplements during that week to lavish praise on him. And just so that no one missed the point, those supplements were heavily supported by advertising in a barefaced show by Japanese industry that they supported the pro-Arab side of the war.

It was, needless to say, a hasty and blatant attempt by an energy-dependent nation to curry favour with the man who, seemingly with the flick of a switch, could turn that imported energy off or on.

Even Yamani admits that, had there not been a crisis, he wouldn't have been received the way he was.

'I used to go to Japan almost on a yearly basis and until January 1974 I was never received by the Emperor. At that time the Emperor didn't receive anyone who wasn't a head of state or at least a head of government. It might be more common now but then it was highly unusual. It was, in fact, the first time that any Arab minister had ever been given such treatment.'

105

So the oil weapon – or, if he insists, oil as a political instrument – had scored again.

'Yes, Japan woke up to the Middle East. They were already interested because they depend heavily on oil imported from the Gulf. Now they were becoming involved in the problems we were having. So this was political. It was oil as a political instrument which created that atmosphere.'

In his speeches to the Japanese, Yamani played to his audience, not at all oblivious to the message his hosts were trying to get across to him.

He told them, 'Japan is in a position to have a continuous supply of crude oil from Saudi Arabia on a long-term basis.'

He told them they might be able to get around many of the current trade barriers if they were prepared, in return, to help with various economic development projects in Saudi Arabia.

He told them that King Faisal would move to reduce oil prices, but added, 'if the other five oil-producing nations in the Gulf were prepared to follow suit. We will discuss the matter with other members. We are not individualists and it would be premature to tell you how much prices might be reduced.'

With the Washington Oil Summit less than a month away, Yamani now made a deliberate point of trying to drive a splinter into the bond uniting the oil-consuming nations who would attend.

He announced in Japan, 'Some consumers now have a very strong individual interest in bilateral arrangements with producers. Japan is first and France, Britain and West Germany also have such an interest. Saudi Arabia is therefore prepared to enter into a dialogue with consuming nations.'

That enraged Henry Kissinger.

Yamani had struck a blow to the State Department's strategy of uniting the oil consumers and isolating the oil producers.

It also sent a wave through Opec's Economic Commission, which was in session at the time in Vienna. The members had only recently agreed to maintain prices at present levels until the end of March when the Economic Committee would produce its report on both short-term and long-term crude oil pricing. But here was Yamani suggesting that, if the Japanese, the British, the French or the West Germans wanted their own deal with the Saudis, anything was possible.

'That's true,' he comments. 'I was saying to France, Germany, Japan and England that we could make our own deals. I don't hide the fact that I wanted to split them away from the 13. But it had nothing to do with Opec because Opec has nothing to do with marketing. We were talking about bilateral commercial relationships. What was important

106

at that time was a secure source of supply. The Japanese for instance wanted to assure themselves that they would get so much oil from me. If I could give them that guarantee, that's what they wanted.'

In other words, Japan was being offered a sort of preferred nation arrangement.

'Yes. But don't forget there were two separate issues. On one hand we had the bilateral relationship between Saudi Arabia and Japan. I think that statement was related to this. Then we had the political issue which concerned the whole of the Arab countries. Where that bilateral relationship was concerned, we were looking for help from Japan to build an infrastructure in Saudi Arabia in exchange for our commitment to them to maintain the supply of energy. Where the Arab cause was concerned, we wanted Japan to say, yes Israel should give back the territories. All I wanted to do was explain to them that an announcement like that would put Japan in a different category.'

* * * *

It's a good bet that before 16 October, 1973, very few Americans, very few Europeans and very few Japanese had ever heard of Opec.

Fewer knew anything about Oapec.

And fewer still would have recognized Sheikh Yamani, even if he had come up to them on the street and introduced himself.

But a lot of things changed when that war broke out.

Opec and Oapec and especially Zaki Yamani became front-page news.

Edward Heath, who knew Yamani well during those years, says he was always impressed by him. 'He's immensely able, well balanced and had a grasp of the world situation.'

Feelings must have been mutual because on one occasion when Heath was in Switzerland to conduct an orchestra – a favourite hobby – and heard that Yamani was also in the country, Heath personally invited Yamani to come to the concert, and he did.

However, an interesting aside from Heath is that while he felt he could always deal with Yamani . . . 'perfectly well' . . . it's understood by politicians in the west that Yamani was 'below the salt' in Saudi Arabia. What Heath means is that westerners could not help but notice how Yamani was forever being reminded by certain members of the royal family that, in spite of his relationship with Faisal, he was not and would never be a member of the royal family.

Below the salt perhaps in Saudi Arabia.

But in the west it was different because, as long as Faisal was alive, there was never any doubt that whatever Yamani said was what the king would say.

As one Aramco official observed, 'Every time we had any sort of argument with Yamani while Faisal was alive, we'd want to go see the king. Everytime we asked for that, Yamani was always happy to arrange it. He knew what the king's reaction would be. He knew Faisal would always support him all the way because the two thought exactly alike.'

Someone else who knew Yamani during those days was Sir Alan Rothnie, the then British Ambassador to Saudi Arabia.

'When I first got there it was midsummer 1972. In those days Yamani had a tiny house next to the king's palace on what was then the seafront in Jeddah, although it's no longer on the seafront because there was a lot of fill-in. He'd already been in office 10 years. It was really only with the quadrupling of oil prices in 1973 that he became a figure on the world stage. And then he emerged as such a very important figure.'

It's fair to say that, until Yamani came along, the all-too-common attitude in the west was to consider the Mediterranean Arabs as the advanced ones and the Gulf Arabs as the backward, feudal Bedouins of the desert.

It's also fair to say, Yamani changed that.

He was viewed as the man responsible for seeing that the political decision to use Arab oil in the war against Israel was translated into effective action.

He thinks he changed some attitudes too. 'I believe I changed the image that the Arabs had in the west and especially in the United States, as savage, ignorant people. When I was talking to the Americans, I did not appear as a savage, nor as ignorant. This reflected on the so-called backward Bedouins of the desert.'

The instant he says that he's reminded of the 'I am just a simple Bedouin' quote.

He responds with a broad smile – much too polite to scream, you just won't let me live that one down. 'In reality, I came from that part of the world. I grew up there. I have my roots there. So maybe the Bedouins are not all that bad.'

But come on, he's told, you're hardly a 'simple Bedouin'.

He answers, 'I'm comfortable in the west. Very much so. I wear my Arabic clothes sometimes to relax in the west because they're more comfortable than western clothes. But I don't know, maybe if all Bedouins had a chance to live in the west they might grow as comfortable here as I am.' Then he pauses and the smile returns, 'You understand, we Bedouins are very adaptable people.'

* * * *

Kissinger's game plan was to confront the oil producers by grouping the oil-consuming nations into an organization which would protect certain commercial and financial arrangements. Collective negotiation with Opec was not ruled out but it would be postponed until the consumers' cartel had a chance to organize.

Set for 11–12 February, 1974, the guest list for the Washington Oil Summit included the nine EEC members, Canada, Norway and Japan, as well as the Secretary General for the Office of Economic Cooperation and Development.

If it accomplished nothing else, it certainly made the Arabs sit up and take notice.

'Of course we opposed it,' Yamani says. 'I personally opposed it violently. Kissinger was very disturbed by my attitude. He wanted to line up all the consumers, whether they be from the developed nations or the developing nations, to have a united front against Opec. There was no way that I wanted the meeting to take place because it meant putting the oil producers on one side against the whole world. I told the nations who planned to attend that this meeting would disturb us.'

If it appeared to Yamani that America might somehow rally the troops and find an effective way to stop the oil weapon from doing any more damage, that's pretty much what Kissinger had in mind. In his opinion, if the oil-consuming nations didn't do something, the world – and that would include the Arabs – could be plunged into an economic depression.

Because the west took this seriously, everyone who got an invitation showed up.

And perhaps something could have come of the meeting.

Except that the French representative, a minor-league politician named Michael Jobert, got in the way.

Setting the tone of France's cooperation with the other nations present, Jobert refused to speak in any language but French. English was to be the language of the meeting and as it happens Jobert speaks acceptable English. But he insisted on his right to speak French . . . the world is out of step with me . . . so delays occurred while translators and interpreters were arranged.

Then, when the United States proposed a joint effort to confront energy issues, Jobert found that his Common Market partners, who were in favour of the agreement, were again out of step with France.

Put to a vote, all of the conferees – except France – agreed to coordinate national policies in the conservation of energy and restraining demand, a system of allocating supplies during a severe shortage, support for national development of additional energy sources, plus the acceleration of energy research and development programmes.

Former British Prime Minister Lord Home, then Sir Alec who was serving as Foreign Minister, remembers the conference. 'Jobert was rather apt to do what he did. I'd been at a number of conferences with him at which he'd almost always insisted on French. It would have helped a great deal if France had cooperated but I wouldn't say that we could have made a stand. The French attitude made it very difficult for us all. Although I can't say that anything very different would have happened had France come along with us.'

Nor did France's refusal to cooperate with the oil summit in Washington come as a surprise to Yamani. 'Anyway, even if they had been successful in agreeing to a proposal, I don't think they would have been able to do anything. We were always able to talk to the developing countries. They weren't. France was consistent in their policy because they also refused to be members of Kissinger's International Energy Agency (IEA). They refused the theme of Kissinger's confrontation. They wanted some sort of cooperation. So they were really in a like mind with Saudi Arabia.'

Traditionally, the French have always believed that they, alone in Europe, hold a privileged place when it comes to western relations with the Arabs. But their memory runs short. They colonized North Africa, spreading their influence through Morocco, Algeria and Tunisia. Yet they were thrown out of North Africa and their oil interests were nationalized in Algeria. They also believed they had a special in with the Iranians when the Ayatollah went into exile and they offered him shelter in a villa outside Paris. Yet when the Ayatollah returned to Tehran, France was not on any 'special favour' port of call for Iranian oil tankers.

That they were trying it on with the Saudis is obvious.

Although Yamani is too diplomatic to say as much.

He prefers, 'Yes, they were getting oil from Saudi Arabia. But they were also getting oil from several other producers. I don't really agree with you that their cooperation in this case, or lack of it in the case of the Washington Oil Summit, was based on the motives you suggest. I prefer to think that they simply had a different philosophy about the third world.'

The result of the Washington Oil Summit was proof that Europe had, in spite of all the exemptions, fallen victim to the oil weapon. Europe's power and unity were a myth. Europe's wealth, foreign trade and enormous population didn't add up to much in terms of political power.

When asked if he was pleased to see that the Washington conference became something of a fiasco, Yamani is fast to answer, 'Of course. Because we were heading for confrontation and it wasn't good for the producers or the consumers. But then when you consider a superpower, like America, I can't blame them for doing what they did. Or thinking the way they thought.'

He says he understands how it could be a tough pill for the Americans to swallow, finding themselves in a position where small nations were trying to tell them what to do. 'I don't blame the Americans for thinking that those small nations have to be punished. If they thought Opec was looking for a fight, then okay, I can see why they acted the way they did. But I don't think Opec was looking for confrontation. The problem for America was that the producers were, for the first time, taking the decision for the price of oil into their own hands. Did that look to America like the producers wanted a confrontation with the consumers? Yes, I suppose it did.'

Always thinking long term, Yamani says he tried to look beyond the point of confrontation and hoped that the crisis might somehow be used as a catalyst to get the industrialized world to sit down and talk to the developing world.

'We did not want confrontation, the way Henry Kissinger wanted it. We wanted cooperation. We wanted to have different groups talking together, like the north-south divide.'

As a direct result of the Washington conference, the Algerians called for a special session of the United Nations to discuss the economic problems of the south, including energy.

Saudi Arabia sent a special delegation, headed by Sheikh Yamani.

Seeing that the UN General Assembly was really no different than an oversized Opec conference, Yamani resorted to character and started personally lobbying members to sort out their views. He spent his first few days in New York on the phone or in private meetings, eventually coming to the conclusion that the Algerian approach, to put these matters before the General Assembly, would merely water down the issues.

'This was my chance to take the developing nations away from Kissinger and bring them into our camp. But let's be frank, once you go to the United Nations you never reach an agreement. You wind up with nice speeches and that's all. Nothing much gets accomplished. I felt that this issue, the energy discussion, was a very vital and important one. Too important to leave to the General Assembly.'

Addressing the General Assembly, Yamani asked for a special conference to be convened between the north and the south where all of their problems could be discussed, including energy. He even specified that it begin with a special meeting for a group of ten nations who would prepare the agenda for the general meeting.

But America strongly opposed it.

'I wanted some sort of real cooperation. Kissinger was looking for confrontation. Definitely. The Washington conference did not give him what he wanted so he started the International Energy Agency.'

However, the day after Yamani made his north-south proposal, he was approached in New York by the French Ambassador who expressed interest in the idea.

As a result of their discussions, French President Valéry Giscard d'Estaing contacted King Faisal and suggested that both France and Saudi Arabia work together to call for the preparatory meeting according to the ten-nation Yamani list.

Shortly thereafter France and Saudi Arabia did just that.

However, unbeknownst to Giscard d'Estaing, Yamani had advised King Faisal not to let Saudi Arabia be active in the invitations.

'It would have been difficult for political reasons both inside and outside Opec. I felt it was not a good idea for Saudi Arabia to appear in the limelight like that. We were the real power behind it but I wanted to remain quietly in the background. France agreed and that was the way it was done.'

The North-South Conference eventually happened, although it was plagued with problems from the start.

The Americans objected to the conference on the grounds that it was nothing but an attempt to upstage the IEA at the very moment of its creation.

In Britain the conference was thought at best a duplication of efforts already under way, at worst a hindrance.

The ten nations came up with an agenda that outlined four areas of discussion: raw materials, transfer of technology, international debt and energy.

Within two years the whole thing was so fragmented that it faded away.

Giscard d'Estaing proclaimed it dead with great regret. He'd adopted it as his own. So if it was a failure, the failure belonged to him.

Yamani, standing quietly in the wings, had very shrewdly allowed the French President all the glory.

If nothing else, it took some of the headlines away from Kissinger's IEA.

'Kissinger set up the IEA for the purpose of confrontation,' Yamani relentlessly insists, 'which was why we in Opec refused to talk to the

IEA. Even today, while the character of the IEA has changed, it's still a sin in Opec to talk to them.'

Officially.

What you do in the limelight is one thing.

What you do in the shadows is another.

'I will now admit that I was committing that sin. Not in public. But in a closed room. Throughout the 1970s I often met with the head of the IEA. Confidentially. When I was the chairman of the Long Term Strategy Committee in Opec, I also established a relationship with the EEC. That wasn't supposed to be done but I knew that we couldn't ignore them. They were too important. Not at the beginning, but when they finally became established and had something to offer, I was always willing to listen. Naturally, I had to proceed carefully with the IEA because Saudi Arabia is after all a member of Opec and we would never do anything publicly that would annoy some members. That's politics. But yes, I used to meet with the chairman of the IEA. Maybe we would have lunch. Maybe we would just meet quietly and talk. It is often very useful to keep open certain informal lines of communication.'

9

Kissinger Fails in the Middle East

YAMANI'S OFFICE in Riyadh was on the first floor of an unremarkable, buff-coloured building half way between the airport and the city centre.

In the outer offices, male secretaries in white Arab robes shuffled slowly back and forth along a hallway decorated with large colour photos of oil refineries and oil wells and the oilfields of the desert.

In the anteroom there were always at least a dozen people waiting to see the minister. Men in Arab dress and men in western business suits staring at the ceiling or looking at the floor or smoking cigarettes or just checking their watch, wondering how much longer Yamani would be.

His own office was magnificent . . . a huge, panelled corner suite where the centre piece was his enormous French empire desk.

There was more French empire furniture scattered around . . . lots of chairs and tables . . . and large Arab couches too, covered with multicoloured cushions the way the Arabs love multicoloured cushions.

There were plenty of telephones that never seemed to stop ringing, a shortwave radio he talked on every now and then and long sheets of telex printouts with oil prices from all over the world that piled up on his desk throughout the day.

As is always the custom in the Arab world, anybody who finally made it past the anteroom and got into the office was automatically offered sweet mint tea or cardamom coffee.

If you'd ever been there before you knew to accept.

Drinking tea or coffee was something to do while Yamani juggled phone calls.

* * * *

In early November 1973, with the oil embargo in full swing and oil prices fixed at $5.12, a minor event took place that received little or no notice outside the oil world.

There was an auction sale of a single lot of Nigerian crude.

Even though the world shortfall, owing to the production cutbacks, was only something like 7 per cent below the September pre-embargo levels, bidders at the auction let panic get the best of them.

The Nigerian crude was sold at $16.

When the Shah saw that, he decided to give the market a second test. Iran's economy was in trouble. Foreign debt was overextended. He wanted to implement a very ambitious five-year development plan. He needed cash.

In early December Iran held an auction where prices hit $17.40.

Because he could see what was coming, Yamani urged his colleagues not to be influenced by the auction prices. He argued that to a large extent they reflected the effects of the oil embargo and the production cutbacks. He warned, 'Since these measures are of a political nature, they should not have an economic effect.'

The Shah, however, had ideas of his own.

Three weeks later, the ministers of the six Gulf member countries met in Tehran.

The Shah took advantage of the reduction in output and the extreme nervousness of the market and announced to the ministers that he wanted to raise his government's take to $14, which would put the price of oil at nearly $23 a barrel.

Yamani had no doubts that such a drastic hike would send the western economy into a tailspin. Sharp increases like that weren't healthy for the producers either. On the other hand, the west could absorb less severe price increases, so he proposed that the price for Saudi Arabian Light, the Opec market crude, be raised to no more than $7.50.

With the militants of his side, the Shah's compromise position put the price of oil at around $12.

Yamani wanted to hold out, but he felt that, with the crisis at a head, a split now with other producers – especially the Arab producers – could endanger Opec.

The Shah asked Yamani for an answer.

Getting up from the table, Yamani explained that he couldn't take a decision without consulting the king. He excused himself, left the meeting and went to a phone. He put in a call but didn't get through. So he tried again. Nothing. He tried a third time. Still nothing.

The Shah pressed him again for an answer.

After several more futile attempts at reaching Riyadh, Yamani was forced to second-guess what Faisal would have wanted.

'It was a very critical moment,' he remembers. 'It was a decision I had to take very reluctantly. I was afraid the effects of such a price rise would be even more harmful than it turned out to be. But I didn't know that then. I was afraid that such a severe rise in prices would create a major depression in the west. And I knew, as I have always said, that if the west went down, we would go down too.'

His choices were obvious. He could either hold out against the Shah and risk splitting Opec into two camps, or he could go along with the Shah and try to bring prices down eventually.

He opted for the latter.

It was only when he returned home that he discovered Faisal would have been against the move if he'd been consulted.

Oil was now $11.65 a barrel.

Prices had quadrupled in a matter of months.

At a press conference after the meeting, the Shah showed his colours as the leading price hawk in the Gulf. He proclaimed, 'It will do western consumers good to learn to economise. Eventually all those children of well-to-do families who have plenty to eat at every meal, who have their own cars and who act almost as terrorists and throw bombs here and there, will have to rethink all these privileges of the advanced industrial world. And they will have to work harder.'

The Shah sounded disquietingly like a man with a grudge.

Even if he didn't come right out and say as much, a good part of his hostility was aimed directly at Yamani.

'The Saudis always got in the Shah's way,' notes a US State Department observer. 'Because he took his Peacock Throne so seriously, he would never publicly criticize a so-called friendly monarch. He wouldn't go after Faisal, for instance. Especially Faisal. So he used Yamani as a whipping boy. Yamani was fair game for the Shah's hostility towards the Saudis in general and King Faisal in particular.'

James Akins agrees. 'Yes, the Shah did hate Yamani. There was a personal antipathy. But part of this was contrived. The Shah didn't like to attack the Saudi government or attack the king. And so when the Saudis would take a position on oil prices, to keep the prices from going up for example, the Shah would then launch into a long attack, not on Saudi Arabia and definitely not on the king, but on Yamani.'

It's the same story from Ian Seymour at the *Middle East Economic Survey*. 'The Shah didn't like Yamani?' He chuckles, 'You're putting it very mildly. Yamani was fronting for the Saudi regime and so he got the hammering from the Shah as the guy who was responsible because the Shah didn't want to say Faisal or Khaled was responsible. He was putting the whole thing on Yamani. When he called Yamani a tool of the imperialists it was really just a way of saying, you're not allowing Iran to get its way. If anybody was a tool of the imperialists it was the Shah. And sure he and Zaki had different ideas. What Yamani was saying was that Saudi Arabia was reserving its right to have a bit of the imperialist booty.'

When pressed, Yamani, ever the gentleman, couches his feelings in typical diplomacy. 'I don't know exactly how the Shah felt about me but it was obvious that he didn't necessarily like what I was doing. Then, too, it was also easier to criticize me than to criticize the Saudi royal family.'

Actually, while Yamani and the Shah had a definite adversarial relationship in public, especially where Opec was concerned, it doesn't seem to have been anywhere near as hostile in private.

In the 1960s, when the Shah was on his honeymoon at the Mark Hopkins Hotel in San Francisco, Yamani also happened to be staying there. Yamani spotted the Shah and his bride across the lobby one day but didn't want to disturb them. Late that night, just as Yamani was falling asleep, his phone rang. In a daze he heard someone on the other end say, 'Zaki, it's Reza.' It took him several seconds to realize who was calling. The Shah wanted to know, 'Why are you avoiding me? I saw you in the lobby today. Please dine with us tomorrow.'

Around the same time, on a trip to Tehran, Yamani tried to purchase some grape vines for his orchard in Taif. He was told that export of Iranian vines was forbidden. He wanted them badly but never mentioned that to anyone in the government, and certainly not to the Shah. He simply let the matter drop. Thirteen years later, after an especially gruelling Opec meeting, a bunch of those vines was sent to him as a gift from the Shah. It seems the Shah had known all along and suddenly decided he wanted Yamani to have them.

* * * *

As prices shot up, oil was news and the story was covered from every angle.

An especially unique view came from the Pulitzer Prize-winning columnist Jack Anderson. He believed that the Saudis, with their 100-year supply of oil, feared that if prices got too high it could destroy oil as a product before they could get rid of one-tenth of it.

He wrote, 'In the maneuvering before the Tehran meeting, the Saudis and the new American Ambassador to Riyadh, Jim Akins, tried to get Kissinger to put pressure on the Shah, using U.S. leverage as Iran's arms supplier. But nothing came of it beyond a routine letter from Kissinger, which the Shah ignored, and the Nixon administration kept unsullied its record of never having used muscle to keep down foreign oil prices.'

When asked if that sounds accurate, Yamani is quick to say, 'Yes. King Faisal asked Kissinger on several occasions to talk to the Shah. But this implies that Faisal did not know that Kissinger wanted a high price of oil. Because this is how you ultimately reduce your dependence on foreign oil. With a really high price you encourage exploration, you encourage development of alternative sources of energy and you gradually reduce your dependence on imported oil. That's what Kissinger wanted. He was looking to reduce the Arabs' power because the real power the Arab had was derived from oil. Kissinger wanted to take away that power. It takes some time, but it does not happen except through a high price of oil.'

That being the case, Kissinger and the Shah might both have had reasons to go for a higher price.

At least Hamed Zaheri, an Iraqi-born Iranian who spent a decade as Opec's press spokesman, is convinced that's true.

'Iran wanted it to buy more arms. And in those days Nixon and Kissinger wanted to arm Iran. They wanted to have a strong Iran. The only way for Iran to get the money was by increasing oil prices. I have reason to believe that the bug was put into the Shah's ear by Kissinger. Raise the price and buy the planes.'

So he, too, believes that the 1973 price increases were stage-managed by the Shah with the backing of the Americans. 'But I believe there was another factor as well. After the Vietnam era, the US economy wasn't functioning well, vis-à-vis the Japanese and the Germans. The only way to slow down the Japanese and the Germans was to increase the oil prices on which they were so dependent. It was the Shah and Kissinger who came up with that. Do you honestly believe the telephones didn't work? No, the Iranian government started to play a game and somehow kept Yamani from getting through. It was to their benefit that he didn't reach King Faisal in time. So they pulled the telephone plug. It was definitely a strategy which was well played by the Shah with the support of the Americans.'

Perhaps not as far-fetched an idea as it sounds, there is now good reason to believe that King Faisal had serious reservations about Henry Kissinger.

In fact, Jim Akins insists, his apprehensions bordered on distrust.

'Because Henry Kissinger lied to him. Before Kissinger first came out, Faisal was very apprehensive. I talked to the king at length and said, look, he's the American foreign minister. He has a sense of history. He'll be doing all the things that will advance America's interests, not

Israel's interests. You can deal with him. I was probably more responsible than anybody else for getting a reasonable relationship between Kissinger and the king. Then Kissinger started playing fast and loose with the truth.'

At this point it's only fair to explain that Akins and Kissinger have not remained the warmest of friends over the years.

That's an understatement.

Akins was assigned to Saudi Arabia towards the end of 1973. But Akins didn't play the game by Kissinger's rules and Kissinger recalled him within a very short period.

By most accounts, the Akins-Kissinger clash was two-sided. Says a long-time Kissinger associate and close personal friend, 'Jim thought he knew the Arabs better than Kissinger, better than anyone else, and when he disagreed with policy he didn't always follow Henry's directives. At the same time, Henry was always undercutting his ambassadors. He was a great one for that.'

So when it comes to talk about Kissinger, Akins' comments have to be put into a proper perspective. As one of his fellow ambassadors suggests rather pointedly, 'Jim Akins is sometimes very emotional for a Quaker.'

George Ballou contends that Akins is 'one of the most arrogant people you'll ever meet. Anything you get from Akins, you've got to remember that Jim is carrying this grudge which has influenced him. He's bright and aggressive. But he told me even before he went out there that he was going to get fired. That said, Henry Kissinger did lose credibility with the Arabs. The '73 war ended up with Kissinger's shuttle diplomacy. And the Arabs still feel they were done in by Kissinger. From their point of view, I think they were.'

The way Akins sees it, Kissinger's mind operates the same way Metternich's did. 'Metternich was able to tell one story to the Emperor, another story to the King of Prussia, another story to the King of France and so on. By the time they compared notes, things had changed. Kissinger didn't seem to understand that the world had changed since Metternich. And he was not able to get away with it. People compared notes very quickly. The initial reaction was as Kissinger had calculated it. They thought, "we must be mistaken. The American foreign minister could not be lying to us." But very quickly they concluded that Kissinger was lying. By the time of King Faisal's death, if Kissinger had said, "I guarantee that the sun will rise in the east tommorrow", the king would have said to his advisers, "We better wait and see".'

John West, the former Governor of South Carolina and Jimmy Carter's Ambassador to Saudi Arabia, says there's a lot of truth in Akins' appraisal of the Saudis' feelings towards Kissinger.

'His method of operation was to tell each side what he thought they wanted to hear in a sufficiently clever way that they couldn't actually say it was an outright lie. But none of the Arabs trusted him. They respected his capacity, but they didn't trust him.'

Part of Kissinger's problems with the Arabs, according to that long-time associate and close personal friend, was that Kissinger always remained as much a European as he was an American. 'He never quite absorbed the American sense of discipline about telling the truth. For Americans there is usually a very distinct line between the truth and a lie. For Europeans and the Arabs the distinctions can be less clear. Telling different things to different people goes against the grain with Americans. However, it isn't necessarily viewed the same way by the Europeans or by the Arabs. I think Akins exaggerates a bit when he compares Kissinger to Metternich, although it's certainly true to a degree. But, then, maybe Faisal just didn't like Kissinger because he was a Jew.'

Yamani objects. 'That had nothing to do with it.'

He confirms the fact that neither he nor Faisal was necessarily Kissinger's biggest fan, but he insists he never heard the king say anything about Kissinger's religion.

'Not at all. That wouldn't have bothered Faisal and that never bothered me. You know, I respect intelligent people and Kissinger is extremely intelligent. You can see it in his eyes. Whether you have differing views with someone or not, when you are dealing with an intelligent person, you enjoy that. It becomes a challenge. I never felt that he was completely neutral. But that doesn't mean I was worried about dealing with him, because, after all, he was the only person to deal with.'

On a Kissinger trip to Saudi Arabia in early 1975, it seems he spent considerable time going through all the motions of diplomatic politesse, praising Faisal to his face. But when he returned to his hotel suite and was alone with his staff, he spent just as much effort referring to the king in extremely unkind terms.

The Secretary of State's diatribe surfaced in a CIA report, suggesting that the room was bugged.

That unnamed long-time Kissinger associate and close personal friend finds the story amusing. 'Kissinger thought it was fair game for the Americans and the Russians to bug people. And we all knew that the Saudis had hired experts to bug rooms. We had reason to believe that all the palaces were bugged. Probably still are.'

But here Yamani raises an eyebrow. 'I really don't know. It was not a normal practice during the time of Faisal to bug a hotel room like that. Kissinger's comments could have been reported somehow, but I honestly don't think the room would have been bugged. No, not during the time of Faisal.'

After Faisal?

He shrugs, 'Could be.'

On Akins' comment that Kissinger played 'fast and loose with the truth', Yamani acknowledges, 'Akins was in a position to know because he got the reports. I wasn't involved in Kissinger's discussions with the Egyptians, Syrians or the Iranians. But Akins told me several times that Kissinger had lied to the Arabs. He didn't say it while he was the Ambassador because as such he was not in a position to say it. But we were told the same thing by many other people. Now, don't forget that Faisal was extremely intelligent and sometimes I felt he could read minds. If he had discovered that Kissinger was lying to us, he never would have shown it. He was shrewd enough to play that game. Although it would have changed his attitude towards policy decisions. Yes, it definitely would have affected his thinking.'

It is therefore just possible, Yamani suggests, that Kissinger's attitude did serve to harden Faisal's position on peace in the Middle East when the two men met for the final time.

It was in February 1975.

The Saudi Foreign Minister had just died, so Faisal asked that Yamani receive Kissinger on behalf of the goverment.

Yamani met the American at the airport and brought him to the king's office.

They talked as they rode into Riyadh and Yamani thought to himself that Kissinger seemed very tense.

It was Kissinger's aim to see another disengagement agreement between the Israelis and the Egyptians.

But when he explained his plan in the king's office, Faisal said no. He said the second agreement should be between the Israelis and the Syrians.

Kissinger tried to convince Faisal to let him go ahead and get this agreement between the Israelis and the Egyptians and after that, he promised he would go for an agreement between the Israelis and the Syrians.

Faisal said, 'No. I will oppose that.'

Kissinger promised, 'We will undertake to work very hard to see that an agreement between the Israelis and the Syrians take place immediately after this one.'

Again Faisal said, 'No. I will oppose that. The second agreement must be between the Syrians and the Israelis.'

The meeting went on like that for some time.

Kissinger kept trying to change Faisal's mind.

Faisal would not budge.

Every time Kissinger spoke about a second agreement between the Egyptians and the Israelis Faisal said, 'I will oppose that.'

Yamani explains that Faisal was looking for an overall settlement. 'That was very important because, without an overall settlement, the dispute will continue. The first step was those who fought. Egypt and Syria. We're talking about disengagements, which would have been a preparation for the final settlement. Then there would have to be talks with Jordan, for instance. But the first step was Egypt and Syria. Faisal wanted the Americans to insist that Israel sit down with the Egyptians first and the Syrians next because it was the only way to bring about the beginnings of peace.'

The way Faisal saw it, Kissinger's plan was too limited. 'Faisal understood that if you only solved the Egyptian problem, you would isolate the Egyptians from the Arab camp and the problem with the Syrians would remain. Of course, isolating the Egyptians from the Arab camp was what Kissinger wanted to do.'

When the meeting ended, Yamani took Kissinger back to the airport.

Yamani says Kissinger still seemed very nervous in the car. He kept saying, 'Now we will not have a second agreement with the Egyptians.' He knew that as long as Faisal opposed the second agreement it would not go through. Egypt would never have signed it over Faisal's opposition.

Then, one month later, Faisal was assassinated.

And Kissinger got his agreement between Israel and Egypt.

This is not to suggest in any way that there's a relationship between the two events. Not at all. Although there was talk at one point that the CIA was behind Faisal's assassination.

Yamani instantly shrugs off that idea. 'You always hear all kinds of talk. But there has never been anything to substantiate that.'

Even James Akins is willing to stand up for Kissinger when it comes to that. 'Henry Kissinger had absolutely no credibility in Saudi Arabia or anywhere else in the Arab world by the time of King Faisal's death. But because the young murderer had just come from the United States where he had serious trouble with the police and was almost put in jail, the belief grew that he was recruited by the CIA and that Kissinger or the CIA was responsible for King Faisal's death. I'm scarcely one to be defending Henry Kissinger, but this was one of the problems I had when I was out there. I still tell people that there is no truth whatsoever in that story. They think that because Kissinger thought Faisal had outlived his usefulness and as he could no longer manipulate him, he decided to get rid of him. This is one of the problems you have in dealing with the Arabs. They jump early to conclusions. They're strongest in deductive reasoning and tend to think it equates to proof.'

That the Middle East situation is still so volatile, Yamani holds, goes straight back to Kissinger's motives. 'I think the important question is whether the Americans, under Kissinger, wanted an overall settlement or simply wanted to water down the fire, to reduce the heat of the situation and keep things pending until some time in the future and there would be no settlement. That way Israel could continue its occupation of the territories taken in 1967 and annex them. These are my feelings and I think I share them with everybody who follows the problem of the Middle East.'

When Gerald Ford took over as President, Yamani says, nothing changed. Kissinger was still the architect of US foreign policy.

'I met with Ford the first time when he was Vice President in early 1974. He wasn't necessarily well informed about the oil business. But then I never expected him to be very knowledgeable about oil. He was still only learning about the Middle East. The clever one in those days was William Simon [Energy Czar under Nixon, Secretary of the Treasury under Ford]. He was a very hard-working man and we used to mix very well. I even stayed at his home in Washington. I remember waking up one morning early and looking down into the garden and Simon was sitting there with a huge stack of files, already working.'

By 1976, with Carter's election to the White House, Kissinger was out. 'We thought at the time that everything now depends on Israel's attitude. If they were serious about peace, then Carter's initiatives could be a step forward. If they were not serious, it would be a step backwards.'

The result of Carter's efforts was the Camp David Agreements, a September 1978 accord between Egypt's Anwar Sadat and Israel's Menachem Begin. The decisions made at the presidential retreat in the Maryland mountains that autumn laid the foundations for a peace treaty which Egypt and Israel signed the following spring.

The world hoped it might work.

Yamani, ever the pragmatist, realized it couldn't.

'You see, Camp David was designed to isolate Egypt from the Arab world and weaken the Arabs' united front. Israel could then relax and stay on the West Bank until some day when they could annex the territories and make them officially part of Israel.'

The only positive result he can see coming out of the Camp David talks was the return of Sinai. 'But nothing else. I think history will prove that the return of Sinai was definitely a net gain while the isolation of Egypt from the Arab camp was a net loss. Whether Israel will realize one day the importance of an equitable and peaceful settlement, especially to the Palestinian problem, remains to be seen.'

What he means by 'an equitable and peaceful settlement' starts with the return of all the territories taken in 1967. 'But it doesn't stop there because the most important thing is satisfaction to the Palestinians. Whatever will satisfy them as human beings. They want to feel again that they are a nation, whether as part of a federation with Jordan or as an independent state. Whatever they will accept should satisfy the problem.'

There is, though the additional problem of Jerusalem. 'If Jerusalem is not liberated, if the Moslems do not have the right to go there without restrictions and to pray in the Mosque, then something is missing. I would like to see the Israeli occupation of East Jerusalem removed so that Moslems from all over the world would then be free to worship in the holy places alongside any other religious group who considers Jerusalem a holy city.'

At the time of Camp David talks, there were rumours that Saudi Arabia, under King Khaled and Crown Prince Fahd, actually tried to encourage the Egyptians to accept the agreements as a first step towards peace. But the more militant part of the Arab world wouldn't stand for it. They object. And the Saudis backed down.

'So many people have had that reading,' Yamani says, 'but we officially denied that. I'm afraid where this matter is concerned, I have nothing else to contribute.'

10

Boomtime

THE EMBARGO ended in the spring of 1974.

Arab oil started flowing again to the United States.

In Saudi Arabia this was the beginning of boomtime.

It was the start of an unprecedented era of economic euphoria.

However the actual decision to call off the embargo put Yamani in some personal danger.

'It was a very serious matter to end the embargo,' he says. 'But the Americans started moving in their efforts to help find a peaceful solution to the Middle East crisis and there were disengagements. As I've told you, it wasn't our intention to seriously hurt anyone.'

An American source suggests that Sadat had approached Faisal following the first disengagement agreements, urging Saudi Arabia to end the embargo. The hint is that Sadat had promised Kissinger he would intervene on the Americans' behalf to help relieve the oil crisis.

Yamani confirms this. 'Sadat wanted to lift the embargo almost immediately. I personally carried his wishes to King Faisal. But the king refused because he believed it was much too early.'

It wasn't until February 1974 that Faisal felt the time was right to normalize relations with the west. He then arranged for a summit in Algiers with Sadat, Algerian President Houari Boumedienne and Syria's President Hafez al Assad. Only after they agreed was it decided that the actual plans for putting an end to the embargo could be handled at the ministerial level.

A meeting of the Arab oil ministers was scheduled to convene in Tripoli.

Then, out of the blue, Colonel Qaddafi decided that he was against ending the embargo and refused to let the ministers meet in Libya.

He said that removing the embargo was contrary to the Arabs' interests and he did not want such a decision to be made on Libyan soil.

So Sadat said the ministers would be welcome in Egypt.

The venue was officially moved to Cairo.

As soon as it was, Qaddafi changed his mind again. He insisted they meet in Libya.

Yamani says the reason was obvious. 'He wanted us in Libya so he could put pressure on us to maintain the embargo. He was going to try to force us to keep the embargo intact.'

Just before leaving for Tripoli, Yamani received disturbing news from Sadat that Egyptian intelligence had unearthed a pair of plots.

The first was that the Palestine Liberation Organization was planning to hijack a KLM plane and destroy it the moment the ministers removed the embargo against Holland. In November 1973 they'd already hijacked a KLM jet on route to Japan. On 3 March, 1974, the day the meeting was moved back to Tripoli, they hijacked a British Airways jet over Yugoslavia, forced it to land at Amsterdam's Schipol Airport and blew it up on the tarmac. So yet another PLO hijacking had to be considered a real possibility.

Even more upsetting to Yamani was the second alleged conspiracy.

Sadat claimed that the Palestinians were plotting personally against him and the Kuwaiti oil minister, although their precise intentions were not clear. Egyptian intelligence couldn't establish whether they planned to hold the two for ransom or execute them for their part in lifting the embargo. However, the Egyptians were convinced that a plot had been hatched. Sadat's exact words to Yamani were, 'They are planning to hurt you.'

The meeting in Tripoli was set for 13 March.

On the night of 12/13 March, Yamani slept badly. He was suffering from the first stages of the flu and his health would have been a perfect excuse to postpone his trip. But he felt obliged to attend the meeting. Anyway, he convinced himself, Qaddafi would never allow any personal harm to come to an Arab minister on Libyan territory.

Or would he?

In his plane the next morning on the way to Tripoli, Yamani opened his newspaper to see that the police had arrested a group of Palestinians trying to smuggle weapons on board a KLM flight.

The thought haunted him that at least half of Sadat's information was accurate.

'What I didn't want was for the other part to be true as well.'

He knew it was too late to back out now, even with his flu. So in the event that there might be trouble, Yamani ordered his pilot to refuel the plane right away and stay with it. He told his pilot he wanted to be able to leave at a moment's notice.

Throughout the morning and well into the afternoon, the Arab ministers discussed the merits and pitfalls of lifting the embargo completely, of maintaining it and of all the permutations in between.

Interestingly enough, just at critical moments, a message would be delivered to the Libyan minister who'd then get up and leave the room. He'd be gone for 15 or 20 minutes before returning to expound on Colonel Qadafi's opinion about their discussions. After the first couple of times he was called away, it became pitifully obvious to everybody there that Qaddafi and his number two, Major Jalloud, were in a nearby room somewhere, listening to what was said.

They'd bugged the room.

Not that hidden microphones particularly bothered Yamani. It was, he says, par for the course. 'Yes, there were bugs, but so what?'

The thing that did worry him was a gnawing premonition that the longer he stayed in Tripoli the more likely it was that someone might try to take him hostage.

He began to think about his exit.

It would have to be graceful.

No one could suspect what he was up to.

The meeting dragged on through the afternoon and into the evening. The group was finding it more difficult than they had imagined to make the final decision to lift the embargo. So over dinner the idea was suggested that they might postpone the decision until the Opec meeting in Vienna in three days' time.

The Algerian minister, Abdesselam, who was presiding at the time, thought that was a good idea. But there were Colonel Qaddafi's feelings to consider. No one wanted to make the postponement look like an insult. So Yamani and Abdesselam and a few others decided the most diplomatic way was for the Syrian minister to ask formally for the postponement on the grounds that he had to talk to his President.

When he did, the Libyan minister seemed indifferent to the postponement.

That's when Yamani decided it was time to make his move.

Ever casual, he passed a note to his secretary that he wanted his car out front immediately.

After waiting a few more minutes, making small talk around the table, Yamani stood up, politely excused himself and walked out of the room as if he was going to the bathroom. But instead of turning left down the hall he went right out of the door, climbed into his car and ordered the driver to take him to the airport.

He wasn't certain how long it would be before Qaddafi and Jalloud would realize what was happening and try to stop him. But he knew he didn't have all that much time. After all, not only would this be a de facto postponement of the meeting, his abrupt disappearance would also upset any plans the Palestinians might have had. If they got angry, who knew how they might react. So too the Libyans. Walking out like that could be seen as a great insult.

Arriving at the airport, he hurried towards his plane.

But the Libyan authorities stopped him.

Yamani demanded to know what they wanted.

An officer answered that he wanted to see Yamani's passport.

Yamani knew he didn't have time to lose so he confronted the man. 'What? In Libya, the main advocate of Arab unity, you would insist on seeing my passport?'

There was an awkward moment as the Libyan officer decided how to handle the situation.

Knowing that the best defence is a strong offence, Yamani was relentless. 'You know who I am, don't you? You know that I am an official representative of the government of Saudi Arabia. And you ask for my papers?'

The officer probably should have called his superiors, and given half a chance he might have.

But Yamani never gave him that chance.

'Perhaps, Excellency,' the officer quickly backed down, 'perhaps it will be enough just to sign your passport.'

Yamani glared at the man.

The officer took Yamani's passport, scribbled across a page, then quickly handed it back.

Yamani hurried onto the plane and told his pilot, 'Take off right now.'

The pilot wanted to know where they were going.

Yamani said, 'Just take off. We'll decide where we're going once we get up in the air.'

As they climbed out of Libyan airspace, Yamani's flu went straight to his ears.

Within a few minutes he was suffering very badly.

He told the pilot to go to Geneva.

But the pilot soon came back to tell Yamani that Geneva had a curfew on night flying and that the airport was closed.

Now Yamani suggested, go to Rome.

But when the pilot contacted Rome he was told that the airport was closed because of a storm.

'Then I said, go to Athens. I had to find someplace because I was in terrible pain and we certainly couldn't go back to Tripoli.'

So the pilot headed for Greece.

He called Athens on the radio, but before the authorities would grant permission to land there they insisted on knowing who the passengers were. The pilot only said, 'They're Arabs.' The Greeks asked if the Arabs held current visas. The pilot checked with Yamani and then had to radio back to Athens, 'No.'

The authorities refused them permission to land.

But along with rank and world fame comes privilege.

Now the Saudi oil minister said to his pilot, 'Tell them it's Sheikh Yamani on this plane and that I have a terrible earache. Keep heading for Athens. Tell them you have a patient who needs to land there.'

Within half an hour the Greeks decided Yamani was welcome.

The Greek Foreign Minister and the Minister of Interior were both at the airport to greet him.

They even brought along a doctor.

* * * *

In 1970 King Faisal moved Sheikh Hisham Nazer out of his job as Yamani's deputy and made him Planning minister.

Nazer's office had big ideas but a relatively small budget. The ministry was out of money before the end of the year.

However, boomtime changed everything and by 1974, Nazer had enough cash to finance the building of that national infrastructure to the tune of £33 million ($77 million) per day!

From 1974 until well into 1976, with oil flowing like manna from heaven, Saudi Arabia was the California gold rush in spades.

The Saudis couldn't spent their money fast enough.

Although with a wish list that included water, food, schools, hospitals, cement, steel, roads, telephone networks, electrical grids, ports, a railroad and dock space for imports, they gave it their best shot.

'It was an extraordinary and unprecedented period in our history,' Yamani says. 'King Faisal always believed that it would be dangerous to push the west too far. His thinking was, let's be careful not to give consuming nations the idea that they're in a captive market. Then we found ourselves in this era of prosperity. Among other things, we realized our own prosperity could be used to strengthen our relations with the west. We had money to invest, so we invested it heavily in the west. It stands to reason that when you invest in a country, the way we did in the United States, then the prosperity of that country becomes your concern. The prosperity of the United States and the prosperity of the west became our concern.'

Sir John Wilton was Britain's Ambassador to Kuwait for the first four years of the 1970s and arrived at his Embassy in Saudi Arabia in 1976.

'Saudi prosperity manifested itself in a total blockage of the ports. It was an incredible sight, hundreds of ships queueing off Jeddah, waiting to unload. That's also when you heard all those stories about piles of merchandise, rusting, rotting, being eaten by rats on the quayside. It actually reached crisis levels. The whole import programme of Saudi Arabia was distorted by their sudden enormous wealth and yet frustrated by the fact that they couldn't get the stuff in. They bought all over the world and they sent the goods home and then they couldn't get anything off the ships and into use.'

Boomtime brought tens of thousands of foreigners into Saudi Arabia, modern forty-niners rushing west to pan gold, all yearning for a fast score, all anxious to cash in quickly on the Saudis' sudden riches. Hotels appeared over night. Restaurants for western tastes flourished. There were construction derricks wherever you looked. Culture shock set in.

Paradoxically, while the Saudis could afford almost anything, they couldn't always make it work. For instance, the King Faisal Hospital was by 1976 stocked to the brim with the most up-to-date, state of the art, hi-tech medical equipment. From that standpoint alone it ranked among the world's most advanced medical facilities. But they had to staff the place with foreign doctors because there weren't enough Saudi medical students graduating every year.

This new-found prosperity created a new entity on the international business scene – the extremely visible Arab middleman.

In polite circles, they are sometimes called 'an intermediary'.

When politesse gives way to the bottom line, they are more accurately referred to as 'a fixer'.

Of course the middleman is an ancient Arab tradition. But when boomtime arrived a handful of very enterprising Arabs gave up camel trading and afternoons at the souk to go off in search of really big money.

Adnan Khashoggi led the pack.

His father had been an occasional court physician to Ibn Saud, so certain amenities were available to Khashoggi as a youth. He used that access to earn his original stake as an agent, putting two parties together and taking a commission from the middle. As the deals got bigger – usually arms on a multi-billion dollar scale – he built himself a power base important enough to become, at least for a while, one of the richest men in the world. When he was flush, he reportedly spent in excess of $330,000 a day on his personal lifestyle. That's $120 million a year!

In the early 1940s Suleiman Olayan was driving a truck for Aramco, supposedly earning no more than 300 rials a month. But in 1947 he got himself into the import trade. With royal family backing he had all his ducks lined up when boomtime hit. The money that poured into his business in the early 1970s was immediately reinvested in US banks – among them Mellon and Bankers Trust – and before long he became a major shareholder in Chase Manhattan, second only to David Rockefeller.

Nor was Akram Ojjeh born to money. A Syrian, he was educated in the Lebanon by French monks who convinced him to study law in Paris. After befriending Prince Mansour, Saudi Arabia's first Defence Minister, he too started dealing in arms. But it took a subsequent bankruptcy and a generous helping hand from Khashoggi to put Ojjeh into the big time. They were partners for a while, until Ojjeh decided that Khashoggi liked having his name in lights and Ojjeh didn't. Yet boomtime was so good to Ojjeh that he quickly acquired serious interests in a regional French airline, the Credit Commercial de France bank and the Dumex construction group. In 1977 he used $16.5 million in spare cash to purchase the ocean liner *Le France*. He then filled it with antiques and sold off everything for a huge profit.

Add to them men like Gaith Pharoan, the son of a Saudi court physician, Minister of Health and special adviser to Kings Faisal and Khaled, who parlayed his contacts into a wheeling/dealing career. And Mahdi al-Tajir, who used his friendship with Sheikh Rashid of Dubai and Sheikh Zayid of Abu Dhabi to create the Customs Service for the United Arab Emirates and cut himself into the middle of astronomically large deals.

As long as everyone else was getting rich, the Saudi royals figured they might as well get richer.

While Ibn Saud was alive, the idea of a royal going into business was frowned upon. He often said, 'There are two things which do not mix. Making money and running the government. If you run the government, you must concern yourself with spending money for the good of your people, not making money for yourself. If you do not compete with the merchants then they will not compete with you.'

The old man's philosophy quickly fell by the wayside as one of his own sons started a business.

It was Prince Talal who broke the ice for the royals, asking for and finally getting a subvention from Ibn Saud to open a cement factory. Ibn Saud's chancellor, Abdullah Suleiman, managed to convince the king that a prince in private business could set a good example. And even though Ibn Saud tried to find a compromise by letting Talal set up the company and then insisting that he be only one of many shareholders, the Ibn Saud equivalent of a royal vow of financial celibacy was instantly forgotten.

That Talal, leader of the Free Princes, should have been the first royal in business is amusing. That it was Abdullah Suleiman who helped convince the king that royalty in business was kosher is actually funny. Suleiman would have been the last person to call the kettle black. His own hands were elbow deep in every coffer within arms reach, including a much publicized tanker deal between the government and Aristotle Onassis that wound up as an embarrassing scandal.

Faisal remained a modest man, but his brother-in-law Kemal Adham did extremely well in a long business career of putting people together.

King Khaled, who followed Faisal, was always more interested in falconing than in business.

The current Crown Prince, Abdullah, makes a point of not doing business in Saudi Arabia. Although he got himself involved with the Hunt Brothers when they tried to corner the world's silver market and, along with them, he too lost a fortune.

However Fahd and his business dealings is another story altogether.

Having blown millions at gaming tables in his carousing days, he has since more than recouped his losses. Together with members of his own family, including his 15-year-old son, Prince Abdul Aziz, and his favourite brothers-in law, Abdul Aziz al-Ibrahim and Khaled al-Ibrahim, Fahd has managed to acquire fabulous riches.

He is reliably said to be the second wealthiest man on earth, only surpassed in riches by the Sultan of Brunei.

One interesting side of his business interests comes in the highly profitable form of a Greek-bearing-gifts connection with the mysterious John Latsis.

An Athens-based shipping magnate who obsessively shuns publicity and particularly detests being photographed by the press, Latsis is said to have begun life as a baggage handler on ferries across the Aegean. Yet in July 1971, with offices in Athens, London and New York, Latsis had enough stashed away through shipping and oil trading to offer $3 million to the Greek government to help support the military when the United States voted to cut off aid to the Greek Colonels. Latsis' donation was politely refused.

In September 1979, with oil prices heading for the roof, Latsis became the official assignee of the Greek government with the express purpose of buying oil from Saudi Arabia.

At the same time, he personally worked out a series of construction/barter deals with Fahd, building ports in Saudi Arabia in exchange for oil. That's about the time that Latsis bought the yacht *Atlantis* from Stavros Niarchos reportedly for $35 million, which he then gave to Fahd as a gift. Renamed the *Abdul Aziz*, it is often described as the most opulent yacht in the world. An opulent thank you perhaps for the then Crown Prince's help in their then mutually beneficial business affairs.

So boomtime made a lot of people very rich.

When he was first named minister in 1962, Yamani was put on a salary of 12,000 rials a month. That was then about £950 ($2,665). Before too long, because times got temporarily tough for the Saudis, King Faisal cut Yamani's salary to 10,000 rials a month. Then the good times began to roll and his pay cheque steadily rose until October 1986 when he was earning 50,000 rials a month plus an additional 400,000 rials annually, for a total salary of somewhere around £325,000 ($500,000) a year.

Today, as a former government employee, he's on a pension that amounts to 100 per cent of his final salary.

But even if you add up all the money he earned over his 28 years in government, it still won't come anywhere near his reputed wealth.

Enter here the Saudi system of gifts.

An integral part of life throughout the Arab world, a gift of land is the traditional method used by the Saudi royal family to reward loyal servants. It's the way the royals say well done and thank you.

'Over the years,' Yamani explains, 'King Faisal was extremely generous to me. I received from him huge parcels of land which were mine to do with as I chose. Later King Khaled was also generous to me. But King Faisal treated me very very well and between 1974 and 1976 I was able to make my fortune in real estate.'

In the beginning, when Yamani started receiving parcels of land, you could buy real estate in Riyadh for next to nothing. One American businessman who was there during the early 1960s seems to recall 2 rials per square metre as the going price. Says he, 'They were giving it away.'

When boomtime came, prices went wild.

'It was so easy to make a lot of money during those years,' Yamani continues, 'and there was so much money to make. I would be given some land, or I would buy some and then sell it. Then I would get more land and sell it. I got in and out, in and out. I was lucky to make as much money in land as I did. But I was also lucky to get out before the collapse came in 1976.'

He parlayed his Saudi land wealth into an international real estate portfolio. Today he has land holdings in Saudi Arabia, Italy, Switzerland, the Lebanon, France and England. He maintains homes in Riyadh, Jeddah, Mecca and Taif, outside Beirut, on Lake Geneva, in a Swiss ski resort, in Sardinia, in London's Mayfair and in the plush fields of suburban Surrey.

His law practice has, since the early 1960s, been one of the most successful in the Gulf, with offices now in Riyadh, Jeddah and Bahrain and with associates in Switzerland, Britain, the United States and Japan.

He also has financial interests in several businesses in Saudi Arabia, including clinics and a paper goods company that manufactures, among other things, sanitary napkins.

Finally there are certain international business investments, like his controlling interest in the Swiss watch manufacturer Vacheron Constantin and his founder's stake in Investcorp, an investment banking group with interests in New York's Tiffany jewellers, People's Department Stores, Bertram-Trojan-Riva boats, Club Car golf carts, Dellwood Dairies of New York and Muller Fire Hydrants.

About as far away from the Khashoggi wheeler/dealer image as any international businessman can be, Yamani goes to work every day, 'because I have to. I must manage my investments. They don't take care of themselves. I have to work to maintain my lifestyle.'

'Obviously gifts got him started,' Wilton comments. 'But he's a shrewd enough businessman that he was able to use those to earn the rest. Of course there are always stories of corruption and wheeler-dealing with so many Arab businessmen and other Arab ministers. But I can tell you categorically, I've never heard anyone say that Zaki was involved in this or that deal. Sure, people will say, well Zaki's very rich, hah hah, and wink. But that's not any kind of evidence at all and I was always sad to hear that kind of insinuation because Zaki always struck me as a very upright sort of man.'

In an off-beat feature article about Yamani's personal fortune only three months before he was fired, one British newspaper quoted an international oil company executive who described Yamani as 'a tough son of a bitch but as honest as the day is long'. To that the paper added, 'He lends credence to the comforting idea that, with enough time and money, "they" will become like "us".'

Another of Yamani's international investments is a share in the Saudi European Investment Corporation, parent company of the Saudi European Bank in Paris. And a recent addition to the board of directors is Yamani's son Hani.

Part of the group's holdings include shares in a US-based company called Gotco.

Originally the trading arm of the Gulf Oil Corporation, Gotco was split away in a $39 million management buy-out when Gulf was sold to Socal in 1983/4. At the time, Yamani's name was bandied about as one of the principal backers. But then, much like Howard Hughes, his name has often been discreetly dropped by certain parties interested in bringing new investors into the fold. You know . . . pssst, Yamani is in on this too. The bigger the deal the more discreet everyone involved knew they had to be. The more discreet everyone was, the less possibility that Yamani would ever find out his name was being used like that.

'Let me tell you something,' Yamani leans forward to show his concern about this particular point. 'In all the time that I was Minister of Petroleum I never once dealt in oil.' He pauses to emphasize that this is very important. 'Not even once.'

It was widely reported in *Platts* and other oil journals that at one point Hani was ready to buy into an American company called US Oil.

But Hani explains his father wouldn't allow it. 'I went to him and told him my plans and asked his advice and he stopped me from making the deal. He told me that as long as he was Minister of Petroleum none of us would have anything personally to do with the oil business. And that was the end of that.'

However, Yamani could have traded oil for his own account. It would not have been illegal.

Yamani himself confirms that. 'No. It would not have been against the law in Saudi Arabia.'

So, you could you have done it had you wanted to?

He says, 'Of course. It would have been very easy for me to make a great deal of money.'

Then why didn't you?

He says, 'Because I felt it was wrong.'

*   *   *   *

It took the dramatic events of 1973 and 1974 to put the issue of oil into its true perspective.

'Oil had been taken for granted,' Yamani maintains. 'The consumers, assured of the availability of cheap, abundant energy were complacent. The oil companies were happy with the excessive profits they made. The producers, due to a combination of market conditions and an inability to assert their rights, were acquiescent.'

Late in the summer of 1973, certain Opec members had convinced themselves that doubling prices and indexing them to an annual 10 per cent inflation factor would suit their purpose.

However those prices fell short of the mark and they were increased again in January 1974.

With the true picture blurred by the oil embargo, Yamani points out, it wasn't until March 1974 that normal conditions were restored.

'The market mechanism is the final arbiter of the soundness of human judgements with respect to economic trends. The discernible decline in world demand we saw after January 1974 was undoubtedly a direct consequence of the sharp increase in prices. What prompted Saudi Arabia to call for lower oil prices was our belief that the sharp and sudden increases would have adverse effects on the world economies. And while our efforts did not succeed in bringing prices down, I am totally convinced they did prevent prices from shooting up.'

Although they were fast becoming masters of their own destiny, getting ever closer to their goal of owning Aramco, Yamani feels that Saudi Arabia's interests continued to parallel those of the consuming nations.

'The theme for consuming countries has always been security of supplies and cheaper prices. Our theme has never been dissimilar. We too have always wanted to see a secure supply. But in addition, we've been concerned with adequate reserves. Oil is a non-renewable resource and constitutes the greatest source of our livelihood. It's therefore understandable that we should concern ourselves with the rational utilization of our natural resources.'

When the meeting that was adjourned in Tripoli reconvened in Vienna in March 1974, the embargo against the United States was formally lifted.

Four months later the embargo was lifted against Holland.

Throughout the summer of 1974, with oil prices hovering around $11.65, the bad taste of the oil crisis lingered in many western mouths. Even now Yamani is well aware that a great deal of bitterness remains, especially in the United States. 'I think it's only natural. Yes. I can understand that.'

But as Saudi Arabian oil policy had become increasingly tied to Middle Eastern politics, the Saudis found themselves constantly butting heads with the Iranians.

The Shah still wanted $20–$25 oil.

It was Yamani, as the Saudi spokesman, who stood in his way.

Yamani was by this time skilled enough with the media to be courting an ever-growing army of journalists. But he now realized the odd predicament they had helped to create. The more the press wrote about him, the more vulnerable he became to criticism at home, particularly from certain members of the royal family who didn't care to see a commoner dwarfing them in international stature.

At the March 1974 Opec meeting in Vienna, while failing to bring prices down, Yamani was able to get his colleagues to agree to a three-month freeze on prices. But in June, when Opec met in Ecuador, the matter of oil company profits was raised. The cartel was upset by the 'excessive profits' earned by the oil companies during the first six months of the year. They also criticized the industrialized west for not containing 'the alarming trend of inflation'. To right the wrongs, Opec decided the member states should increase their royalties by 2 per cent, which effectively added 10–11 cents per barrel.

Feeling that this could be the thin end of the wedge, Yamani temporarily dissociated Saudi Arabia from the increase, using the rather obscure excuse that it could somehow get in the way of the not yet concluded Aramco takeover arrangements.

Having bought time, he now plotted to bring prices down. He decided to use the same method the Shah had chosen to take them up. He announced that Petromin, the Saudi state oil company, would host an auction.

When the Shah tested the waters in November 1973, there was sufficient hysteria to get a price well above going rates. But auctions in other Gulf states in early 1974 had failed, averaging 10 per cent under market prices. Encouraged by that, Yamani's idea was to offer a small parcel of oil to a limited group of bidders, confident that none of them would pay over $11.75.

He knew that if he stage-managed it properly, the Opec fixed price would come tumbling down.

What he hadn't counted on was terrific public praise from the United States for his idea.

The Americans loved the possibility of lower prices.

But that didn't sit well with his fellow producers.

Firstly, they didn't want lower prices. And secondly, they didn't like the idea of Yamani and the Saudis constantly playing into the hands of the Americans.

Right or wrong, that's what they saw happening.

Iran and Algeria joined forces to protest directly to King Faisal, warning him that, in the face of the threat of lower prices from Saudi Arabia, they would band together to decrease production and in so doing keep prices from falling. The Algerians even lobbied the Saudis to cancel the auction.

Yamani strongly argued its merits.

But when Prince Fahd threw his weight behind the side objecting to the auction, Faisal conceded.

Yamani spent the rest of the year quietly busying himself with the plans for the final takeover of Aramco.

Despite Yamani's rhetoric about secure supply and safeguarding natural resources, and despite King Faisal's repeated assurances that Saudi Arabia longed to maintain strong, friendly ties with the west, by the end of 1974 there was grumbling in the United States about the way the oil companies had behaved over the previous 15 months and also about the way certain American allies, namely Saudi Arabia, were continuing to behave.

At the same time, certain members of the Saudi royal family were showing distinct signs of irritation with the way Yamani was behaving.

To some people, Yamani appeared to be caught between two different worlds.

To many oil producers, specifically Iran and Libya, Yamani was a tool of the Americans.

To many consumers, among them the United States, he was the man who engineered the oil crisis and who now kept promising that prices would fall, except they were still going up.

Yamani finessed his way through the final stages of the Aramco takeover and, as some American diplomats in Saudi Arabia at the time believed, he tried to make his peace with Fahd, Sultan and Salman.

Then Faisal was murdered.

Now it was an odds-on bet that Yamani would go.

11

King Faisal's Murder

OIL IS the world's biggest business.

In terms of both volume traded and monetary value, it has no equal.

It's a business that touches absolutely every country on earth and every person on earth. The only exceptions are, possibly, lost tribes in darkest Africa or the remotest jungle dwellers of New Guinea.

Gold might be the closest any other commodity has ever come to being a political force. But gold won't turn factory turbines or make planes fly. Gold has never come close to matching oil as a political commodity.

Nor has any other commodity ever been so effectively managed by so few people.

Maybe the Ecuadorians can control the world's banana market. And maybe the South Africans can control the world's diamond market. And maybe the best red wines in the world can only come from France. But in the end, none of that really matters.

The world will survive if the last banana tree should ever become extinct.

The same is not true of oil.

Not these days.

The Saudis, who own nearly one-third of the entire free world's oil reserves, are basically a conservative lot who believe that oil was a gift from Allah.

It was a reward for their devout belief.

Ever thankful, they see no reason to deny the teachings of the Koran. They believe that they must therefore never waiver from their devotion to Islam. At the same time, God has given them oil wealth which is to be translated into money as a means by which they can modernize. But one should never interfere with the other.

It is, to say the least, a dangerously narrow contradiction.

Success for Saudi kings therefore lies in cautious change.

When Faisal decided the time had come to educate girls in Saudi Arabia, he skilfully brought about the change even though the population was largely opposed to it. Until then, school was for boys and very much the domain of religious leaders who were traditionally against higher education if by that you meant anything except the study of the Koran. So Faisal appointed one of these old educators to set up the new system.

In 1965, with the introduction of television in Saudi Arabia, some staunchly traditionalist Moslems protested that this was too radical a step towards modern western decadence and therefore a blatant insult to any fundamentally conservative interpretation of Islam.

So Faisal, concerned with the powerful religious elements of Saudi society, set down certain rules. For example, love scenes in films must be edited out. Even smooching in cartoons was banned. Still, Faisal said, television was vital for the education of his people and it was going to happen in Saudi Arabia regardless of the most extreme Islamic elements.

One of those who considered television as something akin to heresy was an off-balanced born-again fanatic named Khaled ibn Musaid.

What made his views slightly troublesome to the royal family was that, as the son of Ibn Saud's 15th son, he was King Faisal's nephew.

Even then, Khaled was only a minor nuisance . . . at least until he led an armed attack on Riyadh's new TV transmitter.

The police arrived instantly to quell the disturbance. But Khaled and his followers refused to disperse.

The moment the police officer in charge realized that the man leading the rioters was a Saudi prince, he sent word to the Chief of the Security Forces who rushed off to inform Faisal.

The king was fully briefed.

The Chief of the Security Forces awaited instructions.

Faisal considered the situation for a long time. Then he answered, it doesn't matter who the man is. He said, no one is above the law. He said, 'If the prince fires at you then you must fire back.'

It was the Chief of the Security Forces himself who shot and killed Khaled ibn Musaid.

A few years later Khaled ibn Musaid's brother Faisal went to study in the United States. He started at San Francisco State, transferred to the University of California at Berkeley and then went on to the University of Colorado at Boulder. But his years there were marred by drug taking and a 1970 arrest in Colorado for conspiracy to sell LSD.

Although King Faisal refused to intervene personally on his

nephew's behalf, when word of the arrest reached Washington, bells went off at the State Department. Because of the boy's royal connections the Colorado judge was informally asked by the government to be lenient. He allowed the boy to plead guilty, gave him a suspended sentence and placed him on probation.

In 1971, once the boy returned to Saudi Arabia, the king banned him from leaving the country.

Yet somewhere along the line, the 27 year old had picked up some radical views on Saudi politics, an American girlfriend with whom he lived for five years and the idea that his uncle had to die.

*   *   *   *

For Zaki Yamani, 25 March 1975 was supposed to be just another day.

He got up early, washed and went through his morning prayers. Then he ate a bowl of special fibre porridge while he read through whatever urgent matters had come in over night.

He sat in the small livingroom of his private wing at the Yamama hotel and quietly went over the message traffic, until about 8:30 or quarter to nine. Then he dressed, called for his chauffeur and drove the few hundred yards to his office.

As usual, there was a full schedule of meetings that morning.

As usual, there was already a queue of people waiting for him.

Had it been just any other day, he would have stayed in the office until 3:00 or 3:30 before going back to the Yamama for a late lunch of yoghurt, nuts, dates and fruit.

Had it been just any other day, he would have returned to the office at 5:00 or 5:30 for more meetings, or perhaps a session of the Council of Ministers, which often lasted until after 9:00.

Had it been just any other day, depending on what he then had to do, he might bring files home to read. Or play cards with friends. Or he might simply stay in his room, sprawled across his big bed, talking on the phone to friends around the world while watching a video. He has always had a regular supply sent to him from the States and England. He still does. Programmes taped right off friends' television sets, complete with commercials. Everything from last week's '60 Minutes' to reruns of 'Charlie's Angels'.

But on the morning of 25 March, Abdul Mutaleb Kazimi, the new oil minister from Kuwait, was in Riyadh. It was on Yamani's calendar to escort Kazimi and his party into the royal offices at the working palace and introduce them to the king at a 10:30 courtesy call.

He left his office at 10:10 for the short drive to the palace and greeted Kazimi in an anteroom of the king's small office.

It was 10:20.

'Kazimi introduced me to everyone in his party, including one young man whom he called "brother" Faisal bin Musaid. I didn't recognize him. But I was amazed because the name is a Saudi name of the royal family and yet he spoke with a Kuwait accent. What also struck me was that he was nervous. Very nervous. Yet he obviously knew Kazimi well and he seemed to belong with the group so I thought nothing more about it.'

While waiting for the king, Yamani promised the Kuwaitis that at exactly 10:25 Faisal would enter his office. Yamani assured them, 'He is so precise. You could adjust your watch to him because he's more accurate.'

And right on cue, at 10:25, Faisal walked into his office followed by his one bodyguard.

From where Yamani was standing in the anteroom he could see Faisal in his office. He excused himself and left the Kuwaitis in the company of the Chief of Royal Protocol while he went to speak privately with the king for a few moments.

The king's modest office was a narrow room at the far end of a corridor, taken up by a simple desk, two straight chairs facing the desk, two couches facing each other beyond that and a single window looking out at a garden.

Yamani explained the reason for Kazimi's visit, but the king was in an especially good mood that morning and spent several minutes joking with Yamani. Then they walked together from his office to a reception room. It was larger than the king's office but it was still a very modest room with cushioned couches along three of the four walls.

A television crew was already set up to tape the gathering, which was to last not more than 10 or 15 minutes. It was to be just enough time to say hello and share a coffee.

When Faisal was ready to receive his guests, Yamani took his place next to the king. The two of them were facing the television crew.

The door opened and the Chief of Royal Protocol ushered the Kuwaitis in.

Kazimi was first.

The others in his party waited their turn in a queue.

Faisal welcomed Kazimi.

Just as he did, the young man with the Saudi name and the Kuwaiti accent started running towards the king.

It all happened very quickly.

The young man got right up to Kazimi before anyone noticed him.

Now he was only a couple of feet from Faisal and Yamani.

And now he pulled a .38 pistol out from under his robes and started shooting.

It was 10:32.

He fired three times.

'I didn't know what happened. I heard the gun shots but I didn't know who was shooting. Then the king fell down. I came down with him.'

Panic erupted in the room.

Yamani raised his head to see the king's bodyguard grab the young man.

They were struggling for the gun.

The guard had a grip on the boy's wrist, forcing his hand up towards the ceiling.

But the boy was staring directly at Yamani.

There were more gun shots.

'He looked straight into my eyes. He stared directly at me and fired into the ceiling.'

Now more guards rushed in to wrestle the gun away from the young man.

And now Yamani raced outside to scream for help.

He screamed for a doctor.

Other people were screaming too.

There was noise and confusion as everyone crowded around Faisal, who lay sprawled and bleeding across the carpet.

Yamani ran back into the room, pushing his way through the crowd. He bent down next to his king and stayed there until the ambulance arrived.

Medics rushed Faisal to Central Hospital.

But the first shot had ripped open the king's jugular vein.

Over the next few hours, with very little information being released about the incident, official silence merely served to create a good market in rumours.

The first news was that the king had been shot twice in the head and three times in the chest, at close range. The young prince was said to have easily talked his way past the palace guards.

Next came the rumour that the king had merely been wounded.

When the official announcement was finally forthcoming, when Riyadh Radio announced that Faisal was dead, the palace claimed that the assassin was 'mentally deranged', and had been acting alone.

It was obvious that the Saudis were determined to put to rest any rumours that there had been a conspiracy or that the young prince had been a tool for any sort of uprising against the king.

Next came the announcement that Crown Prince Khaled had

assumed the throne and that the Minister of Interior, Fahd, would be Crown Prince.

As Khaled had not taken a very active part in his duties as Crown Prince, the moment he became king it was assumed, correctly, that Fahd would be the country's chief executive, while Khaled would handle the more ceremonial details.

Years before, Faisal had realized that Khaled was not capable of ruling, that he much preferred hunting and spending time with the desert tribes. So Faisal took the unprecedented step of naming Fahd to be Second Deputy Prime Minister.

However, once enthroned, Khaled had his own ideas.

There was even talk at the time of a minor rift between Khaled and his Crown Prince.

If there was any real antagonism between the two, it remained very private, as those things are wont to do among the ruling brothers of the Saudi royal family.

The new king personally spent hours questioning the murderer. And it was Khaled who learned that when the young prince stared into Yamani's eyes and fired at the ceiling, he honestly believed the gun was aimed at Yamani. He was convinced he had killed Yamani too.

It was only after Khaled decided there was 'no external motive for the crime', that a medical panel was allowed to rule that the nephew was, 'although mentally deranged, sane at the time of the murder'.

On 18 June, Prince Faisal bin Musaid was led into the middle of the main square in Riyadh, in front of the Palace of Justice, where a soldier paraded him before the gathered crowd.

The unsteady prince wore white robes and a blindfold.

The soldier pushed the prince to his knees in front of the execution block.

Then a man with a huge sword came up behind the boy and in one smooth swing beheaded him.

The prince's head was placed on a stake and displayed for 15 minutes before an ambulance removed it and the body.

Now, there are some people who believe the boy was simply avenging his brother's death.

Others say he was carrying out a single act of terror in some sort of organized concert towards world revolution.

There are those who contended then and still believe today that it was a CIA plot.

Or that Qaddafi had a hand in it.

What's known is that while the young prince was at Berkeley he became interested in radical Arab causes, such as the PLO, and in various fringe Marxist groups. He was a staunch anti-Zionist and frequently told his American friends that his own family was too weak on the question of Israel.

Immediately after the assassination, a New York newspaper quoted one of the prince's friends as saying, 'He often remarked that his family was one of the major obstacles to progress in the Arab world. Many times he said that the Saudi Royal Family was interested primarily in cooperation with American oil interests.'

Yamani is, these days, firmly convinced that the young prince was not just avenging his brother's death. 'He was from the other side. The brother was very religious. This one was anti-religion.'

He believes that the nephew merely wanted to change the regime.

'I must admit I don't know that for sure. But some months later, when I was with the terrorist Carlos, he told me that he knew the nephew. He said he used to tease the nephew's American girlfriend. He used to ask her how she could go out with such a reactionary. And the girlfriend told him, he is not a reactionary. The girlfriend told Carlos, he will do something very soon which will prove that he's a hero.'

* * * *

Because Saudi Arabia is such a highly complex society, the key to ruling the country is not, as some people believe, in somehow stitching together the various interest groups and factions. Rather it lies in the less easily clarified talent of keeping those interest groups and factions from ripping apart.

Government is therefore a delicate balancing act.

Generally speaking, Khaled represented the traditionalists, with the roots of his power base in the tribal areas. Fahd was known as a champion of the technocrats and, at least in Saudi terms, a progressive.

Unfortunately, as one journalist spelled out at the time, 'It is Fahd who has inherited the problem. But he hasn't inherited the talent to deal with it.'

Not that there was open dissension among the two factions in the royal family. Instead the royal family conducts its affairs with a some-what mysterious oriental discipline. Decisions are privately argued out amongst themselves behind the shut doors of their palaces. They rarely if ever hang their laundry out to dry in public. Shooting one radical nephew and publicly beheading another doesn't count. In 1958, when King Saud bankrupted the treasury through sheer extravagance and Faisal was assigned the task of rebuilding the state and Saud eventually left in exile and everybody pretty much knew the whole story . . . that was a rare exception.

Now, with Faisal dead and Khaled on the throne, there was obvious jockeying for position. Khaled was devout and well loved. But he'd had a serious open heart operation in the United States in January 1972 and was still in frail health. Believing that Khaled was not well enough to rule for very long, the Al Fahd moved as one block to take control.

'Watching Yamani', the British *Sunday Times* said in mid-April 1975, 'will tell us what is happening between Fahd and the king.'

They pointed out that over the previous year Yamani's relationship with Fahd had become strained. 'Fahd doesn't appear to like Yamani's freewheeling attitude with the western press. Yamani's power lay in the complete confidence shown him by Faisal. Neither this, nor his dazzling success endeared him to the Saudi establishment.'

Maybe that was why, they theorized, 'Throughout the past year Yamani went out of his way to ingratiate himself to Fahd.'

Maybe that was why, as so many Saudi watchers started to agree, Yamani's position had become uncertain.

The announcement that he'd be replaced was expected within a matter of weeks.

When it didn't happen, the pundits remained confident. They assured anyone who asked, it will later this year.

When it still didn't happen, they said, but it will one day soon.

That day turned out to be more than 11 years away.

Yet James Akins asserts, it wasn't quite so obvious to him that Yamani would be the first to go. 'He's extremely clever. Extremely intelligent. He knows his field very well. And before the king was assassinated he'd made his peace with the other members of the royal family. Fahd and Abdullah [Crown Prince under Fahd]. When the king was assassinated there really wasn't any question of getting rid of him.'

But many other people aren't so sure.

One Aramco senior executive puts it very plainly. 'It's amazing that he worked for the royal family as long as he did because there was always a lot of jealousy on their part. And some things did clearly change for him after Faisal died. For instance, Zaki could no longer speak with the same authority. It wasn't a very obvious change. It was extremely subtle. But it was a change. Deep down there was always the hint that he couldn't second-guess Fahd the way he could Faisal. Still, after Faisal's murder, when it was Fahd who was running the country, Fahd and the Sudairi group somehow managed to push aside their jealousies and Yamani stayed on. They didn't necessarily love him. But I guess Fahd and the others understood that they needed Zaki more than Zaki needed them.'

Former British Ambassador Sir John Wilton adds to that view. 'The problem in Saudi Arabia is always power. Who has it and how much they have of it. There's no doubt at all that Fahd was jealous of Yamani's relationship with Faisal and the power he had under Faisal. But Fahd was shrewd enough not to let that get in the way. Now it was Fahd who had the power and he could share it out as he liked.'

Wilton, however, is not convinced that Faisal's assassination changed the course of the country as much as it might have changed the course of Yamani's life. 'One remarkable thing is the swiftness with which the Saudi system adapts itself to the changes which are necessary. When Ibn Saud died people naturally said, how can you replace a man of that stature. Well, Saud took over. It was perfectly smooth. The machine changed gear and went on. Then Saud was seen to be quite impossible and eventually the family said we must get this chap out. After incredibly patient manoeuvring over a period of years by Faisal, Saud was edged out and Faisal took over. When Faisal was assassinated the next chap was there ready to take over. The committee continues. The next chairman is always there.'

With King Khaled, the chairman was Fahd.

Wilton continues, 'Everybody said, we know that Fahd doesn't like Yamani as much as Faisal liked Yamani so Yamani is on very thin ice. You see, instead of doing the football pools in Saudi Arabia they guess about cabinet reshuffles. The great national pastime, especially during Ramadan, is saying, as soon as Ramadan is over the king is going to reshuffle the government and Yamani is going to be out and Sultan is going to be this and Abdullah is going to be that. You hear this every year. Usually nothing happens. The number of cabinet changes in Saudi Arabia is infinitesimal. There are still chaps in government today from Faisal's time. In fact, after Faisal's assassination, there wasn't a significant change in ministerial office for years. Yes, the Minister of Communications dropped dead and had to be replaced. And the Deputy Minister of Defence [Prince Turki] offended his brothers by what they thought was an imprudent marriage and he was required to retire from public life. But apart from that the same team went on and on. Sure, Yamani was on thin ice with Fahd. But thin ice in Saudi Arabia tends not to crack for a decade or so.'

James Schlesinger, then US Secretary of Defense, sees it another way. 'After Faisal's death, Yamani became just another technocrat who had to work with a slow-moving and ponderous Saudi machine. He couldn't speak for Saudi Arabia after Faisal's death the way he could before.'

The reason why is suggested by Sir James Craig, another former British Ambassador to Saudi Arabia.

'Look at the personalities. Faisal was a deeply intelligent man. He never had a formal education but he was travelling the world and meeting prime ministers as a child. He came to Britain when he was 13 and met with Lloyd George. It would be easy to see how he and Yamani would get along. Khaled was a very simple man. A very likeable man, but he was a dotty old chap and I suspect he'd been a dotty old chap since the age of 10. He certainly wasn't capable of understanding inflation. He wouldn't even know what the word was in Arabic. And the notion that he sat there and solemnly discussed the Saudis' five-year development plan is quite absurd. Fahd did all that. Fahd normally took the chair at meetings of the Council of Ministers. Khaled only went there for ritual purposes.'

Craig accepts that some people say Fahd was jealous of Yamani, but he believes that's putting it too strongly. 'There was I think resentment. Not of Zaki's intellectual attainments, because Fahd wouldn't understand what that meant. It's like, if I don't understand music and don't get any pleasure from it, can I feel jealous of someone who does? But Fahd would be resentful of Yamani's prominence. Of his publicity. That rather silly but naturally human resentment would get a bigger push from the fact that it had political repercussions. Why did Zaki last so long under Fahd with whom it was well known he had bad relations from the start? My answer is, because to sack Zaki Yamani carried with it the danger of throwing open the whole world oil market. I believe the establishment in Riyadh felt in 1975 that Zaki was so well known, was such a pillar of Opec, a pillar of the world oil economy and to a certain extent of the general world economy, that they were nervous. That if there was a visible row leading to his dismissal, the repercussions could be incalculable.'

Prefacing his remarks with, 'It would be difficult to say just how intelligent Fahd is because intelligence depends to a large extent on cultivation, on education,' Craig does stress, 'he's no intellectual. But he had a great deal of native shrewdness and astuteness and years of experience of very high politics on the national and international stage. That rubs off. Even if you're stupid you learn. And he is not stupid. Fahd proved himself capable of understanding, not necessarily fully and profoundly understanding, but understanding for practical purposes things like inflation, economic development policy and oil policy. I think for most of his reign he's been following Zaki's advice. In 1975 he needed Zaki. But he eventually came to the point where he felt able to take decisions against Zaki's advice.'

However, he says, that's not to take away from the fact that Yamani also happens to be a survivor. 'There were stories every six months that Zaki was going to be sacked. I once said to him, I've heard the stories that you're going to be leaving and you've probably heard them yourself. He laughed and said, look, these stories come up every year.

But none of the rumours have been true so far and when it does happen, if it does happen, I suspect I'll be the last to hear.'

As it turned out, he was.

When one leading Saudi businessman was told in 1975 that Yamani might be fired, he replied, 'Well maybe. But not today. I happen to know that it took Fahd two years to fire his cook.'

One of the most obvious things that changed with Faisal's death was a style of leadership. Yamani has always said that Faisal could never be compared with anyone else in Saudi Arabia because he was such an exceptional man. But he adds, 'As far as my own work as a minister was concerned, there was no change.'

That's not quite the case.

Some American oilmen working in Saudi Arabia who had close contacts with Yamani claim that, in more mellow moments, he even said he would be finished with government once Faisal was gone.

These days Yamani denies it. 'I never said that. Maybe it is true from a sentimental point of view that I thought such things. And yes, it was very difficult for me to continue. But I did continue. It took me a great deal of time to get over Faisal's death. Even today I still feel a great personal void. The amount of respect I have for the man is still so great.'

Asking Yamani what else changed with Faisal's death gets you a long, hard stare that shows how reluctant he is to make a list.

Question: 'Was there a change in what you could or could not say?'

Answer: 'Maybe . . . yes.'

Question: 'About oil policy?'

Answer: 'No, not really. When it comes to issues other than oil policy.'

Question: 'Such as?'

Answer: 'You know, I used to discuss all sorts of things with Faisal at length. I could always tell exactly what he had in mind. So I sometimes felt I could reveal certain things.'

Question: 'What about your relationship with King Khaled?'

Answer: 'It was very cordial and warm. He was a man with a good heart, who cared about people and their welfare. He used to follow what was happening in the country. If someone was ill with heart trouble for instance, he'd send him abroad for an operation. He was that type of a man. He loved his people and he was greatly loved by his people.'

Question: 'Had Faisal not been gunned down, had he lived say another six years to the age of 75, what would or would not be different today?'

Here Yamani's first reaction is to say he never speculates on such things. So you have to cajole and say, go ahead, go on, until he gives in and is willing at least to hazard a guess.

'If Faisal had lived I don't think we would have seen the Camp David Agreements. He was so very respected by all the leaders in the Middle East that if he was against something they would not do it. He would go to an Arab summit conference and the minute he took the floor to speak, you could see everyone in the room paying great attention to what he was saying. His opinions were not challenged. Also, I don't think we would have seen a higher price of oil. What happened in 1979 might not have happened. There was pressure put on us to raise the price of oil in 1979 and I don't think Faisal would have succumbed to it. Inside he was a very strong man, strong enough to resist those pressures.'

That inner strength was not the only thing which made him special. Yamani says, 'Faisal also had a special talent for dealing with all of the forces of Saudi society. He could manage it for several reasons. First, because his mother was from a famous religious family, the al-Ashaikh. It enabled him to deal with that group. Second, because he himself was respected as a religious man. None of the religious groups would challenge him. Third, he had a sense of the country's need to move forward, so he was respected by the progressives. Believe me, he was very powerful.'

Now Yamani is asked, 'What about Fahd?'

And he answers flatly, 'He's loved and respected by his people.'

* * * *

On 23 March, two days before Faisal's assassination, Yamani had a small ceremony at the Grand Mosque in Mecca to conclude the marriage contract with Tammam al-Anbar.

As the daughter of a wealthy Saudi businessman, a former Chief of Royal Protocol and a former ambassador to several countries, a traditional Moslem wedding ceremony and parties were planned.

But all of that changed on the 25th.

Once the ambulance took Faisal to the hospital, guards attended to Yamani. They drove him back to the Yamama. They literally had to carry him inside.

He was sheet white, overwhelmed by the murder, in a state of total shock.

Over the next few days, as the reality of Faisal's death sunk in, he couldn't sleep. And he had no appetite.

In the weeks that followed, his own health deteriorated.

His utter horror at Faisal's murder slowly turned to a deep and consuming grief.

'I was in very bad shape. I was really suffering from his death. A part of me died with him that morning.'

Under those circumstances there was no question of having a large wedding ceremony or any of the festivities that go with it.

Everything was cancelled.

However, according to the marriage contract, he and Tammam were already married.

'So she agreed to forgo a wedding party in the normal sense. She wanted to come and take care of me. We eventually had a quiet and private ceremony on April 14.'

There have always been rumours that King Faisal's last will and testament stipulated that Yamani was to be treated by the rest of the royal family as if he'd been Faisal's own son.

But Faisal probably didn't leave a will. Or if he did, Yamani knows nothing about it. 'I don't think this is true.'

Nevertheless, while Faisal was alive Yamani was indeed treated like a son.

'I was with him most of the time. But he was my boss.'

Here Yamani is not being totally straight. Their relationship was obviously much closer than employer and employee. When Faisal was in town, Yamani would not leave town except on official business. Other ministers weren't necessarily on call like that. But it was known that Faisal had once asked that of all his own sons.

Throughout that spring and into the summer, Yamani's grief did not subside.

The only comfort he found was in his family, with Tammam, in his faith and sometimes in his work.

It was already, without any doubt, the worst year of his life.

He prayed everything would be better soon.

Tammam got pregnant with the first of their five children.

And now the two of them shared a hope for the future.

But the year wasn't over.

At the very end of 1975, Tammam nearly became a widow.

12

Kidnapped by Carlos

BY 11:00 that Sunday morning, Vienna was still only just waking up.

There wasn't much traffic on the street.

Although the Christkindlmarkt was open.

So were the cafés along the Ring where you could sit inside, out of the cold and drink hot coffee while you read a newspaper you took off the large rack of newspapers that you always find in good Viennese cafés along the Ring.

It was 21 December 1975.

Christmas was only four days away.

There were holiday lights strung along the streets and nativity scenes in department store windows. There were baubled Christmas trees in hotel lobbies and cardboard signs in shops that spelled out 'Gut Yule' in large cutout letters.

On the first floor of the building at 10 Karl Leuger Ring which Opec shared with the Canadian Embassy and the Austrian headquarters for Texaco, in the large windowless conference room where a glass wall looked out to the hallway, 11 oil ministers and their deputies and their secretaries and the Opec general staff began their meeting.

The agenda contained a discussion of price differentials and quotas and the planned establishment of the Opec Special Fund which would provide interest-free loans to developing nations.

Before the morning was out the agenda was revised to include murder.

Yamani was due to make a speech in Britain on Monday. He'd planned to stay at the Opec meeting only long enough to see it get under way. He intended to be back at his hotel by mid-morning, to pack, make some calls and catch an early afternoon plane.

But the debate that morning was especially good. Two of the

ministers were really going at each other. Yamani looked at his watch and saw that it was just about 11:40. He thought to himself that he really ought to leave. But this was too good to miss so he decided to stay a little while longer.

Had he left five minutes earlier he would have been in the UK for his speech the next day.

Had he left when he was supposed to, taking the stairs instead of the lift the way he always did, he might have been murdered then and there.

Because at precisely 11:40 five men and one woman casually walked into the building through the main door, wearing long coats and hats and carrying sports bags.

They passed some journalists in the small lobby who were waiting there with a pair of plain clothes Viennese policemen and headed briskly up the stairs.

More curious than suspicious, one of the policemen politely asked where they were going.

None of the six took the time to answer.

Now they ran up the stairs.

And when they got to the first floor all hell broke loose.

Led by a man with a moustache and goatee, wearing a brown leather jacket, a light grey roll-necked sweater, khaki trousers, short brown boots and a brown beret, the gang yanked guns out from under their coats and started firing in all directions.

One of the men, a German, went straight for the switchboard, took his gun and blew out the telephone lines.

A policeman grabbed for the automatic pistol held by the man with the beret.

The girl, dressed in a grey wool cap pulled down to her eyes, raced over to the cop, shouted at him, then put her gun up to his throat and pulled the trigger.

Four of the gang rushed down the hallway towards the conference room.

The shooting continued.

An Iraqi bodyguard stepped out of an office and lunged at the girl. She opened fire.

A young Libyan got in the way.

He too was killed.

To cover their rear, one of the terrorists rolled a hand grenade down the stairwell, just in case anyone had any ideas of following them.

By then the man with the beret and most of the others had burst into the conference room.

There was screaming and there was panic as the gang started shooting at the ceiling, running off rounds from their guns and pistols.

Lights were shot out and the stench of gun powder quickly filled the darkened room.

Yamani threw himself under the conference table.

'My first thought was that the attackers must be Europeans protesting against the rise in the price of oil. I thought they came to avenge themselves on us.'

The man with the beret yelled that he wanted everyone to lie down on the floor.

The others kept shooting at the ceiling.

The man with the beret continued yelling.

And the gang never stopped until the man with the beret was firmly in control.

Trapped, with no possible escape, men and women sprawled out along the floor, hovered in corners and cowered under tables. Chairs were overturned. Tables were shoved aside. Papers flew about. Some of the people in the room prayed out loud. Some of the people in the room wept openly. One secretary was crying so uncontrollably that the man in the beret just let her leave. But everything happened so quickly that most of the people in the room were simply stunned into a trembling and shocked silence.

'When the shooting stopped there was dead silence for a short time. Then I heard someone ask in English, "Have you found Yamani?" My heart sank.'

One of the terrorists crawled along the floor with a flashlight, shining it into everyone's face. He looked at everyone hiding under the table, and when his eyes met Yamani's he gave an ironic salute.

'He told the others he had found me. I suddenly realized that I was going to be murdered. That I was going to die.'

Almost as soon as they were in control, the terrorists placed dynamite charges in each corner of the room. They'd brought everything they needed in those sports bags. Within two minutes they had the room wired.

By the time the terrorists had neutralized the conference room, the Vienna police had been alerted. They arrived with sirens blaring. First they cordoned off the neighbourhood. Then, all along the street and on nearby rooftops, anti-terrorist officers with bullet-proof vests and automatic weapons took up their positions.

The moment police commandos approached the front door, the terrorists guarding the entrance to the corridor rolled more grenades down the stairs and down the elevator shaft too.

In an exchange of gunfire, one of the terrorists was wounded.

When both sides were finally dug into positions they thought they could hold, the man with the beret demanded that their wounded colleague be taken to a hospital.

The police insisted that they be given any wounded hostages as well.

A deal was struck and the wounded terrorist was handed over, together with a Kuwaiti who had been shot in the shoulder.

Then the police retreated.

And a long wait began.

As soon as they could locate him, the Austrian Chancellor, Dr Bruno Kreisky, was notified of the siege. He'd gone skiing for the weekend. Told that 11 Opec ministers had been taken hostage and three men were already dead, Kreisky returned to Vienna for an emergency session with his cabinet.

Inside Opec, the man with the beret allowed the Iraqi Embassy attaché to act as his go-between with the police.

And it was the man with the beret himself who told the Iraqi, 'You will have heard of me already. I am the famous Carlos.'

If it was true, Opec headquarters had been seized by the most wanted man in Europe.

Born in Caracas, Venezuela, on 12 October 1949, the pudgy faced, brown-eyed, brown-haired, 5'11" Ilyich Ramirez Sanchez was the son of a wealthy lawyer with long-standing and very active communist party affiliations. So dedicated a communist was Sanchez père that he actually named his other two sons Vladimir and Lenin.

An introverted, fat and socially self-conscious child, Ilyich is believed to have done his basic training in terrorism in 1966 at Camp Montanzas, in the hills overlooking Havana, where Cuban and Soviet agents taught the art of subversion. A few years later he was shipped off to Patrice Lumumba Friendship University in Moscow for a six-month course designed to train militant students from the third world in the ways of Soviet-style communism. But before he graduated the Russians expelled him for anti-Soviet activities of the extreme leftish variety. Whether they decided he was uncontrollable or just used his deportation as a whitewash to send him into the cold, no one knows.

Returning to South America, he soon got into trouble with the Caracas police. Charged with inciting a student riot he was jailed for a couple of months.

From Venezuela he went to France, where he played a role in riots in Marseilles.

He next showed up in London, where his parents had taken up temporary residence. He worked for a time, teaching Spanish at a secretarial school in Mayfair. Assuming the guise of a rich young economist, he joined the Latin American social set, made the rounds of parties and settled on a nom de guerre. He started calling himself Carlos Martinez.

Somewhere along the line he hooked up with Popular Front for the Liberation of Palestine. This is the same group that claimed credit for the murder of the Israeli athletes in the 1972 Olympic Games in Munich and the massacre at Tel Aviv airport that same year. Little is known about Carlos's training with the PFLP except that he was sent for his indoctrination either to a camp in Jordan or to one just outside Beirut.

No one knows for sure.

Where he trained is immaterial.

It is what he learned there that matters.

He obviously completed his degree with honours because, over the next few years, the PFLP credited Carlos with at least six major operations in Europe. Among them were the bombing of Le Drugstore in Paris where two people were killed and 34 were injured, the seige of the French Embassy in Holland, a bazooka attack on a DC–9 at Orly Airport in Paris and the near fatal shooting of Edward Sieff, head of Marks and Spencer's, in London. That one was a particularly daring act. Carlos forced his way into Sieff's home in north London, found him on the toilet and shot him with a 9mm pistol before easily managing his own escape.

The name Carlos didn't mean much to anyone at the time of the Sieff shooting. It was two years later, when police stumbled across the gun he used in a Bayswater flat and officers from the anti-terrorist squad at Scotland Yard also found what has now come to be called 'the death list' – a handwritten selection of men Carlos planned to murder. Included were prominent British businessmen such as Lords Sainsbury and Goodman, playwright John Osborne, actress Vera Lynn, MP Tony Benn, disc jockey David Jacobs, concert violinist Yehudi Menuhin and, yet again, Edward Sieff.

Also on the list was Sheikh Ahmed Zaki Yamani.

The Saudis were alerted and they dispatched a pair of secret service officers to Libya, demanding that Qaddafi arrest Carlos. But Qaddafi denied knowing anything about Carlos and the two Saudi agents returned home unsuccessful.

Then, acting on a tip-off from inside the PFLP in the spring of 1975, French counter-intelligence officers raided an apartment at 9 rue Toullier in Paris's 5th arrondissement, the student quarter. Carlos himself answered the door. In the ensuing gunfight, the PFLP informer and two detectives were killed by Carlos who managed to escape.

In spite of further Carlos sightings in France and Spain, there is reason to believe to came back to London, where he hid for several months while planning his attack on Opec.

From London he went to Baghdad, where it is known he had discussions with the PFLP.

Eventually he made his way to Switzerland, where he left a communiqué with collaborators and finalized his plans.

More than two and a half years after the Opec seige, one of the terrorists revealed to a German magazine that the six of them arrived in Vienna on 19 December. He bragged that they were so laden with pistols, machine guns and hand grenades, 'we could hardly sit down for all the stuff we had', as they rode the near-empty tram car to the Karl Leuger Ring that Sunday morning.

Describing Carlos in *Der Spiegel* as being terribly vain and chiding him for always taking showers, then powdering himself from head to foot, the terrorist claimed that overall command for the operation was left to Wadi Haddad, a Palestinian terrorist now believed to be dead.

Until that point there was speculation that Carlos might have once again been acting for Dr George Habash, leader of the PFLP, who had often gone on record as saying that by breaking up Opec he could sabotage any moves by certain pro-western members – meaning Saudi Arabia and Iran – who might be inclined to try to force through a peace settlement with the Israelis at the expense of the Palestinians.

Rumours of another possible connection suggested the less well-known Northern Front of Rejection, a group supported largely by Syria, Iraq and Libya, who were dead set against allowing the 'capitulation' of Saudi Arabia, Iran and even Yassir Arafat's Palestine Liberation Organization in a peace settlement.

In this case, however, at least occording to *Der Spiegel*'s source, 'the idea for the attack came from an Arab president'.

Although he did not say who that was, the betting man's favourite has always been Libya's Colonel Qaddafi.

In this case, Haddad was merely in charge.

Actually, Haddad's original idea was to kidnap the Pope. That was ruled out when he concluded that no Arab nation would ever allow the Pope's abductors to run around free. His second choice was Mahdi al-Tajir. Some time in early 1975, Haddad drew up a list of wealthy international businessmen and put Tajir's name at the top, believing the Bahraini could be held for as much as $25 million. It was Carlos who vetoed that one when he found out that Tajir, then said to be worth $13 billion, was constantly surrounded by armed bodyguards.

When the unnamed 'Arab president' suggested kidnapping all of Opec and the possibility of murdering Zaki Yamani, Haddad and Carlos finally had a mission they could agree on.

157

Now in Vienna, playing for huge stakes regardless of who was financing the operation. Carlos and the others fortified their positions inside the conference room.

They divided the hostages into four groups.

The ones Carlos labelled 'friendly' – the Algerians, Iraqis and Libyans – were grouped almost directly in front of the door, along the glass wall that bordered the library.

He put the 'neutrals' – the Nigerians, Kuwaitis, Ecuadorians, Venezuelans and Gabonese – in the middle of the room, opposite them.

All the Opec employees were placed just inside the door, to the right, in the front of the room.

Farthest from the door, crammed into the rear corner where the glass wall met the back wall, were his 'enemies' – Saudi Arabia, Iran, the UAE and Qatar.

Everyone was tied and gagged.

The 'enemies' were also corralled in by dynamite charges and one of the terrorists sat facing them sadistically holding two wires barely apart.

Never one to miss an opportunity for publicity, Carlos sent a message to the police announcing that he and his gang were part of the 'Arm of the Arab Revolution'.

Until that moment no one had ever heard of the group.

The police announced the name of the organization to the press.

The press quickly released it to the world.

Just as quickly, the PLO disowned the terrorists. According to them, 'Undoubtedly American imperialism and Zionism are behind this which is aimed at undermining Opec.'

The PFLP did not comment.

In stating his demands to the Austrians, speaking through the Iraqi middleman, Carlos said he wanted a plane made ready to take him and his hostages anywhere in the world. He explained that he had undergone this operation to confront a high-level plot aimed at legalizing the Zionist presence in Palestine. He said he intended 'to confront the conspiracy, to strike at its support and to apply revolutionary sanctions to all personalities and parties involved'.

The text in his *raison d'être* was contained in a seven-page letter, which he turned over to the authorities at just about the same time that an anonymous telephone call came into the press headquarters of the United Nations in Geneva saying that a letter, in English, could be found in the men's lavatory there.

It was the communiqué he'd left in Geneva before coming to Vienna.

As soon as it was found it went out over the press wires as part of this unfolding drama.

The hidden letter was in fact a clever little insurance policy on Carlos's part, showing just how sophisticated his thought process was in matters like these. No one knows who made that phone call alerting the press to its existence. It could have come from any of several sources, as the Carlos gang was said to have had loose connections with other international terrorist organizations like the Japanese Red Army, Germany's Baader-Meinhof group, the Turkish Popular Liberation Front, the Basque separatists and all the various Palestinian liberation factions. The point is that some Swiss-based associate of Carlos would have signalled the location of the letter whether or not Carlos had succeeded in taking hostages and staying alive. In other words, Carlos had assured himself of being heard even if he failed.

The text of Carlos's message was a typically laborious emotional accounting of a terrorist group's motives. It labelled Iran as 'an active imperialist tool', and called Egypt's Sadat, 'one of the leading traitors'. There was, however, praise for Iraq, Syria and the Palestinians as 'progressives' who demanded sovereignty when it came to handling oil reserves, 'for the benefit of the Arab people and other peoples of the third world'.

First, Carlos insisted that his letter be read out over Austrian radio.

Then he said, 'A bus with curtained windows must be made available to bring us to Vienna airport at 7 o'clock tomorrow morning. There, a fully tanked DC–9 with a crew of three must be made ready to take us and our hostages to the place we decide.'

In addition, he asked for two dozen metres of rope, five pairs of scissors, several rolls of adhesive tape, 100 sandwiches and as much fruit as the police could get.

Speaking mainly in English, with smatterings of Arabic and lots of Spanish thrown in for good measure – the Venezuelan oil minister did the translating – Carlos threatened that unless his demands were met he would shoot Yamani's deputy, then Amouzegar's deputy. If the demands were still not met, he would continue by killing Amouzegar then Yamani. If he still didn't get his way, he'd blow up the Opec building and kill everyone else.

The Austrian government retreated to consider their next move.

From the time the gang came into the building until about 2 o'clock, Yamani wondered who they were and what they wanted. He personally found it difficult to believe that they were Palestinian commandos because their leader was not an Arab.

The girl was German and they called her Nada. She was later identified as 25-year-old Gabriele Krocher-Tiederman, a former sociology student who earned her terrorist reputation with the German 2nd of June Movement. The second-in-command said his name was Khalid and that he was Lebanese. There was one Palestinian who called himself Yusef. The one who was wounded was a German. While Yamani says the last had a slight accent, as if he came from North Yemen.

According to investigative reporters Christopher Dobson and Ronald Payne, who went to enormous lengths to study Carlos and wrote the definitive book on him, some of the Arabs in the conference thought at first that they were being attacked by an Israeli hit squad. When someone told him that, Carlos supposedly replied, 'Can I help it if I have a Jewish-looking face?'

Yamani, understandably frightened, spent most of that day trying to calm himself by repeating passages from the Koran. 'At one point two of the terrorists left the room and were replaced by two others. The girl, who was in her twenties, came into the room and said to her boss with a slight smile, "I killed two." He replied, "I killed one myself." Then she asked, "Where's Yamani?" And he pointed to me. When we were told this was Carlos, I was quite shocked. I knew about the death list. I had also been informed that when the French police raided the flat in Paris a few months before, they came across papers and documents, that included a well-organized plan to assassinate me. Carlos and his gang knew all the details of my movements and my way of life. They even had lists of places I liked to visit in various towns.'

Somewhere around 4 o'clock, Carlos took Yamani into a nearby room to speak with him alone.

Carlos sat behind a desk.

Yamani took a chair facing him.

It was dark in the room.

Carlos said in English, 'You will be killed.'

Then he said he wanted Yamani to know that what they were doing was not directed personally against him.

Carlos said, 'We respect you. But you will be killed because what we are doing is directed against your country.'

Yamani immediately felt that Carlos might be bargaining for something. 'After all, it's not normal to say to someone, we respect you and we like you but we're going to kill you. So I said to him, "Now tell me what you want." I said, "Tell me what you're driving at".'

Carlos answered, 'Why do I have to drive at anything? I have my gun and I could kill you right now. What could I want from you? You are under my mercy.'

Yamani agreed that Carlos's power over his life was obvious. But he told Carlos that what he was saying was not logical.

'It was odd, but by that time I had calmed down considerably. I wasn't as worried at that point as I had been because I could see that he wasn't crazy. That may sound like a strange thing to say because yes, he was very cold-blooded. And yes, he was in complete control of everything. But he wasn't crazy. I didn't get the impression he would do something totally irrational. I could tell that he wasn't going to kill me then and there.'

Perhaps not then and there, but Carlos did outline his plan to Yamani, which ultimately included murdering him.

He said, 'Unless the Austrians agree to broadcast my demands and get me a plane, I will have to start the killings.'

He even fixed 6 p.m. for the time of Yamani's assassination.

He said, 'I hope you will not feel bitterness towards me. I would expect a man of your intelligence to understand our noble aims and intentions.'

Yamani wanted to know, 'How could you possibly expect me not to be bitter? You are trying to pressure me into something.'

Carlos laughed. 'Why should I put pressure on you? I am pressuring the Austrian government to try to get out of this place.'

If the Austrians came across with the plane, Carlos said, they would fly to Libya where the non-Arab ministers would be released, with the exception of Amouzegar. The Algerian and Libyan ministers would also be set free in Tripoli. Then they would go to Baghdad to release the Iraqi and the Kuwait. Their final stop would be Aden.

'Once we arrive in Aden,' Carlos promised, 'we will kill you and Amouzegar.'

That said, Carlos escorted Yamani back into the conference room to await the Austrians' decision.

If they said no, Yamani would be dead in an hour.

He took a pen and some paper and began writing a last note to Tamman, to his mother and to his children.

'I cannot deny that waiting for death is a frightful and painful thing. But the human soul is strange. When the hour was 5:00 and the Austrian government had not yet broadcast the communiqué, Carlos with a smile on his face came to remind me what would happen. My feelings had changed and there was less terror in my heart. I began to think, not of myself but of my family, my children, my relatives and those for whom I had responsibility. I wrote a farewell letter to them, explaining what I wanted done.'

Late that afternoon, Carlos untied everybody and got them off the floor. He let everybody sit on chairs. He said people could talk if they wanted to, and even move around a bit – everyone except the 'enemies'. He warned them that if any of them moved off their chairs, they would be shot.

At precisely 5:20, Vienna radio began to broadcast Carlos's statement.

And the government sent word into Carlos that they'd placed an aircraft at his disposal.

For Yamani it was a temporary stay of execution.

Under the circumstances, the Austrians decided that capitulation was their only course of action. They explained their behaviour in a terse press release. 'The terrorists have explosives, hand grenades and many guns in there. They have shown they are prepared to use them. We think that by letting them leave with their hostages the danger will be reduced. It is a gamble.'

Even then, Kreisky only gave in to Carlos on two conditions. First, he said, all Austrians must be released. Second, any foreign hostages who were to accompany the terrorists on the getaway plane must declare in writing that they were doing so voluntarily.

The terrorists agreed, adding their own stipulation that the gang member who'd been wounded and taken to the hospital must be released to accompany them on the plane.

At this point the Shah announced that if Carlos's plane were to fly over Iranian air space, he'd order his air force to destroy it.

That didn't help much to comfort any of the hostages, although knowing they'd live at least until they landed in North Africa some time the following morning was better than nothing.

Tension in the conference room subsided at bit.

Then food arrived.

The police did the best they could to collect enough to feed everyone.

But they sent in a stack of ham sandwiches.

And, of course, Moslems don't eat ham.

More food was demanded.

That evening there was supposed to have been an Opec reception at the Hilton and 500 guests were expected. Someone inside the room remembered the Hilton banquet and suggested the police go over there for food. They did and transported most of the banquet for 500 back to the 70 hostages and their five captors.

That night, in spite of the terrorists' radios which kept crackling and blaring, a few people managed to get some sleep.

But not Yamani.

His chair had been pulled away from the wall. There was nothing he could rest his head on. There was no way he could fall asleep.

It was probably just as well.

The terrorist holding the two wires apart which would set off the dynamite started to doze. Yamani watched as the boy's eyes closed and the two wires came closer.

Now Yamani called for Carlos. 'This one is about to kill us all.'

Carlos shouted at the boy and told him to get away from the charges. He then taped the ends of the wires to keep them apart and assured Yamani that the problem was solved.

Still Yamani couldn't sleep.

By morning the atmosphere was different again.

Exhaustion had dulled everyone's nerves.

Many people seemed resigned to their fate.

An Austrian post office bus arrived at dawn and parked at the rear of the building.

Curtains across all the windows were drawn shut.

At 7 a.m. Carlos started to usher his hostages, group by group, downstairs and through the back door. It took him nearly half an hour to load the bus. And then there wasn't enough room for everyone. So Carlos released all the Opec staff members and some of the various delegation members as well.

Now, with just over 40 hostages, Carlos was escorted to the airport by the ambulance bearing the wounded terrorist and two police cars.

Arriving at the airport, Carlos shook hands with Austrian officials. He smiled and waved to the television cameras which carried the story live.

Once the Austrian Airlines DC–9 was airborne, around 9:15, Carlos announced that they'd been invited to stop first in Algiers and so, instead of heading directly to Tripoli, that's where they were going.

After a while Carlos came down the aisle and sat next to Yamani.

He explained, 'You see, Algeria is a revolutionary country and I could not refuse. Despite the fact that I do not cooperate with the Algerians, they cannot obstruct my plans.'

Yamani asked how long they would stay in Algiers.

Carlos told him, 'Two hours. I will release some of the hostages there, the ones I originally planned to release in Tripoli and then we will go on to Libya.'

'It was odd,' Yamani recalls, 'but as we sat together and talked, it was almost as if we had become friends. He was telling me so much, knowing that I would die. For instance, he said he thought the Syrians were deviationists and dangerous. He said that he fought in the 1970 civil war between Jordan's King Hussein and the Palestinian commandos but that he'd grown disenchanted with the Arabs. He said he could not understand how the Jordanians could love their king. He seemed very bitter about that. He told me that he'd known King Faisal's grandson. You know, I still believe what he told me because it's easy to give your secrets away to someone when you know he won't reveal them.'

Carlos then told Yamani what to expect when they got to Libya.

He said, 'When we arrive in Tripoli the Prime Minister will be at the airport to greet us. There will also be a Boeing 707 waiting for us which can take us to Baghdad non-stop. In Baghdad we will set free some of the ministers. Our next stop will be Kuwait and there we will set free the rest of the hostages. Everyone except Amouzegar and you. Then we will go to Aden.'

He repeated that once they got to Aden he would kill Yamani and Amouzegar.

From there, he said, he planned to go to an African country.

Possibly heady with his success so far – after all, he was still alive and he had the Opec ministers as his hostages and he was obviously getting the press attention he sought – Carlos began to act like a star. He even gave one of the hostages an autograph – 'On flight Vienna Algiers Carlos 22/XII/75'.

He also handed a letter to the Venezuelan oil minister which he asked the man to post. It was addressed to Señora Ramirez Sanchez, his mother.

But when the DC–9 landed at Dar al Beida airport in Algiers three hours later Carlos's jovial mood had changed.

Yamani says, 'He got nervous. He made everyone pull down their window shades and warned that if anyone opened theirs while we were on the ground they would be shot.'

Everyone sat quietly and waited while Carlos positioned the other terrorists throughout the cabin with their guns aimed at the hostages should the police or the army try to storm the plane.

The rear door was opened and Carlos, armed with a machine gun, took up his post there.

Suddenly, Carlos screamed, 'Get out.'

Everyone on the plane froze with fear.

'Get out,' he yelled again as the Algerian Foreign Minister approached the plane and started to climb the rear gangway.

The man backed away.

For the next 15–20 minutes Carlos negotiated with Belaid Abdesselam. The Algerian oil minister was finally allowed to leave the plane to carry Carlos's message to the authorities.

He returned several minutes later to escort Carlos personally into the airport.

When Carlos left the plane the rear door was shut and another round of waiting began.

Without Carlos, the guards on the plane were more nervous, more jittery than before.

Yamani says he couldn't stop thinking that one of them might do something stupid, might get over-excited and react to someone or something, and ignite the whole situation. 'We sat there for a very long time in silent horror.'

Carlos spent most of the afternoon talking to the Algerians who, it was later learned, tried to convince him to release everyone. They agreed to give in to all his demands if he let everyone go. But Carlos refused. Abdesselam then tried to get Carlos to stipulate that he would not harm either Yamani or Amouzegar. Again Carlos refused, although he did promise 'to do my best not to harm them'. Next the Algerians suggested that Carlos drop all his hostages in Baghdad and then return to Algiers where they promised to grant him asylum. This was an idea that appealed to him. So he said yes, all right, but added, 'unless I receive orders while in Baghdad to continue on to Aden'.

Returning to the plane with the Algerian Foreign Minister, Carlos released all his non-Arab hostages, except Amouzegar.

He also set Abdesselam free.

Then he left his nervous colleagues in charge while he went again to talk to the Algerians.

The hostages sat all day on the tarmac.

Inside the DC–9, with very little air and no food, uncomfortable in the narrow cramped seats, Yamani and the others silently prayed that their captors would keep their cool until Carlos came back.

He returned at around 5 p.m., accompanied by Abdesselam.

Despite Carlos's protests, the Algerian oil minister insisted on staying with his Arab colleagues.

The rear door was shut and the pilot was given orders to take off for Tripoli.

There were now 20 hostages on board, including six ministers.

Once they took off, Carlos allowed them to raise the window shades.

They'd taken food on board, so everyone was fed.

While Yamani ate, Carlos sat down next to him and hinted that the Algerians had tried to save him and Amouzegar.

It was a two-hour flight to Libya.

During the trip Carlos wrote another letter and gave it to one of Yamani's aides. It was addressed to an old classmate of Carlos's from his days as a student in London. The classmate was working in Yamani's ministry. It was that letter which was later used to help firmly identify Carlos through handwriting and fingerprinting.

The terrorists were considerably more relaxed now than they had been since the whole thing started on Sunday morning.

Carlos seemed so sure of himself that when the plane landed in Tripoli no weapons were aimed at the hostages. He even allowed them to keep the shades up.

But when Carlos was informed that Major Jalloud was not yet at the airport, he ordered the plane door kept shut.

Outside it was raining and cool.

Inside it was cramped and stuffy and the air smelled stale.

They waited in the closed plane for another hour and a half.

When Jalloud finally arrived, the Libyan oil minster left the plane with Khalid, the second-in-command of the gang.

For the next hour, while Carlos waited for them to return, the plane door remained open and everyone was free to move about inside or go to the lavatory without asking permission.

Yamani asked Carlos, 'Why didn't you go to negotiate?'

Carlos responded, 'Because of the Libyans' mentality. They insisted that the negotiations be conducted by an Arab. In any case, it is all easy to arrange and without complication.'

Khalid returned with the Libyan oil minister and Major Jalloud who walked up and down the aisle, talking to the hostages. But when Jalloud got to Yamani and Amouzegar he gave them a chilly welcome. He offered them his hand to shake but turned his head away.

Finally Jalloud huddled in the front compartment with Carlos.

He explained that Carlos and his hostages might have to stay at Tripoli airport for some time. He told Carlos that the Boeing 737 they had planned to supply was at Tobruk airport.

But Carlos knew a 737 couldn't have taken them non-stop to Baghdad. He knew that a 737 would have to refuel somewhere, like Damascus.

The discussion grew heated.

Carlos did not hide his feelings.

Jalloud did not even try to calm him down.

Carlos demanded the Libyans live up to their part of the deal.

Jalloud said he would try to charter a 707 from an international company or another Arab airline.

There was little else Carlos could do but wait.

'We sat there, with the rain storm outside, watching as Carlos grew more and more anxious. The others too. They all started to get very nervous. None of them had slept. They were exhausted. The girl burst into tears. Khalid got ill and started to vomit. Carlos sat next to me and tried to hide his worries by talking about himself. He told me about his childhood, his studies, his family, his love affairs.'

By midnight, when there was still no sign of a 707, Carlos unleashed his fury with the Libyans. 'No one can cooperate with these people. They are not up to helping me.'

Now he announced that his plan was to take the DC–9 to Tobruk, to pick up the Boeing 737 there and go on to Baghdad. Even though the 737 could only make it that far with a strong tailwind, Carlos said he was willing to chance it.

However, the Austrian pilot scotched that plan when he explained that he didn't have charts for Tobruk and didn't know the airport.

The Libyans offered to provide charts.

The pilot he said he couldn't adapt them to his DC–9 system.

Carlos, feeling the squeeze, said in that case they had no choice but to return to Algiers and find a 707 there.

Before leaving Tripoli, Carlos released ten more hostages, including Abdessalem and two members of the Saudi delegation.

As they were being led off the plane, one of the Saudis turned to Carlos and said, 'For God's sake, do not harm Zaki Yamani.'

Carlos replied, almost laughing, 'I have received instructions here in Libya from my bosses not to do any harm to him or the Iranian minister. And I can now promise you that they will be safe.'

But as Carlos said that, Yamani remembers, all he could see in the man's eyes was mockery and sarcasm.

Still holding four ministers – Yamani, Amouzegar, Kuwait's Kazimi and Iraq's Karim – plus six others, Carlos told the pilot they'd return to Algeria.

The pilot plotted his course and the DC–9 left Tripoli.

About half way to Algiers, Carlos changed his mind.

Ill-tempered and extremely uptight at what he considered to be a betrayal by the Libyans, he ordered the pilot to divert to Tunis. He said that's where they would go because the Tunisians would help them and anyway he didn't necessarily trust the Algerians.

The pilot radioed down, requesting a new heading and asking permission to land.

The Tunisian authorities called back that permission was refused.

Enraged, Carlos ordered the pilot to land the plane at Tunis no matter what. He yelled, 'They can't stop us. Just land there.'

But the airport was suddenly blacked out.

The runway lights were turned off.

Touching down there was out of the question.

So the Austrian DC–9 went to Algiers.

Again Carlos demanded that the window shades be pulled down before they landed and again, after they landed, Carlos left the others in charge while he negotiated with the Algerians.

This time he was gone for quite a long time.

The others could no longer hide their frayed nerves.

The plane was a tinderbox waiting to explode.

When Carlos finally climbed back on board, he was sporting a most disconcerting grin.

Yamani immediately felt he was hiding something unpleasant.

Carlos went straight to Yamani and Amouzegar and told them both, 'I do not know what I should do. I am a democrat and you two do not know the meaning of democracy. I shall have a meeting now with my colleagues and consult them on what to do about your case. I shall inform you about the decision later.'

That meeting took place in the front section of the plane.

Yamani and Amouzegar could only watch.

When the discussion ended, Carlos came to Yamani and Amouzegar and he lied to them, 'We have finally decided to release you by midday. And with that decision your lives are completely out of danger.'

Yamani's deputy wanted to know, 'Why wait till midday?'

Carlos answered, 'Because I want the excitement prolonged until noon.' He offered to shut off the cabin lights. 'You will sleep peacefully knowing that your lives are no longer in danger.'

At this point Gabriele screamed nastily at Carlos, 'Fuck you.'

Now Yamani realized this would be his last night alive. 'I was certain that they planned to execute us right there in the plane.'

One of the gang offered Yamani and Amouzegar some coffee.

Another brought them sweets.

A third gave them pillows to help them sleep.

The cabin lights were dimmed and the aircrew left the plane.

'The atmosphere was one of choking silence,' Yamani says. 'It was the calm before the storm. I was going to die here. There was no doubt in my mind.'

Then the Algerians called for Carlos and said that they wanted to meet with him.

He left and was gone for two hours.

Yamani sat in his seat waiting to be murdered.

To this day Yamani is still astonished that the Algerians discovered Carlos was lying about setting them free at noon, that he had marked 7 a.m. as the hour of their execution. He says they had somehow bugged the front cabin and had been able to listen in on the meeting Carlos had with the others. It was the chief of security who called Carlos off the plane and told him, 'We know your plans. We have spoken to the President about them and he says, if you kill Yamani you will all die.'

Carlos didn't believe it, so the chief of security rang President Boumedienne and put Carlos on the phone.

At one point Carlos is supposed to have told the Algerians, 'If I release them, I won't get the rest of my money.'

That he might then have struck a deal with Boumedienne is possible.

Yamani doesn't know.

All he's sure of is that Carlos returned to the plane nervous and angry.

He told his gang what he planned to do, gave them instructions, then walked through the plane to wake up the few hostages who were sleeping.

He positioned himself directly in front of Yamani and Amouzegar. In a most vitriolic tone he said that he and his comrades had decided to kill Yamani and Amouzegar and that their decision was final. 'But if you escape death this time, our hands in the future will stretch to wherever you might be. And faster than you might imagine, we will implement our decision.'

He then spent a few minutes personally insulting Yamani and Amouzegar and the policies of their two governments.

When he was finished, he annouced to everyone on the plane that he and the other terrorists were going to leave the aircraft and that once they were gone, everyone was free.

And, just like that, Carlos and his gang walked off the plane.

Yamani and the others waited a few minutes, expecting someone to come for them. When no one did, they stood up and came down the gangway. The Algerian Foreign Minister met them and hurried them into an airport lounge.

At exactly 5:45 a.m. local time, the ordeal was over.

Almost.

The Algerian authorities brought all the hostages into a lounge.

Carlos and his gang were in the next lounge.

They could see each other through the glass that separated the two waiting areas.

Khalid, the Palestinian, said he wanted to speak to Yamani, so the guards brought him over.

He said, 'I want you to know that you will be killed much sooner than you expect. Carlos will not let you live.'

As he spoke, Yamani watched his eyes. 'They were dilated and shifted constantly. And his right hand kept moving across his chest. He was nervous, as if he was planning to do something.'

There was an awkward moment before the Algerian Foreign Minister also sensed that something was about to happen.

Thinking very fast, he handed Khalid a glass of juice.

That distracted him just long enough for the Algerian security guards to surround him, reach under his coat and discover a pistol in a shoulder holster.

Later when they questioned him he replied, 'I wanted to carry out the death sentence against the criminals.'

Yamani believed what Khalid said that morning.

And still believes it now.

Yamani spent that day in Algiers.

Tammam, Hani and Maha were flown in from Switzerland to meet him there. Together they flew to Jordan, where King Khaled was, and then home to Jeddah, where an enormous crowd greeted him at the airport with a televised hero's welcome.

From the time the kidnapping began until he arrived home four days later, Yamani never slept a wink.

Later Khaled welcomed him home again, this time with the gift of a brand-new Rolls-Royce.

For obvious reasons it was a long time before Yamani returned to Vienna.

'Austria is an open country. They don't restrict people coming and going. There is some sort of understanding or gentleman's agreement, if you will, that terrorists will not operate inside Austria. But twice there were terrorist attacks – that time with Carlos, and once, if I remember correctly, terrorists attacked a train bringing Jews from Russia. So that gentleman's agreement wasn't very valid. Vienna wasn't that secure.'

He stops short of actually saying that the Austrian police let Opec down. But Opec had in fact once asked for security. 'There had been a minor incident in the same building. The Canadian Embassy was there and I think there had been a bomb scare or something. So the Opec secretariat asked for security. But nothing was ever done.'

* * * *

Too little, too late, the Austrians filed a formal request to the Algerians for Carlos's extradition.

The Algerians disregarded it and no other country ever followed suit.

Like many people, the Austrians assumed that Carlos had been arrested in Algiers.

He wasn't.

All five terrorists were permitted to leave the airport and go wherever they liked.

Carlos moved into room 505 at the Albert I Hotel.

In 1977, Gabriele Krocher-Tiederman, together with a member of the Baader-Meinhof gang, was arrested by Swiss police after a shoot-out along the German border where two guards were wounded.

Under questioning, she supposedly claimed that a senior member of Iraq's ruling Ba'ath party had been the one to provide Carlos with the intelligence details he needed about Opec headquarters.

Could it possibly be a coincidence that, of the 13-member Iraqi delegation to Opec, only three showed up for the meeting that morning?

A Qaddafi-Iraq connection was certainly what Carlos led Yamani to believe. He told Yamani ahead of time what was going to happen in Tripoli and that was exactly what did happen. It is also now known that the guns Carlos used were brought into Austria by the German terrorist who was later wounded. He'd fetched them in Rome where they'd been sent from Libya in a diplomatic pouch.

Terrorist expert, author Ronny Payne, is equally certain that Qaddafi's hand shows in this.

'I think there's no doubt about that. I'm sure that Qaddafi paid for it and that there was a large bonus afterwards. I got that from an Israeli source.'

The supposed fee was $1 million upfront and a £1 million bonus once the job was done.

As for what happened to Carlos, Payne confirms that he soon left Algeria for Aden. 'They were the only convenient friendlies at that point.'

It is known that Wadi Haddad – who happened to have been in Baghdad during the hostage taking – also had a home in Aden.

That might have been nothing more than coincidence as Payne says that Aden was chosen almost by default. 'There weren't actually a lot of places where Carlos could go. The Algerians wanted to be rid of him and Qaddafi is a bit funny. You never know about him. He's your great friend one minute and the next minute he says, kindly leave the stage. Maybe he didn't want Carlos around because he'd promised Carlos money. He's very slow to pay, from what I hear. Anyway, I'm suspicious of all these stories that he's paying a million pounds to terrorists here and two million pounds to terrorists there. I know he says that he will but there's a lot of evidence to say that he tends to be forgetful about settling his bills.'

Carlos may or may not have surfaced briefly in 1984, during the trial in Germany of Gabriele Krocher-Tiederman who was then serving a 15-year sentence in Switzerland for the border guard attack in 1977. Carlos, or at least someone claiming to be Carlos, threatened to murder the Interior Minister if the trial continued.

Then he was said to have been involved in the January 1984 bombing of Marseilles' Gare St Charles railway station.

But there have also been sporadic reports over the years that Carlos is dead.

Says Payne, 'It's one of the great mysteries. Bits and pieces keep coming in from various sources. There was something from an Israeli source not long ago that one of the Palestinian groups had killed him because he knew too much. But there's never been any confirmation of that. Then I heard from a West German source that Carlos was living in Tripoli and recently got married. How about that, a society wedding!'

Nearly one year after the kidnapping, a set of classified reports was compiled by the Austrian police in cooperation with the Saudi intelligence service. Included was a transcript of a conversation between the German terrorist who'd been shot in Vienna and the Austrian authorities.

In it the German talked about a discussion the terrorists held among themselves when they debated who would kill Yamani. He said nobody was reluctant to kill Amouzegar. They all agreed that any one of them could kill Amouzegar. But the question was raised, who will kill Yamani? No one wanted to do it. It was left to Carlos. They decided it was the job of the leader.

Before long the Egyptian newspaper *Akhbar El Youm* claimed to have proof that the plot against Opec had been masterminded and totally financed by Qaddafi with the help of George Habash and the PFLP.

Habash, as it turns out, just happened to have been in Tripoli at the time of the hijacking.

Certain governments then received information confirming that Qaddafi was definitely the one who financed the operation.

When asked, 'Does that sound true?' Yamani tries to waltz around an answer with, 'I don't know how much anyone was paid.'

When asked, 'But in any case, you do know by whom?' he pauses for a moment, then half-nods, 'Take your best guess.'

13

The Sudairi Conspiracy

CROWN PRINCE Fahd skilfully relegated King Khaled to the status of a figure head.

And, against the odds, Yamani continued to run the Ministry of Petroleum.

Through 1975 and into 1976, as Yamani dealt with Fahd on a day-to-day basis to shape the nation's oil policy, his reputation as a political survivor began to take hold.

'There were all kinds of reasons why Yamani wasn't necessarily liked at the centre of government,' former British Ambassador, Sir James Craig, stresses. 'One of them was perhaps that Yamani was a Hijazi. You know, from the west. I remember talking to an old fellow once who was very high up in the National Guard, and he said to me, "You ambassadors are all the same. You live in Jeddah. You meet all those Hijazis. You all think you know about Saudi Arabia. Well, you don't. I know who you talk to, people like Yamani. But they're not Saudi Arabian. I'm Saudi Arabian because I come from the Nejd." I guess it's like what you find in England. People in the north, like Newcastle, all think that people in London are soft and cheeky and too sharp for their own good. Well, in the Nejd they think the Hijazis are city slickers and reluctant members of the kingdom.'

On the other hand, he says, the Hijazis always think of Riyadh as 'that primitive hick town up there on the desert plateau.'

Faisal spent most of his time in the Hijaz.

But Khaled and Fahd and Fahd's full brothers preferred the Nejd.

'That's possibly one of the reasons', Craig feels, 'Yamani might have been under threat from time to time once Faisal was gone.'

Another reason is jealousy.

There can be no denying that.

Anyone who knows anything about the Saudi royal family knows that men like Fahd, Sultan and Salman weren't naturally drawn to Yamani.

Fahd in particular is by nature an extremely insecure and jealous man. Where Fahd is somewhat slow and clumsy, Yamani is bright and sure-footed. Where Sultan was a favourite kid brother of Faisal and often accompanied him on trips, Yamani was Faisal's 'adopted' son and perhaps his most trusted adviser. Where Salman was often referred to as the most popular man in the country – it was sometimes said that if an election for king were held right after Faisal's death, Salman would have been a shoe-in – it was Yamani who emerged in the rest of the world as the most famous Saudi of this century.

Where none of them has any formal education or worldly sophistication, Yamani is altogether in another league.

'Whatever resentment men like Fahd, Sultan or Salman might have felt towards Yamani while Faisal was alive was not expressed,' confides former British Ambassador Sir Alan Rothnie, 'At least not openly. Faisal would never have permitted it. He was a man whose eye could open an oyster at 60 paces. But after Faisal's death, the brothers wouldn't necessarily have been expected to conceal their resentment.'

While Yamani categorically refuses to discuss any of his problems with the Sudairi Seven, even to the point of denying that personality clashes and personal differences alienated him early on with Fahd and his six full brothers, various sources in Washington – the kind of people who make it their business to know what's going on inside the otherwise closed palaces of Saudi Arabia – claim that Yamani's troubles with the Al Fahd faction are deep-rooted.

'They needed Yamani,' notes an American with heavyweight commercial and personal contacts in the Middle East. 'They needed him because Yamani was the best and the brightest. He was, and still is, heads above anyone else in the entire region when it comes to oil and dealing with the west. Of course everyone believed that his days were numbered the moment Faisal was killed. No matter what he says, he did too. But that's only because everyone thought Fahd might have been foolish enough to put his own likes and dislikes in front of the Kingdom's major source of revenue.'

The reason he claims Fahd didn't do just that was because Fahd knew how valuable an asset Yamani was. 'If Fahd had fired Yamani just after Faisal's death, there's no telling what confusion there might have been over the next five or six years. I'm not only thinking about confusion in the Middle East, I'm talking about the rest of the world as well. Remember that the Shah wanted to run prices sky-high in 1976–1977. It was Yamani who held him back. When the Shah fell and

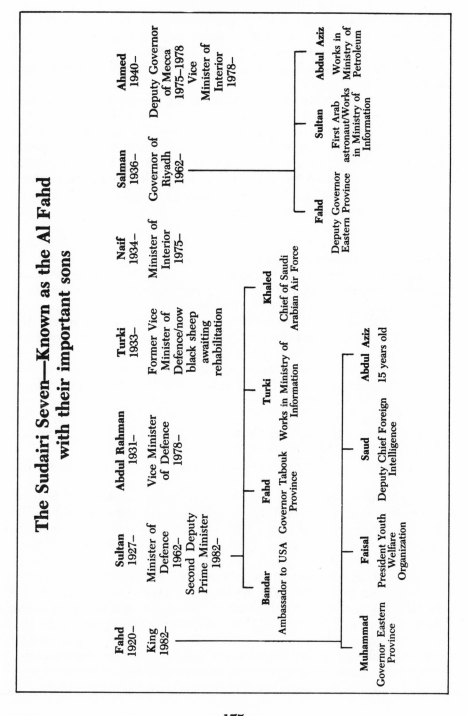

The Sudairi Seven—Known as the Al Fahd with their important sons

Fahd 1920–
King 1982–

Sultan 1927–
Minister of Defence 1962–
Second Deputy Prime Minister 1982–

- **Bandar** Ambassador to USA
- **Fahd** Governor Tabouk Province
- **Turki** Works in Ministry of Information
- **Khaled** Chief of Saudi Arabian Air Force

Abdul Rahman 1931–
Vice Minister of Defence 1978–

Turki 1933–
Former Vice Minister of Defence/now black sheep awaiting rehabilitation

Naif 1934–
Minister of Interior 1975–

Salman 1936–
Governor of Riyadh 1962–

- **Fahd** Deputy Governor Eastern Province
- **Sultan** First Arab astronaut/Works in Ministry of Information
- **Abdul Aziz** Works in Ministry of Petroleum

Ahmed 1940–
Deputy Governor of Mecca 1975–1978 Vice Minister of Interior 1978–

Muhammad Governor Eastern Province

- **Faisal** President Youth Welfare Organization
- **Saud** Deputy Chief Foreign Intelligence
- **Abdul Aziz** 15 years old

prices went through the roof, it was Yamani who kept a firm grip on Opec. When oil went over $36, if there had been no Yamani, prices might have kept right on going. Oil at $45 or $50 or even more would have been a real possibility. God only knows what would have happened.'

There's no denying that the Al Fahd faction are an ever-cautious bunch. They believe first and foremost in a tribal-like loyalty to the princes who keep them in power. Country and government come second. They demonstrate the point almost daily by being openly suspicious of any policies that won't meet with the favour of certain family members. King Fahd is, for example, widely known throughout the kingdom for his inability to make politically difficult decisions.

This is not to say they're stupid men.

Not at all.

The country is run by men, not institutions. Those men trust and depend on other men, who in turn trust and depend on more men, right on down the line. It's the tribal system superimposed on a bureaucracy. Loyalty is more highly rewarded than performance because loyalty is more highly regarded than competence.

But just as the opposite of competence is incompetence, the opposite of trust is suspicion.

Loyalties are constantly put to the test.

Everyone keeps an eye on everyone else.

It is inconceivable that Fahd is unaware of what Sultan and Salman and the others get up to.

And vice versa.

Matriarch of the clan was Hossa bint Ahmad al-Sudairi, without any doubt Ibn Saud's favourite wife.

She must have been something special because he married her twice.

No children came from the first marriage, so he divorced her and she in turn married his brother. That union produced a son. When Ibn Saud realized she could have children, he convinced his brother to divorce her and he remarried her. From the second marriage came seven sons and four daughters.

The eldest, born some time before 1920, is Fahd.

In government since 1953, he served as Minister of Education and in 1962 became Minister of Interior. His promotion was part of the Sudairis' reward for standing behind Faisal in the power play that ousted King Saud. Fahd soon developed a reputation as a lenient minister, albeit one who truly disliked making decisions. Believing that one day he would be king – 'Then the fun will cease,' he was known to say – he decided to amuse himself early on. With no shortage of funds to slow him down, he quickly became known around Europe's swankier fleshpots and gambling parlours.

A frequent visitor to Monte Carlo, among other places, one of Fahd's exploits at the Sporting d'Ete has become a modern Monégasque legend. The story is told that he hit the tables early one evening and by 5 the next morning was $2.4 million ahead. Two hours later, with lady luck having gone home for the night, he was $1.4 million down. In 120 minutes he'd managed to gamble away $3.8 million. That works out to just $520 petrodollars per second!

However, that was Fahd the playboy and compulsive gambler.

Fahd the leader of the Sudairi Seven is quite another man.

Because the Saudi royal family operates on respect and devout loyalty, especially among the Sudairi Seven who continue to meet at least once a week at closed family dinners, Fahd has always been careful to see that the rest of the clan is taken care of.

Sultan, born in 1927, began his career in 1953 as Minister of Communications before moving on to become Minister of Defence in 1962. He is perhaps the wealthiest man in the family, ever-powerful, known to see no difference whatsoever between his own personal bank account and the nation's defence budget.

Much of Sultan's enormous power stems from his ability to use the wealth at his disposal to reinforce his own position. Although exact figures are not available, reports of his giving away to various needy causes upwards of $100 million a year may not be exaggerated.

A favourite of his older brother Faisal, Sultan's fabulous wealth has at times been a minor embarrassment, all the more so since one of Fahd's aims as king has been to reduce the international visibility of the royal family's business rewards in favour of a more dedicated-to-public-service image. Self-confident and outspoken, Sultan's devotion to charity nevertheless remains one of his plusses and because of that he is respected.

Next comes Abdul-Rahman, born in 1931, a successful businessman whom Fahd appointed Vice Minister of Defence.

He is followed by Turki.

Every family has a black sheep and Turki became the embarrassment of the Sudairi Seven.

Born in 1933, he was Vice Minister of Defence until 1978. Although he is a gentle, polite and decent man, he fell out of grace when he married a Saudi woman of Moroccan origin named Fassi who instantly provided the Sudairis with relatives straight out of a soap opera.

Living in Jeddah, the Fassi crowd had a leaning towards anti-regime activities and came into big money very quickly. They spent it just as quickly. Among their indiscretions was the purchase of a huge mansion on Sunset Boulevard in Beverly Hills, the grounds of which were decorated with garishly painted nude statues. The mansion was destroyed in a 1979 fire and the Fassi family was shamed for their nouveau riche mentality. Turki came to believe that the only way he could personally save face was by resigning from the government. He then devoted several years to charitable works as part of what is obviously his rehabilitation and possibly even a return to favour.

Next is Naif, born in 1934, who succeeded Fahd as Minister of Interior.

The youngest is Ahmed, born in 1940, who served as Deputy Governor of Mecca from 1975 to 1978 until he was appointed Naif's Vice Minister of Interior.

In between these two is Salman.

Born in 1936, he was named Governor of Riyadh by Faisal in 1962. His power is based both on his enormous wealth and on his reputation for generosity.

By contrast, bizarrely, he seems to enjoy the public decapitations which go on in the town squares whenever capital punishment has been prescribed. That bit of information comes from a British diplomat with whom Salman once spent the better part of an entire afternoon describing the scenes 'with relish'. According to that British diplomat, 'Looking through the lens of Saudi Arabia you could almost say it was one link he had with the traditionalists.' Salman is also said to be a most vindictive man who bears a grudge for a very long time. Comments a Saudi academic, 'If you fall out with him, you're finished.'

A tall and relatively slim man – where the rest of the Sudairis tend to be on the hefty side – he is said to be closer to Fahd than any of his brothers. That relationship gives him the pivotal role in family discussions.

As the Sudairi Seven tightened their grasp on the nation's ultimate power, the next generation was swiftly moved into place. Three of Fahd's sons hold important government posts. Muhammad is Governor of the Eastern Province, Faisal is President of the Youth Welfare Organization and Saud is Deputy Chief of Foreign Intelligence. Sultan's sons include Bandar, the Saudi Ambassador to the United States, Fahd, Governor of Tabouk Province, and Turki, who works in the Ministry of Information. Salman's sons include Fahd, Deputy Governor of the Eastern Province, and Sultan in the Ministry of Information who became the Arab world's first astronaut when he flew on board a US space shuttle.

The Sudairis are, step by step, taking over the country.

While Khaled occupied the throne during an era of opulence and wealth, Fahd, who ascended the throne in 1982, inherited a taste for opulence and wealth but steadily declining revenues.

Also reputed to be very generous, there are those who claim that's because saying yes is often easier than saying no.

He is neither a firm ruler nor a decisive man.

Although he is talkative.

At a White House dinner in 1985, with the Americans hoping he might shed some light on the political situation in the Gulf, Fahd chose instead to speak proudly and at length about a Saudi Arabian soccer team's tour of the Soviet Union.

He is not, however, known for his punctuality.

Due at the White House that evening at 7:00, he didn't arrive – much to Vice President Bush's shock – until after 9:00.

Prime Minister Fukada of Japan was once forced to sit in a hotel lobby for two hours waiting for Fahd. King Hussein of Jordan was once forced to circle Riyadh airport in his plane for one hour because Fahd wasn't on time to greet him. While the Crown Prince of Kuwait was once forced to wait two days for a scheduled meeting with Fahd.

Nor is Fahd a particularly healthy man.

He is huge.

Standing more than 6 feet tall, he tips the scales at over 300 pounds.

He has, for many years, suffered with back problems. That's been aggravated in recent years by being grossly overweight. He also suffers from respiratory problems, which may in part be due to heavy smoking.

When he came to England on an official state visit in early 1987, the Queen's royal coach had to be reinforced so that Fahd could step out of it without turning it over.

One week later, when he opened the new port of Antibes in the south of France, arriving there on the *Abdul Aziz*, Fahd had to address the crowd sitting down. He simply couldn't stand up for any length of time.

In Paris, he gave a televised speech with President François Mitterand. For a few minutes, on camera, there was Fahd gasping for breath. Then the TV screen went blank and a few seconds later there was Fahd, sitting down, finishing his speech. A reporter in the audience claims Fahd fell and had to be lifted into his chair and that out of pity Mitterand ordered that scene to be cut from the transmission.

Certain members of the western press corps who covered his visit to Europe nicknamed Fahd 'the hunk of beef'.

Besides Salman, Fahd's closest friend is his cousin, Prince Khaled bin Abdullah bin Abdul-Rahman, whose father was Ibn Saud's younger brother. He is perhaps the most professional of the royal businessmen. His partner is the internationally respected Saudi entrepreneur,

Suleiman Olayan. Further cementing the relationship, Prince Khaled happens to be married to one of Fahd's four full sisters.

Once Fahd came to see that his full brothers, sons and nephews were firmly entrenched in key government positions, all but giving the Al Fahd a stranglehold on the day-to-day running of the government's affairs, he found himself one step closer towards his ultimate dream of restructuring the line of succession to the throne.

Ibn Saud had ordained that the crown would pass along the line of all his sons.

It was his intention that each of his sons could be king.

What he did not stipulate was what he wanted to happen once the first generation was gone. He never bothered to say where he wanted the crown to go once all of his sons had passed on.

It's now strongly believed in certain western intelligence circles that Fahd has come up with a permanent solution.

He intends to keep the line of succession tied up within his own branch of the family.

He intends to install the Sudairi Seven as the rightful rulers of their father's kingdom.

However, that's easier said than done because it means eliminating several half-brothers from their right to the crown.

The first move towards that aim was a quiet redefinition of Ibn Saud's decree. The Al Fahd now contend that their father only ever meant to pass the crown to his 'legitimate' sons. As Ibn Saud had several issues out of wedlock, by concubines and slaves, those sons would not be eligible to become king.

There was absolutely no way Fahd, or anyone else, could have stopped Khaled from becoming king. Nor is there any way, short of outright assassination, to prevent Crown Prince Abdullah from one day ruling. Those two have both come from famous mothers whose marriages to Ibn Saud had great political significance.

Several brothers who might otherwise stand in the way of the Sudairis' plan are not in any case eligible. They have either opted out for personal reasons or been eliminated by the family for serious political reasons. For example, the father of the boy who murdered Faisal could never wear the crown.

Yet several brothers further down the line believe they are perfectly entitled by birthright to the monarchy.

It's common knowledge in Saudi Arabia that at least two of the king's younger half-brothers are actively circling their wagons, trying to gather enough family support to ward off the attack on their own right to the throne.

It's also common knowledge in the Gulf that such a change could trigger severely radical reactions from other, as yet undeclared factions, which go to make up the political conglomerate which is modern Saudi Arabia. It's hard to say who or what could be waiting in the wings to challenge the Sudairi Seven. Tribal and religious interests are yet to be heard from. But they cannot be discounted.

How Fahd is going to arrange the Sudairi succession without their consent, no one knows – although he, too, is known to be actively lobbying family members loyal to the Al Fahd to effect an official change. He couldn't possibly alter his father's wishes without their consent. Sources in Washington believe that, if he gets their consent, Fahd will dictate that the line of succession will go only through the seven Sudairi brothers and then on to the next generation, probably starting with Fahd's oldest living son and moving laterally across cousins according to the age of each Sudairi brother.

The unknown factor is Abdullah.

No one, with the possible exception of Fahd, knows whether or not he'd be willing to go along with the Sudairi Seven's conspiracy.

Born in 1923, Abdullah is the 13th son of Ibn Saud. His mother came from the Shammar tribal confederation, which made her marriage to Ibn Saud an extremely important one in uniting the country.

He has no full brothers.

Essentially a man of the desert, Abdullah loves falconry and horses and is said to play a decent game of pool. Fierce-looking with a thick triangular black beard that fully covers his chin, he turns out to be a gentle, almost delicate man, inclined towards innate shyness probably brought about by a bad stammer.

As Commander of the National Guard, Abdullah has been since 1963 the Royal family's insurance policy against a military coup.

His is, to say the least, a very important position.

In 1969, when Crown Prince Khaled hinted that he might like to leave public life, Abdullah voted against it. He said the only way he could accept such a decision was on the condition that Fahd did not then automatically become Crown Prince. Fahd argued that Khaled should be allowed to retire if that's what he wanted. Khaled couldn't make up his mind until Faisal, Abdullah and a few others ganged up on him, insisting that he must accept his responsibility and one day assume the throne.

Faisal obviously liked and trusted Abdullah because he named his half-brother to be Second Deputy Prime Minister when Khaled was Crown Prince and Prime Minister (Fahd was already First Deputy Prime Minister). It was, perhaps, Faisal's way of assuring Abdullah's right to the monarchy, interrupting any plans Fahd might have had to see a Sudairi follow him onto the throne.

181

In 1977, when Khaled was ill and hospitalized in London, there were all sorts of rumours that he would abdicate.

At the same time, Sultan made a bid to incorporate the National Guard into his Ministry of Defence.

The plan was specifically designed to deprive Abdullah of his power base.

It was well known at the time that Fahd did not want to see Abdullah become Crown Prince, that he was openly partial to giving the job to Sultan. But even if Abdullah had certain reservations about one day assuming power, the idea of Fahd and Sultan together in the first and second jobs created such disquiet in the royal family and around the kingdom that Fahd was forced to reaffirm Khaled's tenure on the throne.

As long as Abdullah stays alive he will be the next king.

And Prince Sultan will most likely be the next Crown Prince.

If Fahd doesn't attempt to change the line of succession within his own lifetime it might be because the remaining Sudairi Six have decided to wait Abdullah out.

Don't forget that a seemingly healthy Pope John Paul I lasted only 33 days on his throne.

Whichever way Fahd manages to do it, if indeed he can pull it off, this would be a radical change.

But Fahd must feel that the risks are worth the reward.

Such is the ego of men like Fahd, Sultan and Salman.

When such egos run up against the sophistication and western worldliness of a man like Yamani, there quickly comes a point where jealousies boil over and can no longer be hidden.

American Vice President George Bush and his party discovered the extent of those jealousies when they visited Saudi Arabia in the spring of 1986.

Bush had come to Dhahran on behalf of the Reagan administration to meet Fahd and discuss a number of issues, including oil.

Once all the official greetings had been taped for Saudi television, the Americans took their places along one side of the long conference table, facing the king and his ministers sitting on the other side.

When the subject of oil was finally broached, Bush began telling Fahd what a good meeting he'd had with Sheikh Yamani the day before in Riyadh.

Acknowledging Yamani's presence a few seats away from Fahd, Bush lavished praise on the oil minister, extolling his virtues.

It was too much for Fahd to bear.

He flared into a rage.

His hands trembled.

One of the Americans present says that Fahd made Bush understand, in no uncertain terms, 'When you want to talk to someone in Saudi Arabia about oil, you come to me. No one else.'

Fahd told Bush, 'I am the one who makes the decisions, not Yamani.'

The Americans were stunned.

'We were not prepared for the king's anger and overt display of jealousy,' claims one of them.

They were even less ready for what followed.

According to that American, Fahd turned to his Minister of Information and ordered him to see that Yamani's name and picture be eliminated from any records and press releases of the meeting. He also demanded that the television footage taped earlier be edited so as to make Yamani disappear.

One news broadcast had already gone out, showing Yamani at the meeting. All subsequent showings excluded Yamani.

'The king decided', the American continues, 'that Zaki Yamani was suddenly a non-person. It was an unbelievable display.'

Instead of either confirming or denying that such an incident took place – after all, he could hardly deny it with the Vice President of the United States and his entire party as eye witnesses – Yamani prefers to say, 'I don't remember.'

And the subject is quickly changed.

Yamani is obviously embarrassed about the incident.

That Crown Prince Abdullah is also at times embarrassed by Fahd's occasional childishness is no secret.

When Fahd fired Yamani in a manner that Abdullah found to be excessively abrupt, word circulated through several western embassies in Saudi Arabia that Abdullah phoned Yamani at home the very next morning to apologize for Fahd's behaviour.

The speculation now making the rounds of those same embassies is that, when and if Abdullah becomes king, he might just try to lure Yamani back into public life.

It won't necessarily be easy, as Yamani has, since leaving government, occupied himself with a number of projects well outside the realm of public life.

If Abdullah does approach Yamani, there's no chance at all that Yamani would ever consider the petroleum portfolio again. He's much too proud a man for that. Naming him Foreign Minister is also out of the question, at least as long as Faisal's son Prince Saud chooses to stay in his job. Anyway, that's traditionally a royal's job, as are most of the other large ministries. So the possibilities are not all that great. After all, Yamani could hardly be expected to entertain an appointment that didn't carry with it the highly elevated status he's already enjoyed.

But the gossip around western diplomatic dinner tables in both Jeddah and Riyadh is that Abdullah could try to tempt Yamani with one vitally important post in particular.

In this case Yamani would be ideally suited.

In this case the honour would be great.

And in this case he might just be inclined to accept.

When and if he becomes king, the talk is that Abdullah may ask Yamani to be his Ambassador to the United States.

14

Yamani as a Media Star

ZAKI AND Tammam Yamani settled into married life together and began a family.

Their first child was a boy, born in 1976, and appropriately enough they named him Faisal.

Their son Sharaf was born in 1977 and their first daughter Sarah came along in 1980. Their next daughter, Arwa, was born in 1981 and their third son, Ahmed, was born in 1983.

Because the king commuted regularly between Riyadh and Jeddah, Zaki and Tammam and their children were forever shifting back and forth between the Yamama Hotel and their home in Jeddah – a big house near the Red Sea with a large livingroom that sits just off the indoor swimming pool.

Every year when the king went to his mountain palace for the summer months, the Yamanis moved into their farm in the hills of Taif, some 35 miles southeast of Mecca.

There, in the shadow of the mountains, they've covered a tree with an aviary and stocked it with all sorts of exotic birds. Near the outdoor swimming pool there are fountains with water cascading down a concrete sluice to wash over the cement rocks. And there is astroturf along the pool because a real lawn will not grow.

By this point Yamani's older daughters Mai and Maha were in finishing school in Switzerland. Later Mai studied anthropology at Bryn Mawr on the Philadelphia Main Line and Maha got her law degree from Cambridge. His son Hani soon began studying law at Oxford University but eventually transferred to business administration at the University of Pennsylvania's Wharton School.

Until he married Tammam, Yamani lived alone at the Yamama.

Except alone didn't really mean alone because he had a manservant

185

and he sometimes had his chef there and he also had couple of yappy Pomeranian dogs and two African Grey parrots.

Small dogs as pets were rare in those days.

The Saudis who kept dogs, like members of the royal family, always kept big dogs for hunting.

It was a macho thing.

Lap dogs were a bit too reminiscent of old Victorian ladies sipping tea in their European parlours. Small animals like Pomeranians were not yet part of Saudi culture.

In fact it was Yamani who helped to change that.

He was one of the first people in Saudi Arabia, if not the very first person, to have small dogs, and to breed them, and to make them an accepted part of Saudi upper-class family life.

His two African Grey parrots were also unique.

It seems they had the uncanny ability of mimicking perfectly whatever anyone said. Good words, bad words, in any language, they'd repeat whatever they heard.

The problem was that they'd wait until the person who said something left the room and someone new arrived before they'd do their act.

One learned quickly at Yamani's house never to criticize anyone in front of the birds.

* * * *

Boomtime in Saudi Arabia made a lot of people very rich.

In Yamani's case, it also made him the most visible oil minister in the world and gave him a superstar's status.

'It's obvious why,' says Sir John Wilton. 'Yamani was the man who dealt with the subject that captured the world headlines. He was someone everyone wanted to know. Westerners especially took to him because he was one of the few leading Saudis who entertained informally. He kept more or less open house. Everybody was always welcome. And his wife and children appeared. His family was a part of the business of entertaining his guests.'

Just as an aside, Wilton suggests that being a successful host in Saudi Arabia is a lot more difficult than being a successful host in the west.

'You always have to know who will mix with whom. There were a dozen or so families who habitually entertained the western community where men and women, Saudi wives and western wives, would turn up. It was a thing you had to keep an eye on. When you wanted to have a party where you invited Saudis and their wives, you had to know whose wife went out in public and whose wife didn't. Then you not only had to know which Saudis were prepared to bring their wives, you also had to identify those with whom they were prepared to have their wives seen.'

The most special time of the year, Wilton adds, was during Ramadan. 'You'd get to Yamani's house at about sunset. The prayers would be finished and the dates and water and the coffee would be passed around. The meal eventually appeared and the nearest thing I can compare it to would be a fork buffet. It was that sort of informality. He was always so proud of his own cooking, although I never actually saw him wield a skillet. It was all very different from when the king or the crown prince entertained the diplomatic corps or a visiting head of state. Then it would be a sit-down dinner with placement and no women. Yamani's dinners were infinitely more enjoyable.'

Viscount Tonypandy, the Welsh-born former Speaker of the British House of Commons found himself at Yamani's home one year for Ramadan and simply couldn't believe how fabulous it was.

'King Khaled and seven princes all came to dinner. Zaki had put up a great tent in the grounds of his house in Taif. And he brought in the poor from the area too because when the king comes you must have all the people. I will never forget it. The feast, the splendour and the dignity of Zaki receiving his king. It was "Arabian Nights".'

That much a celebrity at home, he was an even bigger star in the west.

His face adorned two *Newsweek* covers, one *Time* cover and a newspaper ad for a British car manufacturer who promised you'd get 'a run for Yamani'.

Yamani by the way insisted the car manufacturer cease and desist.

Another car manufacturer then tried to name one of their models 'The Yamani', only to discover, again, that Yamani's sense of humour doesn't stretch quite that far.

On two occasions over the years he also received offers from Hollywood.

One film producer planning an epic about the Israeli raid on Entebbe contacted Yamani, offering him the role of the airline pilot. Yamani says he politely refused.

Another dropped him a line to say that if he ever left government and wanted to become a movie star, any number of roles could be his simply for the asking.

That letter has gone unanswered . . . at least to date.

Because Yamani attracted so much attention, he always tried to make certain that it never got in the way of what he wanted to accomplish.

Throughout the 1970s, especially during the second half of the decade, he often visited Washington. Some of those visits were announced. But many were not. To avoid the press, he'd fly into the country without even informing his Embassy, hide himself away in a hotel or at the home of an American official, and go about his business using B-thriller techniques.

'I'd meet frequently with Henry Kissinger but there were times we didn't want anyone to know because we both believed that the less attention our meetings attracted, the more we could accomplish.'

At those times, Yamani's walkie-talkied bodyguards would rush him from his hotel suite to the nearest elevator without being seen, then down to the hotel's garage where a smoked-glassed limousine would be waiting. The chauffeur would deliver him straight into the garage at the State Department, where he'd be whisked into the private elevator that brings you non-stop into the Secretary's office.

'No one ever saw me coming or going except the people who were supposed to know I was there.'

In London he used a slightly different approach. 'I'd come to England to meet Nigel Lawson when he was Energy Minister or to meet Peter Walker when he had that job, and the press never found out. I'd either meet them at home, like I did with Walker, or see them in the office late at night the way I used to do with Lawson.'

On one occasion he also met secretly with Margaret Thatcher.

It took place at Peter Walker's home.

A very private luncheon had been arranged there. Just the Prime Minister, her husband, Yamani and Walker.

No one ever found out about it.

'We could speak frankly knowing that we were free from the press. Not because there was anything to hide but because without the press hounding us we were more relaxed, we could operate more smoothly. If you can do what you have to do in a very quiet manner, without being subjected to too much publicity, it's usually easier to succeed.'

Of course, some of the people he dealt with, especially the Americans, were used to a more open style.

'Zaki is kind of idiosyncratic,' comments a cabinet member who served both Presidents Nixon and Ford. 'He always liked to do things differently. Clandestine meetings with the President would appeal to Zaki. Come to think of it, Richard Nixon also would have loved to meet Yamani surreptitiously if possible. Given the type of man Dick Nixon was, he would have enjoyed that kind of thing too.'

But then, many of Yamani's lessons in dealing with the press were learned the hard way.

When the embargo took hold, the ink that flowed wasn't only about his oil policy.

In January 1974, the western press discovered that his two daughters were on their way to a private boarding school in Switzerland. Wrote one reporter, 'They have both decided not to wear veils at home, instead opting for western style dress.'

Yamani shrugs, 'Is that really news?'

When word came that Yamani had purchased a pied-à-terre in London, Fleet Street jumped on it. They explained that, while it was only a two-bedroom flat, it was in Belgravia and he paid the then extravagent sum of £70,000. This was at a time when the average London flat, albeit not in Belgravia, was on the market at £10,000.

The *Daily Express* pointed out that Yamani quickly redecorated the place with glass, louvred doors and white walls. As a matter of fact, except for the white walls, the place isn't decorated like that. Nevertheless they decided, 'It would be very eccentric if he were an Englishman,' and then quoted a neighbour who suggested, 'Perhaps he will help to improve the central heating.'

In June 1975, the first of several 'Yamani at Harrods' stories broke.

One news hound revealed, 'Harrods agreed to stay open a few nights ago so that Yamani could bring his two teenaged daughters there to shop. The store shut to the general public while staff in selected departments stayed on to cater to Yamani and his daughters who reportedly spent in excess of £35,000 in the 75 minute shopping spree. In the past such "late night" treatment was usually reserved only for the British royal family.'

The second instalment ran in December.

The British press disclosed how Yamani was back at Harrods and had spent £35,000 again with his two teenaged daughters on Friday evening, 19 December.

'Hours later,' they added with great drama, 'he was kidnapped in Vienna.'

The only problem there is that the closest Yamani got to Harrods in December 1975 was Paris.

A year after that the Press Association rehashed the story yet again.

Leading with a rather odd sentence – 'The wife of Sheikh Yamani, one of the world's richest men' – they described Tammam on a 90–minute Christmas shopping spree. When asked why she left empty-handed, her escort, Harrods' store manager, was quoted as saying, 'We will be taking parcels round later.'

On that occasion Harrods supposedly brought so many parcels around later that they wouldn't fit into Yamani's Rolls-Royce so that a coal lorry had to be commandeered en route to Heathrow to help them get everything to the plane.

It was, in keeping with the other episodes of the same story, nonsense.

Yet the PA report concluded, 'Last year the store stayed open especially late so the Sheikh could spend hundreds of thousands of pounds on Christmas gifts. One of his aides said, "He doesn't like fighting his way through the crowds. In fact, he hates shopping so he has sent his wife to do it".'

At this point Yamani roars with laughter. 'I happen to love shopping. But you see how it gets more expensive for me every time?'

His version of the story is quite mundane.

'We were shopping in the food halls at Harrods. I like to go there because I find all sorts of things at their health food counters. Just before closing we thought about looking at some garden furniture. We went upstairs and found something we liked but it was 5:30 and the store was closing. The salesman there said not to worry because at 5:30 they only lock the front doors so that no new customers can come in. He assured us that we would be welcome to stay. We bought the furniture, paid for it, arranged to have it shipped, and we left. It was just after 6:00. The next thing I heard was that the store stayed open late just for us the way they do for the Queen of England and that we spent £35,000 or £75,000 and now you say hundreds of thousands of pounds. I suppose if the papers keep printing the story often enough, it will become the truth. If they print it often enough even I might start to believe it.'

In September 1975, during the Opec meeting in Vienna, the papers found a new angle to the 'Yamani as cult hero' theme.

They vividly described how he held his ground, refusing to give in to the demands of other member states.

The price of oil was then $10.46 a barrel and some cartel members were looking for an increase of up to 20 per cent. But Yamani had gone into the meeting with a directive not to accept more than a 5 per cent price rise. In order to agree to anything over that he'd need the approval of Prince Fahd.

As the discussion grew heated, Yamani supposedly matched the shouts directed at him, shout for shout. The Venezuelan minister, trying to mediate, felt he was close to an agreement on a 7 – 8 per cent increase, with the other members having come down from their 20 per cent increase demand. They were now looking towards Yamani to compromise.

Quite frankly, if Yamani was frustrated at not being able to go beyond his mandate of 5 per cent, it's only fair to say that the other members must have felt a similar frustration, knowing that in the end it was Saudi Arabia, as the largest producer, that held the strongest hand when determining prices and policy. A price increase agreed by the other members would be very difficult to maintain without Saudi consent.

In the heat of the argument Yamani went to the phone to call Saudi Arabia.

When he couldn't get through he went to another room, tried another phone and still couldn't get through.

He then, reportedly, stormed out of the meeting in angry frustration.

Going directly to his car, the papers said, he found that his chauffeur wasn't there. He locked himself into the rear seat to wait and was immediately surrounded by reporters who shouted questions at him through the door.

One ingenious television sound man somehow squeezed a microphone through a crack in the window, into which Yamani supposedly said, 'There is a complete difference of opinion. It is very violent in there.'

When his chauffeur eventually showed up, Yamani was said to have ordered the man to drive to the airport, where he climbed into his private jet and flew off to find a phone box that worked.

In London!

Former Opec press spokesman, Hamed Zaheri, quite clearly remembers the incident. 'I'll admit that Vienna might not have had very good communications in those days. But I wouldn't think he had to go all the way to London just to make a phone call. His Embassy could have easily sent a coded message to Saudi Arabia. No, this just was part of the show. In case you haven't noticed, he's really a very good showman. Whenever he wanted to put pressure on any of the others, his style was to come up with excuses to leave the meeting.'

Still, greatly amused by all of this, Yamani says the way the press reported it was almost the way it really happened.

But not quite.

'First of all,' he says, 'I never shout or raise my voice. I do not lose my temper. Secondly, I did not storm out of that meeting. I have only twice walked out of an Opec meeting. The first time was in 1963 when the Iraqi oil minister said that Saudi Arabia was the agent of the oil companies. I asked for an apology and wanted his comments to be removed from the minutes. He refused, so I left. We then refused to attend any further Opec meetings at the ministerial level. We sent someone as a representative just to sit and listen, but I wouldn't appear.

In the end the Iraqis simply had to give in and apologize. And their comments were removed from the records.'

He cites the only other time as being in 1976 in Bali. 'Again, the Iraqi oil minister attacked Saudi Arabia as the agent of the imperialists. And again I got up and left. I asked for an apology and insisted on having his comments removed from the minutes. President Suharto personally intervened. In the next session the Iraqis apologized. But these were the only two times I've ever walked out of an Opec meeting. I only did it on these occasions because the comments that were made touched the dignity of my country.'

However, he doesn't deny that he flew from Vienna to London just to make a phone call.

'This is perfectly true. It was very difficult to use the phone from Austria to Saudi Arabia. Of course I could have sent a coded message from the Embassy but that's not like a personal discussion. It was only unfortunate someone leaked the information that I was going to London. Otherwise it would have not been known.'

Asked about his comment to the reporters from the back seat of his car ('There is a complete difference of opinion. It's very violent in there'), he shakes his head. 'I left Vienna without anyone knowing. There were no conversations from the back seat of my car. But it's true that most of the Opec meetings were violent. That was nothing new.'

Another favourite topic of the press is Yamani's interest in horoscopes.

'The Sheikh is a devoted astrologer and never goes anywhere without a book of astrology,' announced one newspaper.

Treating him like a rock star or the leading man in a hot new sit-com, they headlined their story, '21 Things You Didn't Know About Sheikh Yamani.'

In addition to horoscopes, other items mentioned were the story of his after-hours spree in Harrods where they said he blew £38,000; that he lives in a tent during the summer months; and that in 1973/4 and again in 1979 he singlehandedly drove up the price of oil fourfold, causing a major economic crisis around the world.

But the astrology entry was the best because they asked, how come, if he knows so much about horoscopes, he didn't know that Faisal would be murdered, that he would be kidnapped by Carlos and that he would eventually be fired by Fahd?

'Astrology', he answers, 'is an important subject in my life. But it's not the astrology of horoscopes in newspapers. I'm interested in the effects of the various planets on human beings, marine life, animals and plants. I'm interested in how the moon's cycle affects our lives. I'm not at all interested in the astrology of predictions, of what will happen tomorrow, the astrology of do this and don't do that. I never look at my horoscope in the newspaper because I don't believe for a moment that anyone can see into the future.'

Many public figures wind up having an odd sort of love-hate relationship with the press. Especially politicians. They cheerfully acknowledge all victories as a demonstration of their own skill while defeats are blamed on a press which has totally distorted their views and misrepresented their cause. A right-wing press. A left-wing press. A world press conspiracy. It's always the fault of the press.

Yet, all too many politicians habitually rely on half-truths and innuendo to escape answering tough questions, as if the Fourth Estate had neither the right nor the responsibility to subject public servants, their words and their actions to the most minute examination. In the same breath, those same politicians then accuse the press of reporting nothing more than half-truths and innuendo.

Case in point, Richard Nixon. As the first President ever to resign from the White House, he blamed most of his Watergate problems on the *Washington Post*. God only knows, he may still believe it.

You'd think that, after a lifetime in the public eye, most politicians would learn how to avoid such confrontations with the media. But very few ever manage that. Most politicians and other public figures who live by the press believe they might die by it too.

Exceptions are rare.

Henry Kissinger is one.

As the story goes, he was in his office one afternoon at the State Department when a panic call came from someone at the front door that the Foreign Minister of some never-before-heard-of African country was arriving. It wasn't on Kissinger's calendar and no one knew anything about it. Statesman to the end, Kissinger headed for the front door to greet the man. On the way, he stopped in the press room and gathered up all the reporters he could find. He put them into a reception line so that the visiting Foreign Minister would think he was being met by two dozen very important State Department officials. That was impressive enough. But what really stuck in the reporters' minds that afternoon was that, while Kissinger was walking the Foreign Minister down the reception line, he introduced every reporter by name.

Yamani is out of that mould.

Comments one old-time reporter, 'You'd be hard-pressed to find a guy who's covered the world oil scene for any length of time and who hasn't broken bread with Zaki or been to his house or met his family or at least been welcomed by him as an old pal the second time they're introduced.'

Zaheri agrees, 'Yes, Yamani definitely knows how to use the media.

193

He's always been most efficient. He knows when to use it, where and how. Amouzegar did also. Actually, in the early 1970s Amouzegar was the more forthcoming. Yamani didn't have so much power to talk, it seems, so it was always Amouzegar who was quoted. Especially when it came to technical things. He knew a lot. After Amouzegar, Yamani became the lone star. He had the right background for it. His English is very good. He's a lawyer. He's intelligent. And don't forget he was in the business for a long time. But it was not only Yamani who wanted to talk to the press. The press also wanted to talk to him because he was the representative of a country with such a high capacity for production. The press was always trying to corner him. So he learned how to deal with them. His was the longest university course in journalism you can possibly have.'

Obviously he graduated with honours.

'Yamani is unfailingly gracious with the press,' says Joe Fitchett of the *International Herald Tribune*, 'and with Henry Kissinger's gift for knowing when to take a journalist apparently in his confidence in order to drop a strategic bit of information. He always put the west and his customers on notice and gave warning in advance of everything the Saudis were going to do. Besides not lying and besides being rather acute and courteous and not saying too much so you'd pay attention to what he did say, he also knew how to use a background. He took real experts, of whom there are only a few, and skilfully used those channels in order to explain a situation.'

The method was based entirely on the mutual trust he'd established over several years with a small handful of reporters who were as knowledgeable about the world oil business as he was.

At select times, when matters had real weight to them, Yamani would supply one of these confidants with just enough inside information to send them off in the right direction.

It was like a journalistic treasure hunt, where he'd provide the clues to help get them to the prize. They, in turn, scooped their competitors while editorializing on Yamani's points in their own voice.

The beauty of the device was that the direct responsibility for bringing the facts to light was theirs. It protected Yamani both against western complaints and also against anybody in the Arab world who wanted to accuse him of having said too much.

'This is a very sophisticated technique,' Fitchett goes on. 'But never forget that he was in a very difficult position. Yamani was trying to represent Saudi interests in a way that would be palatable to the west. However, there were factions in the west which were eager to say that the kingdom was leading an assault on the west in spite of the fact that Yamani always believed there was a community of interest in financial terms, security terms and political terms between the west and most of the members of Opec.'

At the same time, Fitchett says, it's worth noting that Yamani was considered a very polished press performer. 'So formidable in fact, that he was more than once singled out for extensive disinformation attacks against him by anti-Saudi groups. I remember hearing Israeli radio one day report that the name Yamani was a derivation of the word Yemeni and that they had located someone in Israel, a Yemeni Jew, who was claiming to be his relative.'

One of Yamani's long-standing confidants was Ian Seymour of the *Middle East Economic Survey*. 'I always thought he handled the press very very well. He was extremely good at relaxed briefings. But he was also just as good at formal press conferences. I met him some time during his first year as minister. He was a bit diffident when he came into office but it didn't take him long to develop confidence. He had good relations with quite a number of reporters. Although anyone who, either by accident or by design, got on his wrong side, well, that was it.'

One western reporter who got on Yamani's wrong side earned his place by writing about group-sex shenanigans after hours at Opec meetings. He made the drastic mistake of tarring Yamani with a brush too wide. While Yamani won't say whether other ministers might have taken part, other ministers are fast to say that Yamani has never ever been involved with anything of the kind. That reporter, who has since tried to apologize to Yamani but has never been permitted close enough to extend his regrets, discovered the hard way that his best source of information had dried up about as fast as the ink on the offending story.

Another long-time Yamani confidant is Wanda Jablonski, founder of *Petroleum Intelligence Weekly*.

She was one of only two reporters at the first Opec meeting in 1960 and therefore already an Opec veteran when Yamani arrived on the scene two years later.

The way she tells the story, she wanted an exclusive interview with him after his first meeting. Instead he invited her to his press conference. She told him that she didn't go to press conferences. He shrugged as if to say, too bad for you. She then showed her class by walking out, finding a comfortable chair in the hotel lobby and sitting there with a woman's magazine pushed up to her face, knowing that eventually he'd have to walk right past her.

When Yamani finished with his press conference, he headed for the lifts.

And he couldn't help but notice her sitting there.

He also couldn't help but see that she was miffed.

Yet he said nothing and continued upstairs.

A few minutes later a messenger came down with an invitation from His Excellency to join him.

She asked if it was for her interview.

The messenger said, no, that His Excellency was playing cards but if she wanted to join him . . .

She said she wasn't interested.

The messenger went away.

She sat right where she was.

Several more minutes passed before the messenger returned.

His Excellency would be pleased to speak with her.

Yamani gave in.

She got her interview.

Twenty-five years later their friendship is firmly intact.

But then, he works at maintaining friendships and never misses an opportunity to strengthen them, especially with journalists he likes.

Again Wanda Jablonski.

During the participation negotiations, she'd broken the story in PIW about the secret terms Yamani had exacted from the producers and was about to take with him to Kuwait, seeking their approval. The story ran literally only hours after the talks concluded.

Arriving at the hotel in Kuwait to cover the next part of the story, Jablonski received a telex from her office in New York saying that George Piercy was livid that she'd run the story and was hereby cancelling Exxon's many subscriptions to PIW. He was also demanding a full refund for those cancelled subscriptions, which amounted to about $36,000. The telex ended, 'What should we do?'

Jablonski wired New York, 'Give them their lousy $36,000 back but tell them we will continue sending all PIWs until their expiration date because "we honor our contracts".' She explains that was a phrase Piercy himself had frequently used during the negotiations.

A few minutes after she'd sent her answer, Yamani happened by.

He found her holding the telex from New York, still a bit shocked.

'What's that?' he wanted to know.

She gave it to him and muttered, 'What's going on?'

He read it, then reassured her, 'But I like your reply.'

She was stunned. 'How do you know about my reply?'

He grinned, 'I have my ways.' Then he said if, after the meeting, she wanted to go back to Saudi Arabia, there'd be room for her on his plane.

She accepted his offer.

Landing in Riyadh, Yamani was about ready to get off when he spotted George Piercy at the bottom of the steps. Thinking fast, he took Jablonski's arm and her luggage.

Yamani greeted Piercy, handed Jablonski's suitcase to him and asked gently, 'You don't mind carrying Wanda's luggage, do you George?'

As Piercy's jaw dropped, Yamani and Jablonski walked away.

He is equally adept at making new press friendships.

A favourite Opec press corps story concerns a young journalist, a novice on the oil beat, who decided he was going to corner Yamani for an exclusive interview.

Easier said than done. He spent several days trying to get a message through without much luck.

He finally summoned up his courage to head Yamani off at the lifts after a long meeting.

Weary as he was, Yamani sussed out the situation right away. He invited the young journalist upstairs for a chat.

The exclusive interview lasted barely long enough for a coffee and various assorted comments on astrology. The young journalist didn't get his scoop about oil prices, but he had been in to meet the star and that was something to crow about.

It also put yet another marker in Yamani's pocket for a rainy day.

Onnic Marashian of *Platts Oilgram News* has covered Opec since 1962 and he too has always been impressed with Yamani's media skills.

'At the time he became the Saudi oil minister, it's possible he'd never even seen an oil well or had any idea how oil came out of the ground. But Yamani is someone who always did his homework. Right from the beginning you could tell he was a clever young man. He had more hair then and a darker beard. I must also say he was not as sophisticated as he ended up. He wasn't as good in those days at handling the press. But at the end he was very very good. He could draw huge crowds of journalists. He mastered the techniques of how to deal with the press and they threw a huge amount of importance on him. He's always been a nice man and he's always been very correct with people. He's never been rude, although you can read impatience on someone's face and sometimes he grew impatient, especially with the press.'

Yamani definitely grew impatient with Oriana Fallaci when she went to Saudi Arabia to interview him for the *New York Times Magazine* in mid–1975.

But then she says she grew impatient with him too.

They met the first time in London.

Fallaci says she thought the interview would take place there.

'It was the birthday of one of his daughters. He was having a big dinner that evening. We went to a very expensive place and he was, as usual, very gracious. I said, okay, tomorrow we will make the interview. He said, no, tomorrow I must give a lecture. You will come and listen to me so you can hear what I have to say. I told him, okay. But the lecture was very technical and didn't interest me very much. When it was over I said, okay, shall we make the interview now? But he said, no, we shall do it in Saudi Arabia. He kept his word. I went to Saudi Arabia but I had to wait 15 days there for my interview.'

She says she flew to Jeddah and saw Yamani there. But each day he'd say he wasn't yet ready to do the interview.

'I grew more and more impatient. You don't stay somewhere for a week to see the person every day without getting the interview. Finally he said we will make the interview in Taif. He has a big house there in the middle of nothing. It's newly built. There's a smaller house next to it, with lots of India fig trees. It's the guest house. It's like a little hotel, very neat, very clean, with lots of small rooms, with beds and closets built in. I was there for four or five days. Then Yamani started again, putting me off. I remember I said to Tammam, he is making fun of me. Tammam raised her eyes to the ceiling and said, I don't know, I'll tell him.'

Fallaci adds here that she liked Tammam and found her 'very *simpatica*. But she's more at ease than him. With him you don't know if he's relaxed or not. She's smart and she's a modern girl for an Arab. You know what? She was always dressed in western clothes like me. I never saw Tammam dressed as an Arab woman.'

Over the course of the next few days Fallaci says she and Zaki and Tammam and all the children had lunch together and dinner together and even took long walks together.

But still no interview.

'I don't understand that man. I feel very uncomfortable with the Arabs because this is a world I do not know. And I am very perplexed in my judgement of him. Maybe he was simply scared by me. But then why was he so exaggeratedly polite and kind with his hospitality. He even gave a party for me in Taif.'

But no interview.

'I remember his son Hani was even making fun of me because everybody knew about this story. Everybody knew how he kept me waiting. We would walk together in what he called his garden. It was really an orchard. He had tomatoes and figs. He would pick up a fig and put it in my mouth, which bothered me a lot. I didn't want the fig and I didn't want him to put it in my mouth. But that shows you how he wanted to be friendly and full of affection.'

Eventually, she says, she couldn't stand it any longer.

'I went to him and said, "Listen, I don't understand this game. You are very gracious and so exquisite but I came here to do some work. What can I tell my editors in Milan and New York?" Actually to say gracious is to say very little. He is more than gracious. But he made me wait 15 days. I got the interview in the morning and left that same afternoon.'

She insists that when he was finally ready they went in his study where he did one of the things that offends her the most.

'He put on a tape recorder. I don't like that because the moment you give an interview it belongs to the one who does it. I don't like them to tape my interview. I was taping him and he was taping me.'

His version of the story is very different.

Yamani says that when Fallaci first arrived she announced that she wasn't quite ready yet to do the interview. She wanted to take some time just to observe him. But the date of the interview was fixed, he emphasizes, according to her request.

The day before it, Yamani says, he had a tiring 12 hours at the office. That evening there was a cabinet meeting. He returned home at around 11 p.m., exhausted. And he says, that's when Fallaci announced, 'We'll do the interview now.'

Yamani refused.

Fallaci threatened to leave.

Yamani offered to help her get to Jeddah and on the next flight for home.

But, he says, she backed down.

The next day, as had been planned all along, he matched her punch for punch.

It must be said here that she's known for her especially brash technique.

It must also be said here that her technique happens to produce for her colourful reactions in the people she's portraying.

Her interview with Yamani, all these years later, still stands out as an excellent example of magazine journalism.

After polite talk about his family and of his various homes, she got Yamani to talk about Yassir Arafat.

Obviously well aware that Arafat's reputation in the United States was generally that of a criminal terrorist, she baited Yamani with, 'I expect your opinion of him is an enthusiastic one.'

Yamani said Arafat was viewed by some as a reasonable man, a moderate.

She snapped back, saying that when she interviewed Arafat he was anything but a moderate. He was a man who kept shouting that Israel had to be swept away, wiped off the map.

Yamani parried, 'If Arafat didn't talk that way, the Palestinians

199

would never have a home. Sometimes people have to talk in a certain way and say certain things.'

When they got on to the subject of oil price increases, she prodded him, 'Between ourselves, Yamani, is it really in your interests to push us over the brink?'

He told her that in Saudi Arabia they didn't think so.

He said they knew that that if the American economy were to collapse, Saudi Arabia's economy would collapse as well. The problem was, as he saw it, that some members of Opec didn't believe that another oil price hike would lead to disaster. And that some of them did not particularly care whether the world's economy collapsed or not.

Fallaci mentioned the problems involved with discovering suitable sources of alternative energy, then hit him with, 'When that day comes we'll no longer need you.'

Yamani retorted, 'By that time we'll be so wealthy that you'll need us for other things.'

Now Fallaci suggested, 'You've already got too much money, haven't you?'

And Yamani told her, 'Yes.'

Looking back on the interview, Fallaci concedes it's not one of her favourites.

'There are only a few parts I like. At one point he said to me, I wish we could import water the way you import oil. I said to him that I have a property in Tuscany, in Italy, and there is so much water everywhere. I said, if you want, I'll sell you water. That was fun for me because we were joking. But the rest was not spontaneous. He's extremely polite. Very, very polite. And very diplomatic. I know through some friends that he hesitated to see me. But frankly, my judgement of him is in a kind of limbo. I don't really know what to think.'

15

The Second Oil Crisis

IT WAS the first real vacation he'd taken in 16 years.

In April 1976, Zaki and Tammam Yamani chartered a yacht in the Caribbean.

It was going to be a sort of belated honeymoon.

He promised Tammam he wasn't going to work.

He even took off his wrist watch.

The boat had been arranged for them in Saudi Arabia and he knew nothing about it besides the fact that it was big.

When they arrived at the dock he was told it was Adnan Khashoggi's yacht.

Yamani was not pleased.

He didn't want it to look as if he was Khashoggi's guest.

Nor did he particularly want Khashoggi to think that.

But it was either sail as planned or go home.

They boarded the yacht and for the next five weeks Zaki and Tammam took the time to be alone with each other.

He also took some time to think about his real estate holdings in Saudi Arabia.

And the more he thought about all the money he'd made in real estate over the past few years, the more he concluded that boomtime was an abnormal time.

A few weeks into the cruise he radioed to a friend in Saudi Arabia, 'Sell everything I'm holding.'

Before the year was out, Saudi real estate crashed.

By then Yamani was long gone from the market.

* * * *

Where oil was concerned, the Shah had his own ideas.

He warned the west, don't depend on oil. He claimed that oil was precious. He claimed that the west's standard of living had been entirely built upon oil. He warned the west to look for other sources of energy as oil was not a replenishing asset and the oil-producing nations would one day run out of it. He said oil could be the basis of future developments in petrochemicals but that as an energy source it should not be depended upon.

He told the west he was going to teach them a lesson.

Until this point, most oil producers sang the same sad song when it came to crying that prices were traditionally too low.

For 24 years, they harmonized, the price of oil has remained well below the level that could have been fetched if the forces of supply and demand had been allowed to interact freely. Oil prices did not rise between 1947 and 1971. In the same 24–year period, however, the price of industrial goods and foodstuffs tripled.

Now the Shah took a more novel approach.

To illustrate that oil was underpriced, he suggested a comparison with Coca Cola.

It turns out that when the price of oil rose to $11.65 a barrel – which is 42 gallons – a 12 ounce can of Coke sold out of vending machines for 20 cents. That comes to just a shade over $2.13 a gallon. Multiply that by 42 and you get $89.52.

See, the Shah said, oil is simply too much of a bargain!

'The Shah actually said to me', claims Mahdi al-Tajir, 'that $100 oil was not unreasonable.'

As far as Sheikh Yamani was concerned, it was absolutely unthinkable.

'You must put the situation into context,' he says. 'We, and I'm referring to Saudi Arabia, were very concerned at the time about the economic situation in the west. We were uneasy about the possibility of a new recession and also uneasy about the political situation in countries such as France and Italy where we did not want the Communists to come to power. The situation in Spain and Portugal also worried us. And we were right to be concerned. We wanted to see an economic recovery take place because that had great political significance for Saudi Arabia.'

But not everybody shared his concerns.

When Opec met in Bali in May 1976, eight members of the cartel, not surprisingly led by Iran, pointed out that the cost of goods imported into Opec countries had increased over the past year by nearly 20 per cent.

So they wanted to do the logical thing and up the price of oil by 20 per cent.

Yamani preferred a six-month price freeze.

This was the point where the Iraqis so strenuously attacked the Saudis for their constant pro-western concern that Yamani walked out of the meeting.

It caused an enormous stir within Opec. Yet it won the Saudis some sympathy and a price freeze.

But six months later, with double-digit inflation running wild in the west, the cartel regrouped in Doha, Qatar, and Yamani found the Shah's team dug in for a fight.

Iran wasn't going to accept less than a 15 per cent rise.

Dr Amouzegar pointed out to the other members that Saudi Arabia's reluctance to increase prices was solely because they'd taken it upon themselves to protect American investments.

The remark did not go down well with Yamani then.

Nor does it now.

'My main worry was that if we increased the price of oil too much we would merely reduce demand for it in the future. I have always felt price increases should come in small doses. After all, the economic stability and the political stability of the west is very important for us. Politically, if we have a high price of oil, the Russians will be very strong, while Europe, Japan and the United States will in turn become very weak. But then you must also understand that it is not necessarily how high you raise prices as much as it is how fast you increase them. Sudden and sharp increases disturb the economy of a country. Gradual increases can be absorbed. It's very dangerous for everyone involved when price increases come as a shock.'

Even now he worries that certain ministers from other oil-producing states are not aware of that.

'I really don't know. It seems obvious to me and I think it should be just as obvious to many others. But there are times when their decisions are, well, let me call them, surprising.'

He claims that whenever he formulated oil policy, he tried to take many elements into consideration.

'But you must not forget that we are well off. We have huge reserves. We have a comfortable income. We could always afford to sit down and think objectively. Not every oil producer has that privilege. The Algerians, for instance, are badly in need of revenue. So are the Nigerians. So are the Indonesians. As for the Iraqis and the Iranians, what can I say? If you have a political motivation, even if you can afford to take the time to think, your perceptions change. I honestly believe that Saudi Arabia always acted as internationalists when it came to oil policy. But that's obviously not true of many others.'

Cynics, particularly in the west, wouldn't always agree with him. There are plenty who would seriously question the Saudis' record as internationalists. Most of them, especially Americans, would happily cite dozens of instances, starting with the Aramco takeover and the oil embargo, where Saudi Arabia has obviously put its own interests before anything else.

'Yes, of course we have always considered our own interests. It's only natural that we would. But we've only ever looked after our own interests on a long-term basis. I know I am repeating myself when I tell you again that I am not a short-term thinker in any way. In my public life, in my personal life, in everything I do I think long term. Once you start thinking short term, you are in trouble because short-term thinking is only a tactic for immediate benefit.'

And here he does not hesitate to add that, in the west, the tendency is to think short term.

'For you, it's only natural. It's one of the results of democracy. A politician is elected to serve for four years. So he sees problems and solutions as defined by the time-span of his own term of office. He never goes beyond that. We, on the other hand, can afford to think long term. What the west has never understood is that, whenever there is a contradiction between short-term interests and long-term interests, you must go long term.'

As true as that may be, at Doha he couldn't repeat the success of Bali.

No matter how hard he tried, Yamani couldn't convince the men who faced him that upping the price by 10–20 per cent was short-term thinking.

The Shah was going to get his way no matter what.

Seeing no immediate solution at hand, Yamani flew to Riyadh for a talk with Fahd. He came back to Doha that night with permission to agree to an increase of 7 per cent.

But no more.

Less experienced negotiators might have put that card on the table right away.

As it was, Yamani never played it at all.

Amouzegar had rallied enough support for a plan to increase prices as of 1 January, 1977 by an immediate 10 per cent – from $11.51 to $12.70 – and 5 per cent more six months later, taking the price up to $13.30.

Only Saudi Arabia and the United Arab Emirates held out.

Together they declared they'd only increase crude by 5 per cent, taking the price to $12.09.

Two-tier pricing was born.

'At Doha,' Ian Seymour reported, 'it looked as though Opec, usually so adept at brinkmanship, had finally missed its footing and tumbled over the edge. The majority had finally got fed up with the perpetual tug-of-war on prices and decided to cut themselves loose from Saudi tutelage, while Saudi Arabia was now determined to demonstrate that its views could not go thus unheeded with impunity.'

The split between Opec's moderates and Opec's extremists deepened.

If the Shah was merely annoyed that Saudi Arabia was not going along with his demands for higher prices, then he was outright furious when he learned the next day that Saudi Arabia now planned to up production from 8.6 mbd to as much as 11.6 mbd.

It meant that Saudi and UAE oil would account for nearly 40 per cent of Opec's total output.

It also meant that if any of the other Opec members tried to fight the Saudis by raising their quota, those newly increased prices would tumble.

The Shah directed his vengeance directly at Yamani.

He called Yamani's actions a blatant act of aggression.

Odd as this sounds, there are some people who contend that the United States might have quietly agreed with the Shah.

The suggestion is that higher oil prices in the mid-1970s were a good move for America. To begin with, the argument goes, this surplus money was funnelled back into US banks. Next, it put the Japanese and the West Germans under pressure. Totally dependent on imported oil, their economies slowed down, which in turn made America more competitive. At the same time, increased prices provided funds for all the western oil companies to finance further exploration.

As importantly, there was the matter of arming Iran.

The Shah became obsessed with becoming a major world power. Concurrently, the Americans wanted to see the Shah secure in his role as policeman to the Gulf. Obviously, the best way for Iran to afford more planes and more guns was by increasing oil prices. Armed to the teeth, the Shah would not only be doing America's bidding in the Gulf, but he'd be buying his hardware in the States where the money would recirculate into American industry.

Finally, the argument concludes, the big American oil companies had an interest in all of this too. Their balance sheets flourish with price jumps. They represent both a powerful economic force and an equally powerful lobby with friends in high places. Don't forget, say the exponents of this theory, Kissinger was the Rockefellers' boy and the Rockefeller fortune was made in oil.

Here Yamani endorses the concept that America did not want to see prices come down.

'Yes. The real interest of the United States was in higher oil prices. I do not recall that Dr Kissinger ever mentioned the subject of oil prices with us. Their whole interest was in raising the price of oil.'

In February 1975 Henry Kissinger met with the Shah of Iran in St Moritz, where he told the Iranian leader, 'The United States understands Tehran's desire to secure higher oil prices.'

To be fair, that's a vague enough statement. It does not in any way imply an agreement to cooperate with Tehran.

But it confused Yamani when he heard about it.

'On the one hand the United States said the price of oil was too high and that they could not tolerate the present levels. On the other they imposed new taxes and new domestic measures geared to raise the price of crude on the domestic market. They were contradicting themselves. We would have been willing to cooperate with the United States if we'd been able to discover what their policy really was.'

A few months after Kissinger's meeting with the Shah, Yamani sent a classified letter to Treasury Secretary William Simon. In it he said that Saudi Arabia could not be convinced that America seriously objected to higher oil prices. 'There are even those who think that you encourage it for obvious political reasons and that any official position taken to the contrary is merely to cover up this fact.'

Mention of Yamani's name to Simon these days initially gets you a long string of accolades. 'I think back to my dealings with Zaki with enormous fondness. He was one of the great statesmen of the world. The fact that he was in power in such a critically sensitive post for, what, 24 or 25 years, well that attests to the statement. You know, he stayed at my home in McLean [Virginia]. He even did my horoscope for me. I don't know where it is. I'm afraid I've lost it. But some of the best memories that I have of a very very exciting time in the four and a half years that I spent in government, in all the posts that I held, well, the relationship I had with Zaki ranks right at the top.'

Unfortunately he doesn't remember that particular letter from Yamani.

'We used to correspond quite regularly as far as confidential messages were concerned. We used what we call "back channel" messages. They didn't go through the State Department. It was more private that way.'

However, he does agree that America didn't necessarily appear to want lower oil prices.

'There was a rumour going around at the time that the State Department made a deal with the Shah of Iran. We helped send the oil prices higher to give Iran the wherewithal to build her military so that she could defend the Persian Gulf against the Soviet Union. That was the story. It was never proven but often rumoured.'

At the same time, the United States had various government programmes that depended on investments in alternative sources of energy.

'The thinking there was that people wouldn't make the investment if the oil price came down, which to me was absolutely ridiculous. That's talking out of both sides of your mouth at the same time. Never mind the alternative energy, let's talk about bringing the price down and what's good for the world economy.'

In other words, Simon agrees with Yamani that during the Nixon and Ford years there was a serious contradiction in US government policy where oil prices were concerned.

'In this instance, the contradictions were in how they were trying to protect the domestic oil industry at the expense of the consumer. Oh sure. That's part of the hypocrisy of politics, isn't it? Don't look for a politician to do what's right. You know, they do what's right as far as getting re-elected, that's all.'

What he's then saying is that, in spite of public statements to the contrary, both the Nixon and Ford administrations were indeed in favour of higher oil prices.

'That would be absolutely correct.'

But was William Simon, Energy Czar and Treasury Secretary one of them? 'No. As the man leading the energy side, I was four square in favour of a reduced oil price. Four square.'

Was Dr Kissinger one of them?

'Well,' Simon says, 'that's the question. Was he or wasn't he? He said he wanted lower oil prices but there were parts of his bureaucracy that clearly favoured higher prices. They had all those price support programmes. That's a fact. But then you often find bureaucrats who are working at cross-purposes with the bosses.'

* * * *

Jimmy Carter moved into the White House in January 1977, his election being yet another event in what has turned out to be a long series of overreactions by a frustrated nation to be done with the Watergate days once and for all.

'I found Carter to be an honest man,' says Yamani. 'Maybe even too honest for a politician. In many ways he was more like a man of religion than a politician or a statesman.'

Under Carter, America took an initiative towards finding a peace in the Middle East. But the Camp David Agreements were not to the liking of most Arabs.

In the beginning the Saudis made some secret overtures to help the Egyptians find favour in the Arab world. But when the other Arab nations closed ranks to condemn Camp David because the Palestinians were not included, the Saudis were forced to line up with the rest of the Arabs against Egypt. From the day the agreements were signed in 1979, for a period of just over five years, no Saudi minister 'officially' set foot on Egyptian soil.

The first post-Camp David 'publicized' visit by a Saudi minister to Egypt came in October 1984.

The man to make that visit was Zaki Yamani.

'Camp David isolated Egypt from the Arab camp,' Yamani continues to assert. 'It did not solve the question of the Palestinians. It never would have happened had Faisal lived.'

While Jimmy Carter tried to build a foreign policy programme around the issue of human rights, coincidentally the price of oil appeared to stabilize.

Because it did, two-tier pricing officially ended in July 1977 when Opec met in Stockholm.

Yamani was categorically refusing to return to Vienna – the Carlos incident had shaken him so badly that he now travelled only by private aircraft and constantly surrounded by half a dozen bodyguards. In deference to him, Opec vagabonded around the world, changing sites for each meeting.

It wasn't until 1979 that Yamani showed his face in Vienna again. The Austrian government bribed him back with an honorary doctorate from the University of Loeben. And, just to prove that their security forces were no longer as lax as they had been in December 1975, Chancellor Bruno Kreisky provided Yamani with a specially trained commando squad known as 'Cobra' to mind him while he was in the country.

In Sweden, the group agreed not to implement their planned 5 per cent increase, in exchange for a 5 per cent rise in prices by Saudi Arabia and the UAE.

Five months later, Opec met in Caracas.

Ironically they chose Carlos's home town to 'celebrate' the second anniversary of the Vienna seige.

Predictably, rumours spread that Carlos had been spotted on several occasions inside the city limits and that various members of his group were gathering somewhere in the Caribbean.

Those rumours merely served to step up the vigil.

There were heavily armed troops everywhere. Army units, fully equipped for battle, plus helicopters, plus naval patrol boats, kept watch on the beachside hotel where Opec was meeting, and at the airport and on all the roads and access points connecting the two.

Supposedly they were guaranteeing the safety of all the Opec ministers. In reality they were there to protect one man in particular.

'When our plane landed I noticed armoured vehicles taxiing to the parking spot with us. When the plane's door opened, I could see soldiers lying prone on the ground with machine guns facing in every direction. The military attaché who came to greet us said we were in great danger and he wanted Tammam to fly in a different helicopter from me. He said they were expecting terrorists in the bushes to fire a SAM–7 missile at one of the helicopters and, if we flew separately, at least one of us would survive. Tammam didn't like that at all. She insisted on flying with me. Frankly, I think they might have overreacted just a bit.'

But the Venezuelans didn't think so.

Sheikh Yamani was in town and, because of that, for those few days in December 1977 Caracas was perhaps the most heavily fortified city in the world.

During the Opec meeting there, Yamani announced that Saudi Arabia was seeking a price freeze which could last throughout 1978.

'There was a surplus in the market,' he says. 'It was caused by Saudi Arabia's willingness to produce more than its financial needs.'

It was also caused by a substantial amount of non-Opec crude pouring on to the market.

Before too long, even the Shah had reversed his position and was willing to agree to a price freeze.

He met with President Carter in Washington in November 1977. The result was what the Shah termed 'sympathy and comprehension' for the American stance that the world economy was still too fragile for further oil price rises.

So Yamani and the Saudis got another price freeze.

In May 1978, Yamani announced there was now a 50–50 chance that prices would start to rise again.

'I was predicting that there would be a balance of supply and demand until about 1985 at which time there would be an oil shortage. That's when supply and demand considerations would determine the price of oil instead of Opec. So I suggested that it was important for Opec to come up with a long-term strategy. The result was that we formed a committee made up of Saudi Arabia, Iran, Iraq, Kuwait, Venezuela and Algeria. The job of the committee was to write a report which would serve as the basis for policy recommendations which we planned to put before the Opec Summit Conference in Baghdad in 1980.'

Yamani was appointed chairman and they called themselves Opec's Long-Term Strategy Committee.

As soon as the project was announced, a rumour took hold in the oil community that Yamani would present the committee's report at Baghdad and then retire.

It would have been a most graceful exit for a 50 year old who had reached the very top.

But it wasn't to be, because all of this was happening against the backdrop of two very important political problems.

The first was the continued weakness of the US dollar.

Yamani, Fahd and the US Treasury Secretary Michael Blumenthal all promised at various times throughout 1978 that the dollar was on the road to recovery. There was even talk among some Opec members of abandoning the policy of pricing oil in dollars, although Yamani as Opec's senior statesman easily convinced everyone that such a policy would merely serve both to hasten the dollar's decline and push up inflation.

The second drama was unfolding simultaneously in Paris and Tehran.

The Ayatollah Khomeini had been living in political exile in a Parisian suburb. Now he wanted to come home.

A lot of people in the Gulf, especially those who didn't always have time for the Shah, were now saying to each other, better the devil you know than the devil you don't.

The Ayatollah's return and his fire-brand fundamentalism were not suited to everyone's taste.

Especially the Saudis. But then, they reassured themselves, the Americans will never let anything happen to the Shah.

And they weren't alone in thinking that way.

The Shah not only believed the Americans would always take care of him, he bet the Peacock Throne on it.

It was a fatal misreading of Jimmy Carter's ability to manage world affairs.

Opec was scheduled to meet in Abu Dhabi in December.

The price freeze had held, although once again there was pressure mounting for another increase.

Yamani hoped to keep it to 5 per cent.

But on the way to Abu Dhabi someone put a match to Iran.

On 13 October, 1978, workers at the world's largest oil refinery, in Abadan, Iran, suddenly went on strike. Within a week the movement had spread throughout most of the country and Iran was, to all intents and purposes, out of the oil business. The Shah tried sending in troops and retired oil executives to get the wells flowing again. But Khomeini in France announced, 'To strike in the oil sector is to do the will of God.'

When Opec convened as planned on 16 December, the situation in Iran had thrown the market into such an unusual situation that there was simply no way Yamani could hold the cartel to a 5 per cent increase.

'Wouldn't it be appropriate,' asked the Algerian oil minister, 'if, to celebrate Opec's 20th year, we put the price at $20.'

Yamani answered him flatly, 'I thought you were a realist.'

Opec finally agreed to a 10 per cent rise.

On 26 December, Khomeini declared, 'As long as the Shah has not left the country there will be no oil exports.'

Five days later, John Lichtblau, director of the independent and influential New York based study group, the Petroleum Industry Research Foundation, announced, 'We are completely pessimistic about the present regime's ability to get Iranian oil production going again.'

In other words, the Shah was finished.

Sixteen days into the new year, the Shah and his family left Tehran on what he claimed was just an extended holiday. He vowed to return.

Unlike MacArthur, he never made it.

One week to the day after the Pahlavi dynasty had crumbled, Khomeini landed in Tehran.

The politics of the Gulf will never be the same.

Mahdi al-Tajir says he was one of those who knew the Shah could not last.

'Maybe I saw it coming but not in the way it happened. I was a great admirer of the Shah. I thought he was going to make the necessary changes to stay in power. I never thought he would leave it as late as he did. I didn't think he could be so blind. But maybe he was taken by surprise, you know, by the speed of what happened. Also, I don't believe for a minute that anyone outside Iran wanted him to stay. He had become too dangerous. He'd started to think about what Iran could do. What role the country could play. He'd started talking about becoming a member of the superpower club. He'd wanted a military to equal the five greatest powers on earth. He'd started to use oil to dictate his wishes. I don't think there was anyone outside Iran, including and especially the United States, who wanted him to stay much longer.'

Yamani agrees that the handwriting was on the wall several years before it happened.

He says it was there to see if anybody had taken the time to look for it.

'It's easy with hindsight for anyone to say that he knew the Shah would fall. But some time around the end of 1977 or the beginning of 1978 I started believing that he had to fall. All the signs were there. You could see he was in danger because of his arrogance and his isolation from his people. You could see problems developing with his drive to make fast changes in his society. You could see real trouble brewing in his strong campaign against religion and religious people. He was trying to extract himself from the Islamic roots of his society. All these things put together led me to think he would not last much longer. I didn't know exactly when it would happen but I felt it was only a matter of time.'

What nobody could have possibly seen coming was the astronomical rise in oil prices that followed the Shah's abdication.

Everything went haywire.

One day Iran was producing six million barrels. The next day they were producing nearly nothing.

The Ayatollah said something like, we don't need to export crude because we've got enough money. Then he spoke with his Exchequer and found out he didn't have a dime, so they started pumping again.

But they couldn't get production back to pre-revolutionary levels because the Ayatollah and his gang had the brilliant foresight to throw out all the western companies that worked the Iranian oilfields. Almost universally those fields lost gas pressure and all forms of maintenance. The Iranians had no in-house capabilities themselves.

They'd pulled the carpet right out from under the market.

And the world panicked.

Where crude started 1978 at under $13, by the end of 1980 you had prices reaching $38, $39, $40.

The oil-producing nations under the Opec umbrella continued throughout that period to set an official price.

But with so much action in the market, everything was open to negotiation.

Every standing contract or term supply came under discussion, revision or renegotiation when one of the partners smelled a better deal somewhere else.

Prices for refined petroleum products are determined minute by minute in five major world markets: Rotterdam, Houston, New York, Singapore and Tokyo. A supertanker riding across the seas carries as many as 2 million barrels. As the price of a basket of refined crude products totals more than the cost of the crude plus the various taxes and surcharges the Arab producers add on top, and as the cargo of crude might change hands several times before it gets to wherever it's going, those sudden price shocks in 1978/1979/1980 meant per-cargo profits for a slick enough independent trader could be in the $1–4 million range.

Colossal fortunes were made in oil.

The trick in 1979 was to buy a cargo just before the spot price went up a few cents per barrel and then unload it right away. The danger was that while you were holding on to ownership of the oil the price could drop a few cents per barrel.

The game was all about taking a few small percentage points of a huge sum.

Because the sums were so enormous, you didn't have to do that very often to amass a fortune.

With such easy money to make, the greed factor immediately set in and independents by the hundreds lined up to buy and sell paper cargoes.

It was this artificially exaggerated demand chasing those few cargoes that ran prices sky high.

However, the euphoria ended almost as quickly as it began.

The oil-consuming nations got wise and all sorts of conservation measures went into effect. The fall was orchestrated by the governments. They decided that the situation had got out of hand and finally moved to right it. Within two years the market was back under control.

Independent oil trader David Thieme is one of those who made a fortune trading spot oil during those years. And he says he saw first hand that, while prices were heading for the sky, it was Yamani who tried to be the stabilizing force.

'His role was that of arbiter and mediator. He was very visibly trying to keep the Saudis on top. They've always been the swing producers, the ones who'd pump or cut back when they needed to stabilize prices. And he did what he could to put the skids on prices. Don't forget, if the Saudis had a radical government they could have gone one way or the other strictly for political purposes. They certainly didn't need the money at that point. If they'd been radical, say leftist, they could have cut the oil off and let the prices go crazy. After all, more than two-thirds of all Opec oil comes out of the Persian Gulf and the Saudis are the biggest producers. There was no one down there to equal Yamani in presence, ability and intelligence in those days. And there still isn't. He was a one man band. In that 1978–1979–1980 surge, without Yamani there, prices certainly could have gone upwards of $50, easily.

Ian Seymour at the *Middle East Economic Survey* figures that's about right. 'Even Saudi Arabia at full stretch was not able to bring down the price very much. It's rather difficult to determine where oil prices could have gone to. In a sense, if you have some shortage or even a perceived shortage, that can be enough to send the market right up. It doesn't necessarily increase that much more as you increase the shortage. Yamani was very active in trying to stop the price rise and certainly slowed it down. In retrospect, a lot of the shortage simply wasn't there. It was that people were panicky. A lot of that oil went into stock and of course that made the downturn in prices all the sharper when it came. But if the Saudis hadn't produced as much as they did, I think yes, oil prices could have gone up near the $50 level.'

'A large part of the problem', Thieme continues, 'was that nobody believed crude spot prices would stay as high as they did. Whenever they went up, everyone figured it was just a burp and they'd come right back down again. Except they didn't. There was total panic in the markets. It was extremely volatile. Believe me, the oil business in the days just after the Iranian Revolution was the last frontier.'

So much so that it critically affected the thinking of everyone who had anything to do with oil.

Says Yamani, 'It had to influence your thinking. This was a major political event. It caused oil consumers to panic, but it did not change the pattern of consumption. And that's what made the price chaos so dangerous.'

Even the French, the only people in the world who had their bets hedged, were caught short by the Iranian Revolution. They'd harboured the Ayatollah in the obvious hope that one day, if he ever returned to power, he'd remember them kindly with a favourable oil policy.

'I'm afraid they were disappointed,' Yamani comments.

By mid-February 1979, with the official Opec price for Saudi Arabian Light (the marker crude) at $13.33, the spot price in Rotterdam was over $20.

In April, by the time Opec raised the marker crude to $14.55, the spot price was already up to $21.50.

The Japanese had been largely dependent on Iranian oil and, as the crisis deepened, they came unglued. It was Japan that led the panic buying and by May spot crude leapt up more than 50 per cent to $34.50.

The next big move in the market came in October when spot prices nudged up towards $38.

Then, in early November, 90 people, including 63 Americans, were taken hostage at the US Embassy in Tehran.

The Carter presidency was doomed.

An international crisis with grave military overtones captured the headlines.

Spot crude hit $40.

'Throughout 1979,' Yamani says, 'continued high demand in the west and the peak prices being paid on the spot markets were creating chaos. Oil companies were rushing in to buy. But this wasn't oil they needed. It was for storage. I asked myself why and the only possible answer was that they thought there could be a total cut-off in oil exports from Iran. If that happened, the United States and other consuming countries would be forced to impose rationing as an immediate first measure. So there was all this panic buying.'

Willing to concede that the Gulf is a politically volatile region – 'Anything can happen in our part of the world. It's a boiling area with a lot of problems pending and one crisis can easily lead to another' – Yamani feels now, as he did then, that the panic which led to higher prices could have been avoided.

'There was a solution. Prices could have been held in check. The panic would have ended the moment the oil companies were stopped from trading in the spot market. The US government should have forbidden it. So should have the other governments. After all, oil companies came knocking on our door saying, "Give us oil and we'll pay you $40 a barrel on the spot market." To resist that temptation you would have had to be an angel, or a Saudi!'

Doing whatever he could to get prices down, Yamani had promised in late June 1979 that Saudi Arabia would not yield to pressure from other oil producers to limit production and let spot prices soar.

He repeated often that Saudi Arabia would stick to its policy of 'moderation and wisdom'. So in the midst of all this price chaos, the Saudis honoured their long-term contracts at the Opec marker price and sold whatever they produced above that at the Opec price as well. Yamani points out that Saudi Arabia was not playing the spot market game and its refusal to do so cost Saudi Arabia literally billions of dollars in revenue. But it was a sacrifice it willingly made in the short term to arrive at the long-term goal of getting oil prices down.

Because he could attract so much publicity and so many reporters hung on his every word, Yamani was now being described in the press as 'the man who holds the key to the oil crisis in the west'.

True or not, while spot market traders like David Thieme and John Latsis were only two of hundreds who made fortunes in what has since come to be known as 'the second oil crisis', Yamani saw the Iranian Revolution and the subsequent rise in oil prices as a unique opportunity to warn the western industrialized nations that the worst was yet to come.

'I began speaking about the real oil crisis which I saw coming in ten years' time. The supply and demand situation was very clear to me. When the revolution erupted in Tehran and demand increased, it was obviously not for consumption because once we increased our prices demand did not come down. It should have. That's basic economics. But it didn't. Opec's share in the market was 28 mbd in 1978. In 1979, with a higher price of oil, it should have been less than 28 mbd. But what happened was the opposite. It went above 31 mbd. So it was very clear that the additional oil which came from Opec and the additional oil which came from non-Opec producers did not go for consumption. Even though we kept increasing oil prices, demand did not subside. This greatly alarmed me because I knew for sure that the oil held in stock would eventually have to come back onto the market as a source of supply.'

In other words, the panic buying of 1979–80 would become the glut of 1981–86.

Prices would tumble.

But these things are cyclical.

Yamani says now that, unless the west does something about consumption, unless there is investment in alternative sources of energy, unless serious efforts are made towards conservation, the glut of the mid-1980s will undoubtedly lead to the third oil shock of the mid-1990s.

16

Yamani versus the US Justice Department

As THEIR young family grew, Zaki and Tamman added a pair of rooms to the suite at the Yamama.

But before long the place was far too small. And anyway, by then, the rest of the hotel had been taken over by the United States Air Force and converted into quarters for their flight crews.

So in 1981 the Yamanis built a large, Moorish-looking house in Riyadh, complete with indoor fountains and pools.

Just before moving out of the Yamama they gave a party for a group of US senators on a junket through the Middle East. One of the Americans was checking out Yamani's bookshelves when he spotted Paul Erdman's novel, *The Crash of '79*. The plot centred around a bunch of Arab oil moguls who were out to ruin the west.

'Sheikh Yamani?' The senator picked it up and showed it with ironic amusement to his host. 'Have you read this?'

Yamani nodded, 'Only part of it. I stopped at the point where I was assassinated!'

* * * *

Even before *The Crash of '79* hit the bestseller lists, the American public had become obsessed with the possibility that Arab oil moguls could indeed ruin the west.

Much to Yamani's growing discomfort, a groundswell of public opinion put the issue on the front pages, and a lot of very influential men climbed on the bandwagon.

Among them were:

Jack Anderson, a Pulitzer Prize winning investigative reporter and syndicated columnist.

Frank Church, chairman of the Senate Subcommittee on Multinational Corporations.

Henry Jackson, chairman of the Senate Committee on Energy and Natural Resources.

Benjamin Rosenthal, chairman of the House Subcommittee on Commerce, Consumer and Monetary Affairs.

Howard Metzenbaum, chairman of the Senate Subcommittee on Antitrust, Monopoly and Business Rights.

Edward Kennedy, chairman of the Senate's Judiciary Committee.

And, John Shenefield, Assistant US Attorney General and head of the Justice Department's Antitrust Division.

As an international lawyer with two advanced degrees from American schools, Yamani didn't feel especially threatened by any particular investigation as long as he could meet it head on.

He had lots of cards he could play.

But he wanted to meet each challenge on a one-to-one basis.

Because, as the Saudi oil minister, he had enough experience with Americans to know that the cumulative effect of all these hearings could directly influence western public opinion, where Saudi Arabia was concerned, for years to come.

What neither Saudi Arabia nor he could afford would be to get caught up in a political game with the American Congress and/or the American press where the cards would be so obviously stacked against them that they couldn't as much as break even.

It was, however, equally obvious to him that many Americans believed some serious soul-searching was long overdue.

And it was not without precedent.

In 1951 a Federal Trade Commission staff report, called *The International Petroleum Cartel*, traced the then 22-year history of the major oil companies and their stranglehold on the production, refining, transportation and marketing of crude oil from the Persian Gulf.

The Department of Justice took the report and started to champion the growing antitrust mood of America.

However, Secretary of State Dean Acheson felt that such an inquiry could get in the way of American interests in the Middle East. He knew he'd have to enlist the help of the international oil companies in an effort to reopen the nationalized Iranian oil properties, so the last thing he wanted was a bunch of writ-happy lawyers scaring off the oil companies.

The Justice Department turned a deaf ear to the State Department and proceeded with their case, intending, if they deemed it necessary, to file criminal charges against the major oil companies. But Acheson held a trump card. Unlike those over-zealous Justice Department lawyers, he had access to the Oval Office. So he took his case directly to Harry Truman, who settled the issue by siding with Acheson.

When Eisenhower arrived at the White House and John Foster Dulles took over at Foggy Bottom, there was no doubt at all but that State's views would win out over Justice's criminal case.

That's when the Justice Department changed gear. They started to look at the possibility of a civil action aimed at the Aramco four, plus Gulf. They originally wanted to include BP and Shell but decided it would be pointless as both would argue, with almost certain success, that they were beyond US jurisdiction. In the end the civil case also fell by the wayside since US national security and Europe's heavy reliance on Persian Gulf production were just too important to Eisenhower and Dulles.

It was another two decades before antitrust talk was heard again on Capitol Hill.

Since the earliest days of the Arab oil embargo, from the end of the Nixon years, through Ford and well up to the end of the Carter administration, hundreds of thousands of letters had poured in to Congress, the White House and the Justice Department suggesting that the major oil companies and the Arab producers were somehow in cahoots, that they were openly holding the American public to ransom with tremendous price increases at the gas pumps.

Jack Anderson chided lawmakers, 'For evidence that Aramco secretly encouraged Saudi Arabia to boost prices, the Senate should subpoena the records of all meetings with Saudi Oil Minister, Ahmed Zaki Yamani.'

In January 1974, Senator Frank Church opened his Multinational Corporations Committee hearings on the oil industry, hoping to uncover the trail which led the United States to depend so heavily on Arab oil.

Having just pulled off a resounding success by exposing the sleazy depths to which ITT's management had stooped in their efforts to topple the Allende regime in Chile, Church now concerned himself with the time-frame from the beginning of the participation negotiations in Tehran to the oil embargo. He wanted to re-examine the premise, 'What's good for the oil companies is good for the United States.'

The nine-volume committee report was published in 1975.

Its oversimplified conclusion: 'The critical issue was how well the companies and the government used the two and a half years before the October War to prepare for the crisis which was clearly foreseeable at the time of the Tehran-Tripoli Agreements. The time was not used very well. The US Government had no energy policy.'

Senator Henry 'Scoop' Jackson then got his committee to report on the question of '*Access to Oil – The United States' Relationships with Saudi Arabia and Iran*'.

This became a televised 'inquisition' of oil company executives that delighted an American public sick of queues at petrol stations and worried that the great American economy could be threatened by 'camel drivers'.

'The American people want to know why oil companies are making soaring profits,' Jackson levied his accusations at the men testifying before him. 'The American people want to know whether major oil companies are sitting on shut-in wells and hoarding production in hidden tanks and at abandoned service stations.'

That committee's report, published in December 1977, raised even more issues than it tackled by warning, 'Dependence on oil imports in turn is equal to dependence of Opec oil. To date the Saudis have played a moderating role within Opec. But the Saudis have also indicated their unwillingness to continue to stand alone in Opec councils. They do not like to appear to be opposing other Arab regimes. They have suggested that the United States should ask its other Opec-member friends, that is, Iran, to moderate their price positions as well.'

At about the same time, the State Department drew some disquieting conclusions. In a classified 1977 report by the Bureau of Intelligence and Research titled *Discounts in Disguise: Price Shaving by Members of Opec*, the assertion was made that the multinational oil companies provided essential support to Opec's system of maintaining artificially high crude oil prices – that the multinationals provided individual Opec countries with a mechanism for policing the other members' compliance with cartel prices by providing information on the quantities of oil moved and the prices paid.

'Unless that information is generally available,' suggested Congressman Benjamin Rosenthal, chairman of the House Subcommittee on Commerce, Consumer and Monetary Affairs when he unearthed the report in 1980, ' individual member countries could get away with price shaving or secret discounting to such an extent that cartel unity would be undermined and price erosion would occur.'

That was followed by Senator Howard Metzenbaum's plea to the Justice Department to undertake an immediate investigation into claims that Exxon, Texaco, Socal and Mobil were acting irresponsibly by making up to $7 billion a year in profits by taking advantage of Saudi Arabia's lower crude prices and not passing those lower prices on to the consumer at the petrol pumps.

During a hearing of the Senate Judiciary Committee, Senator Edward Kennedy questioned Assistant Attorney General John Shenefield about Opec's relationship with the major oil companies.

Shenefield: 'It could be argued that Opec is not a cartel and, while Opec may set a price, the actual task of insuring that aggregate output is sufficiently small to sustain that price in the marketplace is performed by the oil companies.'

Kennedy: 'If that statement were correct, would that or would that not be a clear violation of the antitrust laws?'

Shenefield: 'Assuming some impact on the US commerce, which I think we can assume, my off-the-top-of-the-head reaction would be that it would be, yes.'

By this point Church had returned to the battle.

He ordered the staff of the Subcommittee on Multinationals to write a report on Saudi oil production and look into what previously undisclosed understandings might exist between the four Aramco partners and Saudi Arabia.

Over strenuous objections from the oil companies, the committee staff, with the full power of the United States Senate to enforce compliance, subpoenaed and eventually received the documents they were after.

Yamani was furious.

As far as he was concerned, this was Saudi Arabia's business and whatever went on between Saudi Arabia and Aramco was of no real concern to this congressional committee.

He summoned the then US Ambassador to Saudi Arabia, John West, and told him, 'Under no circumstances will Saudi Arabia tolerate this material being made public. The files subpoenaed include Aramco documents and they are the property of Saudi Arabia. Their release constitutes an invasion of national privacy. It doesn't matter what the documents are or what the committee intends to do with the report. This is a matter of principle.'

These days he still thinks he was right to take the position he did.

'In some countries, information about oil reserves and reservoir behaviour are not only classified but to reveal that information is a crime covered by capital punishment. In this case we were singled out from all the oil producers in the world by a group of Americans working for the Zionist lobby. Their aim was to show that Saudi Arabia is not really a country which can solve America's energy problems. Our refusal to be singled out was very clearly a matter of principle. The committee was politically motivated. So we acted in a political manner. We refused to allow a public discussion to be based on secret information about our natural resources, which would of course have been revealed to the media. There is no other country they could have singled out.'

Among other things, the committee was anxious to look at the 1977 agreement that finalized the Saudi takeover of Aramco.

Again, Yamani was unyielding. 'It did not concern the committee. At that point there was only a draft of an agreement. It wasn't yet an agreement. It was a matter not yet approved by the Saudi government. It was not for publicity. It wasn't even for our colleagues in Opec to see. It was only our affair. No one else's.'

West, a former governor of South Carolina, says that he relayed Yamani's concern back to the State Department. 'Of course I kept Secretary of State [Cyrus] Vance informed. I reported back to Washington that Yamani was adamant that the records of Aramco should not be turned over. As he pointed out, in some countries like Iraq and Iran, giving away oil exploration data is a capital offence. It's deemed to be classified for reasons of national security.'

But he was personally in a position to do more than simply keep Vance informed. He jumped the chain of command and went straight to the White House.

'I was in an unusual situation. Much of whatever effectiveness I had as an Ambassador to Saudi Arabia was based on the perception that I had a direct pipeline to President Carter. Which I did. I didn't use it, except very rarely. But I did use it on occasion. On this issue, yes, I did go to Carter.'

Unbeknownst to the committee, the White House took a position. The committee staff had put together a 130–page report, then set a date for the five subcommittee senators to vote on whether or not to make it public.

Suddenly Saudi Arabia's friends stood up to be counted.

Included in the list of oil company executives who lobbied the subcommittee hoping to cool their ardour was Clifton Garvin of Exxon.

'I didn't have to ask anyone to do that,' Yamani responds in a defensive tone. 'They knew our feelings. They knew that we held them responsible if they gave away any information about Saudi Arabia. They knew that their relationship with us would have been damaged. We have, in the past, even refused to give as much as 10 per cent of that information to our partners in Opec. Why should we have supplied such information to a public inquiry in the United States? It was our private business.'

But, he's asked, what if Garvin and Co. had been subpoenaed and forced to testify? He answers sharply, 'That's hypothetical.'

Next came Joe Twinam, the Deputy Assistant Secretary of State in charge of Arabian Peninsula Affairs. He warned the five senators that, should their report be released to the public, not only would it serve seriously to embarrass the Saudis, the Saudis would find a way to retaliate. He reminded the committee that they could always use oil as a political instrument to make their feelings felt.

Then Cyrus Vance personally intervened. He telephoned several members of the subcommittee to say that releasing their findings would impair relations between the United States and Saudi Arabia. He insisted that the Saudis would look upon this as interference in their sovereign rights.

The vote was three to two against making the report public.

That's when Jack Anderson revealed in his column that Saudi secrets were being protected by 'oil moguls' on the subcommittee.

To avoid a nasty public debate on their own motives, the three members who voted against publication of the original 130–page report agreed to release a watered-down version.

It was a mere 37 pages long.

Topics removed from the first draft included Saudi-gathered evidence of Aramco's gross mismanagement, disputes between Yamani's ministry and Aramco officials regarding production levels, accusations by the Saudis that Aramco had overproduced and that Aramco had relied on deceptive accounting to explain reserves.

Quotation marks, names of Saudi officials quoted and the names of the oil companies concerned were also deleted. Nor was it mentioned that the report had been based on documents subpoenaed from the oil companies.

That Yamani and the Saudis got their way with the various congressional committees was one thing.

That they then had to face the US Department of Justice was another game altogether.

Public pressure to take legal action against the oil companies and the never-ending petrol pump price increases was growing. So the Justice Department's Antitrust Division opened an investigation into the supply and pricing practices of the major international oil companies.

Of prime concern here was the possibility that Exxon, Socal, Mobil and Texaco might have had both the incentive and the ability, independent of the Saudi Arabian government, jointly to limit the production of Saudi crude and in so doing increase world crude prices.

John Shenefield headed the Antitrust Division in those days. 'A staff was assembled. There are people whose lifetimes are devoted to disentangling these kinds of things. PhD economists are involved alongside trained investigators, lawyers and accountants. The staff that was assigned to this was at one time or another pretty sizable.'

At one point it consisted of no fewer than 50 people, including 13 attorneys, 4 economists, 16 para-legals and 17 secretaries.

The next step was a massive request for documents from seven American and four foreign corporations. Included within the scope of the investigation were Aramco (addressed in New York), British Petroleum (London), Compagnie Française des Petroles (Paris), Exxon (New York), Gulf (Pittsburgh), Mobil (New York), Royal Dutch Petroleum (The Hague), Shell Oil (Houston), Shell Transport and Trading Company (London), Standard Oil of California (San Francisco) and Texaco (New York).

Of course, as soon as the investigation became known to them, each and every one of the companies concerned protested this intrusion into their confidential business affairs. Mountains of correspondence went back and forth between all of the various lawyers.

Lawyers for the American-based corporations were well aware that the Justice Department could, by using the court system, force the issue and demand that the requested documents be produced regardless of their commercial confidentiality. Yet they also knew that by being 'benignly benevolent' they could stonewall the issue, if need be, for years. Their apparent game plan was to respond to every Justice Department request, asking why certain documents were necessary, asking for clarification on every point, suggesting that these documents were irrelevant, pinpointing obscure cases which supported their opinion, appealing against Division interpretations that did not favour their cause, then asking for extensions to deadlines whenever they were finally forced to hand over documents.

Obviously, by turning the post office into a tennis court, keeping the volley of letters going as long as possible, the corporate lawyers hoped that a change of administration might bring about a change of management at the Justice Department and the whole matter would just disappear. Anyway, because the world also changes, the longer these things are dragged out, the less chance there is that the end product will actually matter.

As for the four foreign-based corporations, they could afford to sit tight, knowing that unless their own governments agreed to cooperate – an unlikely prospect – there was little the US Justice Department could seriously expect in return besides a polite 'sorry, no thank you', reply.

Comments Shenefield, 'Why did we send civil investigation demands [CIDs] to foreign majors when we couldn't necessarily enforce them? Because you never know if they're going to comply. It has always seemed to me, perhaps naively so, if companies wish to do business in the United States they may have some concern about adhering to US law. It seems to me also possible that governments of, say, Great

Britain and France, or other countries that we think of as close friends, will give us, as we give them, sufficient running room for their companies to assure respective governments of their willingness to comply with US law. So it didn't strike me as silly at the outset to proceed on the basis that, yes, we might well get some compliance from them.'

The one company that obviously required some special handling was Aramco. Shenefield knew there were documents in Aramco's files concerning Saudi Arabia. He also knew he could count on Yamani to do everything in his power to prevent Aramco from turning them over.

'No, the Saudis wouldn't cooperate,' Shenefield says. 'We asked for documents from Aramco and the gist of their response was that the Saudi government didn't understand the whole point of this and it was causing them some embarrassment. They wanted further explanation and elaboration about it.'

Further explanations and elaborations were duly sent to Aramco for the Saudis' perusal.

The reason the matter had to be handled delicately by both sides was because both sides realized that, regardless of Saudi objections, the Justice Department could legally demand to see any documents on US soil. But such a demand would undoubtedly bring with it repercussions from the Saudis.

That was a situation Shenefield wanted to avoid.

The seven American companies managed to hem and haw and stall for over a year, until they had no choice but to turn over more than 125,000 documents.

Then in October 1978 Aramco's attorneys notified the Justice Department that Yamani, acting for the Saudi Arabian government, had expressly forbidden the removal from Saudi Arabia of any documents responsive to the CIDs.

By June 1979 the Antitrust Division concluded that additional information would be required, so a second round of CIDs were issued.

For diplomatic reasons, in the face of resistance from Yamani to any documents dealing with Saudi Arabia, the seven domestic companies were informed by the Justice Department that only non-Saudi-related materials had to be complied with during this second round of CIDs . . . at least until the question of the Saudi-related materials could be dealt with.

By coincidence, this happened at the same time that Exxon and Socal were forced to make disclosures about Saudi reserves and production capacity to the Church subcommittee. Because the Antitrust Division did not want to be confused with the Church subcommittee, Shenefield felt he might be able to reason with Yamani and avoid the kinds of problems that could develop if he subpoenaed the materials he wanted.

Perhaps Yamani couldn't recite Kingman Brewster's antitrust law lectures word for word, but he knew what the American antitrust laws were all about, he knew how the Justice Department worked, he had seen the power of the Senate Foreign Relations Committee and there was no doubt in his mind that Saudi Arabia had a fight on its hands.

Yet, like all lawyers, he also knew that the longer you take to put the gloves on, the greater the possibility the other guy will lose interest and just go away.

In November 1979 he met US Treasury Secretary G. William Miller who was on an official visit to Saudi Arabia. Although the trip was totally unrelated to the Justice Department investigation, Miller broached the subject of the investigation. Yamani admitted his concern. At the very least, Yamani said, he would prefer that the investigation not inquire into Saudi oil production, capacity, reserves or pricing policies. Miller tried to reassure Yamani that confidential information would be kept confidential. But Yamani merely had to point to the Church subcommittee to prove that wasn't the case. Anyway, Miller suggested, the materials the Justice Department wanted were already in the possession of American companies and on US soil and could legally be subpoenaed. Yamani remained firm that the CIDs would not be answered.

Shenefield heard about Miller's meeting with Yamani while attending a briefing in the Situation Room at the White House. 'It was just after the hostage-taking in Tehran. By this time I was Associate Attorney General and I was representing the Justice Department at those Situation Room meetings every morning. Somebody from the Treasury reported that they'd just had a contact on this investigation and that Yamani was concerned about it. One of the early issues in connection with the Iranian hostage matter was, were actions that might be taken by the United States likely further to constrict oil supplies in any way? This became relative in that context. No decision was made there about the investigation itself. And none would have been appropriate in that forum. But enough people there realized that we at the Justice Department were quite determined to pursue the investigation.'

Attorney General Benjamin Civiletti then told Shenefield to send Yamani a telex which might reassure him that no precipitous CID enforcement action was contemplated.

That message, hand-delivered to Yamani in mid-January 1980 by Ambassador West, proposed that the Justice Department was willing to send responsible officials to Riyadh to explain first-hand to Yamani the purpose of the investigation and the methods available for protecting the confidentiality of sensitive information.

'The problem here was', explains West, 'that it was too easy to confuse the Church committee's demands with the demands of the Justice Department. The Church committee said they would keep the information they obtained confidential. But everybody knew that was a farce. Nothing that went through a congressional investigation, especially if it could be used as anti-Arab propaganda, was ever kept confidential. So the assurances by the Justice Department that the information they wanted would be treated on a confidential basis were not given much credence by Yamani.'

'What we were trying to do,' Shenefield goes on, 'first of all, was to reassure Yamani that we were concerned about and willing to talk to him about how to protect Saudi interests while getting our own investigation moving forward. We didn't want to take a position that would seem to him brusque and oblivious of his concerns. Secondly, we wanted to open up, if possible, a sort of negotiation, hoping that the Saudis would be, in some respects, responsive to our needs. The telex was a kind of opening round in that negotiation which culminated in a visit to Riyadh to meet with Yamani.'

With three other Justice Department attorneys in tow, Shenefield arrived in Riyadh in March. 'We spent the earlier part of the visit with one of Yamani's subordinates, sitting around in a large circle, drinking coffee and talking about the subtance of the investigation. We went over the CIDs with this subordinate and some of his colleagues, item by item. And we came away from that meeting heartened because there seemed to be some flexibility and a willingness to be discriminating among the various items of the CIDs.'

But first impressions can be deceptive.

A day or so later, Shenefield and the others met with Yamani.

'It's odd because one thing that struck me was that the ministry, for all its importance, seemed to be so lightly guarded. I was amazed by it. There was a checkpoint but, as I remember, there were only two security officials anywhere in evidence with automatic rifles. It struck me that given Yamani's problems in Vienna, at least to the naked eye or to the untrained observer, the place was very lightly defended. Then, you walked down long halls and there wasn't much activity. In the United States, in an office building, you'd see secretaries and people working. There you tended to see men in Arabic dress, sitting around in the offices, smoking and talking and there wasn't much evidence of any work going on.'

Yamani greeted them at the end of the hall and ushered them into his office. 'His office was extraordinarily rich. It was magnificent. He was extremely cordial. And I admit I was absolutely fascinated by him.'

After the usual greetings, Yamani and three of his assistants, all in white robes, sat facing the four Americans, all in dark suits, while servants hovered around them pouring coffee. Yamani was interested in knowing where each of his guests had gone to law school. One had been to NYU. Shenefield's degree was from Harvard. Yamani was very much in his element, so they chatted about that for a while.

'The beginning part of the meeting was taken up with having coffee and light discussion,' Shenefield remembers. 'Our small coffee cups were constantly being refilled. None of us were aware, until we drank a lot more coffee than any of us would have preferred, that there's a way of holding your cup up and shaking it that signifies you've had enough. Until you did that they were just going to pour more coffee. So we were sitting there drinking too much coffee and all the time we were trying to figure out how to cut it off.'

Once they got down to business, Shenefield saw first hand just how difficult a negotiator Yamani can be. 'He was very attentive. He's obviously a very bright man. But he was totally non-committal. We left that meeting a little non-plussed because we seemed to be getting conflicting signals. John West assured us that this was all quite orthodox and that he thought he might perhaps be able to intercede with Yamani and that we might get some further assistance or at least indication of willingness to be of assistance. But time just dragged on. I think there was another letter or two in an effort to pursue the matter, all to no end. The documents were never forthcoming. The companies of course threw up their hands. There was nothing they could do, we were assured, until Yamani spoke. And of course he never spoke.'

In the weeks that followed, several informal discussions took place between West and Yamani. They resulted in a series of letters between Shenefield and Yamani which appeared, at least to the Justice Department, to have narrowed down some of the differences. Concessions to Yamani by the Justice Department included the agreement to drop their inquiry into several sensitive areas such as Saudi oil exploration, reserves, production capacity and government sales.

Believing they'd finally arrived on common ground with the Saudis, the Antitrust Division then requested, in January 1981, that Aramco's lawyers initiate talks with Yamani regarding possible limited compliance with the outstanding CIDs.

But that was the last the Justice Department ever heard about the matter.

Yamani had effectively brought the 'International Oil Investigation' to a halt.

* * * *

Carter left office and Ronald Reagan moved into the White House.

Having gently warned the Carter administration that, unless the potentially embarrassing investigation was terminated, Saudi Arabia would retaliate against the United States, Yamani now let Reagan officials know that the investigation 'was a thorn in the side of US – Saudi relations'.

William Baxter was Reagan's appointment to head the Antitrust Division.

Now a professor at the University of California at Berkeley Law School, Baxter says, 'The investigation had dragged on for a number of years and then gone into a period of inactivity, but it was still officially open. At some point in time I wrote quite a long memo explaining why I felt it was appropriate to close it.'

So it looked as if the Reagan crowd would, in this instance, let bygones be bygones.

Although in January 1983, the four Aramco partners came close to inadvertently scoring an own-goal.

During the first week of the new year, as Baxter was tying up what loose ends remained in the dormant inquiry, a very private dinner took place in Yamani's 18th-floor suite at the Intercontinental in Geneva.

Only five men were present.

Sitting around the large oval mahogany table at the far end of the livingroom were Yamani and the chief executive officers of the four Aramco partners: Bill Tavoulareas from Mobil, Clifton Garvin from Exxon, George Keller from Socal and John McKinley from Texaco.

The dinner table talk that night was that the major oil companies could not continue paying $34 for $30 oil.

Yamani was sympathetic. He too wanted to see the price of oil come down, eventually. But at this point he refused to commit himself to a widely speculated cut of $1.50 in the Saudis' officially posted prices.

'All we did was meet,' Socal's chairman George Keller claimed at the time. 'We certainly did not solve any problems. I hope we did not create any new ones.'

By new ones he meant with the Justice Department.

The Sherman Antitrust Act makes it very clear that competitors who discuss prices together are in violation of the law. And the reporters who heard about the private dinner knew they were on to something as soon as there was an official announcement from the Saudi oil ministry which labelled as 'misplaced speculation' any reports that a price reduction had been discussed that evening.

'We spoke in general terms,' Yamani insists. 'We would never discuss the specifics of pricing. Come on, those four men know the law. I know that if we had started to talk about prices, three of them would have gotten up and left the room. Let me tell you, when it comes to talk of prices, all four of them are cowards.'

John Shenefield believes Yamani's assessment of the four American executives is basically correct. 'There are certain things you can do only with great risk and one of them is to talk price in a setting where you are totally unprotected. Yamani understands that. He might not care about it but he's a man of subtlety and sophistication so he'd understand just how far anyone in the room could go.'

As far as the Justice Department could ascertain, if they didn't talk about price it was because they knew they couldn't. If they did talk about price, none of them would ever admit it.

By the end of 1983, Baxter decided that he could not make a case to suggest that any private agreements regarding crude oil production or pricing had taken place beyond those in effect. He couldn't establish that anything was going on under the table.

Nevertheless, he wrote in his conclusion to the investigation that there was evidence to suggest that between 1974 and 1977, and perhaps even as late as 1979, the four Aramco partners 'may have had' the ability to exercise market power by controlling Saudi crude production within the Saudi government's imposed limits.

Proving it would have been near impossible.

And even if he could have proved it, in the world of 1983, it was probable there was no relief or remedy that would make any sense.

The case was closed.

However Baxter did take the trouble to add in his report, 'It is always possible that a response to the civil investigation demands would have provided evidence of an actionable antitrust violation.'

So could there have been something in Yamani's files that might have produced a different result?

The only person who knows for sure is Zaki Yamani.

And, on grounds of principle, he isn't saying.

17

The Supreme Negotiator

'As a negotiator,' says one American oil company executive, 'Yamani is superb. He is patient and polite and knows variations on every trick in the book. For example, we found that whenever a tight situation arose Yamani would go to the telephone. We all knew that he was not a maker of policy, that he negotiated within a framework, that he was always under instructions. But I'll be damned, as soon as anyone was about to score a point, he'd disappear to the telephone and all the momentum against him would dissipate.'

Adds another, 'Yamani whispers, never threatens. His deadliest tactic is to probe for holes in your argument by calmly repeating question after question until finally you're so weary you'd hand over your grandmother.'

Having finely tuned his negotiating skills in arenas as tough as Opec and the world oil market, Yamani is more than just confident when it comes to explaining his approach, grandmothers notwithstanding.

Call this brief class then Negotiation 101.

Professor Yamani presiding.

'The main thing in any negotiation is to know exactly what you want. To know the bare minimum that you can accept and the maximum of what you are hoping for. Once you've got those two things clearly defined, you must mentally put yourself on the other side of the table and try to study the weaknesses they have. You must try to figure out how much they can give away and how much you can expect from them. It is only in light of what you then conclude about their strategy that you can draw a tactic.'

The key, he says, is patience.

'As any negotiation proceeds, it's essential to be patient. But you must also allow the negotiations to move along. Don't let them bog down. And never lose your temper. Once you lose your temper, that's the end of your ability to negotiate.'

There is, he's told, one old axiom of negotiation that goes, when money is at stake, never be the first to mention sums.

The thinking behind it is that you may be underpricing your views or willing to pay over the odds for theirs.

He thinks about that for a moment before he says, 'Yes, but only as a general rule and not as an absolute. I agree that you should not be the first to mention figures unless you have to. Except that there are times when you must.'

He did in his very first negotiations with Aramco.

'I had to come up with a figure because my predecessor, Tariki, had already stated that he wanted a certain sum of money to settle a particular problem. I started off by naming that figure. But I did that only to make it very clear that I would never accept one dollar less. So there are exceptions to the rule, like when a figure is not negotiable. But otherwise, that's right, don't be the first to say a figure because the other side may offer you more.'

In cases where you have a group of companies or several interest groups working together, he advises, know the various conflicts of interest that might exist and how you can utilize that to your own advantage.

Here Opec is a good example.

'There are some pretty shrewd people negotiating there. You have all kinds of mentalities. You also have lots of conflicts of interests. You have those members with a small oil reserve and a short life-span for their reserves. Their interests are to raise the price of oil as high as they can for the next five to ten years. And they don't care about anything beyond that because they won't be exporting oil after that date. Then there are those with small reserves who want to remain as oil exporters for the next 50–80 years. They want to keep their production low. Finally there are important producers who want to maintain a steady supply to the market because it is their major source of income. But even there you find differences in marketing and value differentials. Negotiating under circumstances where you have so many views to consider requires a lot of patience.'

Again patience.

He says, 'Yes, again patience. Maybe that's why I love to go fishing when I'm on holiday. I take my family fishing with me when we're on holiday because fishing is a great way to learn patience.'

*　*　*　*

Caracas, Venezuela, December 1979.

Opec is at the Tamanaco hotel and the helicopters are overhead and the armed soldiers are guarding the roads.

Negotiations are under way.

All the ministers meet daily around a table in the main ballroom.

Afterwards, only some of them meet the press.

Sheikh Ali Khalifa al-Sabah from Kuwait is fairly good at it.

He's part of the Kuwaiti royal family, born there in 1945. He went to university in San Francisco, so his English is perfect and he understands the western media. He's known by the reporters who cover Opec for being very intelligent, for being the only minister to rate as Yamani's intellectual equal. And some say one day he could challenge Yamani for the starring role. But Kuwait doesn't have the same oil clout as Saudi Arabia. It's rather like saying the Bulgarians never produced a fellow with the same charisma as Stalin. Of course not. They never had the same number of divisions.

Next is the UAE's Sheikh Mana Saeed Oteiba.

He's a few years older than Ali Khalifa and fancies himself a poet. He's a likable enough man who hands his poetry out to anyone who looks like they'd care to have a copy. He enjoys the spotlight. But stars are born, not made. And when the lights are turned on, when the camera is rolling, he doesn't have the presence.

Then there is the minister from Qatar.

Abdul Aziz bin Khalifa al-Thani has been his country's Opec representative since 1973. He's the son of the ruling Sheikh. And he too has visions of stardom. He arrives at this meeting in his private 707, with an entourage that includes his own hairdresser and his own television crew. He doesn't speak a lot in the meeting. In fact, he arrives late and leaves early, the way he always does, just so the journalists will speak to him. Behind his back the Opec press corps call him 'Lifo'. You know, last in, first out.

Finally there's Professor Dr Subroto.

He's the Indonesian minister without a first name. He's always happy to talk to the press.

But in the end they're all second division.

Centre stage belongs to Yamani.

He fields questions at the large noisy press conferences with the ease of Olivier doing Hamlet.

Spot oil has reached $39 a barrel.

Everyone wants to know if prices could go even higher.

The media are looking for a front-page story.

So Yamani gives them their front-page story.

He stands at the podium, half-hidden by microphones, smartly dressed in his perfectly cut dark suit, and announces to the world that there will be an oil surplus some time in the next two years. He predicts that before the end of 1981 members will be fighting amongst themselves and that the price of oil will come under serious threat.

He predicts that the price of oil might even collapse.

It's just about the last thing anybody expected him to say.

You mean, someone asks, come down gradually?

No, he answers, the word is collapse!

Collapse? With prices still going up, it's kind of hard to believe. So some of the press go running off to see if anyone else in Caracas is willing to corroborate Yamani's views. But the Nigerian oil minister says to them, 'Yamani is joking.' And the Iranian oil minister, suggests to them, 'Yamani is out of his mind. We know he doesn't drink alcohol but maybe he's taking drugs.'

* * * *

Dhahran, Saudi Arabia, three weeks later.

Yamani tries again.

This time it's in a speech at the University of Petroleum and Minerals.

Pressure is continuing to build throughout the Gulf to raise the price of oil.

But here the white-robed Yamani tells a fully packed university auditorium, 'There will be a drop in the price of oil and a sharp decrease in our level of production.'

Saudi Arabia is producing nearly 10 mbd.

He predicts before long they will go below 4 mbd.

And now the white-robed audience snickers.

They come very close to laughing at him.

They sit there thinking, Yamani is talking nonsense.

He urges them, 'Just make some basic calculations. The first law of economics is that when the price goes up, consumption comes down. This is a divine law. You cannot change it.'

He reminds them, 'Prices for Arab Light went from $11.70 to $18, then $24, then $28. What has to be the result? A lower level of consumption. In 1979 the Opec share of the market went to a little more than 31 mbd. We were pumping 3 mbd more than the year before. What does this mean? It means there was a huge amount of oil not going for consumption but instead going for stock.'

He asks them, 'All right, so you stock oil, but for how long? That oil must come back one day as an additional source of supply. It means the level of production must drop in Opec, from 31 mbd to 27 mbd, then 23 mbd, then 20 mbd. The producers must fight each other for market share and that brings the prices down even lower.'

But at Dhahran they find it as hard to believe as the reporters did in Caracas.

They should have believed him.

Because as oil climbed from $35 to $39 and then edged over $40 in the spot markets, most of the world's oil producers made the exact same mistake.

They thought the party would never end.

* * * *

When Jim Akins was recalled as US Ambassador to Saudi Arabia by Henry Kissinger in 1974, the State Department sent William Porter. The joke that went around the State Department was that Akins had been too pro-Arab so Nixon sent Porter to Jeddah to get even.

When Jimmy Carter was elected President he replaced Porter with John West, a former fellow southern governor.

Short, stocky and an old school southern gentleman, West met Yamani for the first time in Washington, during King Fahd's visit to the States in May 1977. As West had not yet been sworn in, the meeting was little more than an introduction and a hand shake.

Four or five weeks later, once he'd settled into a daily routine at the Embassy in Jeddah, West felt it was time to call on Yamani.

The Saudi oil minister invited the new American Ambassador to meet with him in a relaxed, informal setting at his summer home at Taif.

They sat outside on the wicker furniture next to the pool, drinking fruit juice, chatting amicably for 10–15 minutes.

Once West felt he'd paid his respects, he stood up and told Yamani that he'd only stopped by to say hello. He told Yamani that he didn't want to take up any more of his time.

But Yamani motioned to West to stay. He said, 'I'm happy to see you and anyway you've already spent more time with me than your predecessor ever did.'

It was the beginning of an especially warm and long friendship.

The two got along so well together that every year on Mrs West's birthday, Yamani would invite them to Taif for the weekend.

'One year my wife and I took our daughter and my secretary along. Now Zaki is a very attractive man. My daughter was then in her 20s and my secretary was then in her 50s. Both of them were unmarried. On the way home my daughter and my secretary said to me, we understand that Saudis can have more than one wife, do you think he'd be interested in us? You know what, I'm not so sure they were joking.'

The friendship was more than just social. It worked on many levels. And because it did, West admits that he owes Yamani a real debt.

'Before every Opec meeting, there were all these task forces back in Washington. The State Department, the Office of Management and Budget, the Treasury, everybody was trying to predict what Opec was going to do. Well, my friendship with Yamani was such that I could go to him and ask, what's going to happen. He'd say, this is what our range will be, or he'd say, I'm sorry but I can't discuss this with you. He was always very frank and forthright. He never misled me in the slightest. It's funny, but because of that I got a reputation of being an oil expert that I certainly didn't deserve.'

During West's four years in Saudi Arabia, the United States found itself almost totally dependent upon the Saudis to keep the price of oil under some degree of control.

So West's easy access to Yamani was a valuable pipeline for the men formulating American oil policy.

Just before the Opec meeting in December 1977, Yamani said to West that talk around the cartel was for a price increase.

West sent that information to Washington.

Back came a cable from Treasury Secretary Blumenthal who said he felt that, in order to control inflation, Opec had to keep its prices fixed.

West relayed that information to Yamani, who answered that a modest price increase of 10–11 per cent might be in order, pointing out that all of the Opec countries save Saudi Arabia and maybe Kuwait were in deficit financial situations.

As inflation had been rising at 8–10 per cent, Yamani explained to West than an increase in the price of that amount would simply maintain the status quo.

West sent that message back to Blumenthal.

But it wasn't what Washington wanted to hear.

Blumenthal must have brought it up at a cabinet meeting because the next thing West knew, Jimmy Carter and Cyrus Vance asked him to make an all-out pitch directly to the king and the Crown Prince, hoping their intervention could get the rest of Opec to keep the status quo.

So West duly requested an audience and it was duly granted.

But when he walked into the king's office, he found himself alone with Khaled, Crown Prince Fahd and Prince Sultan. Yamani was not present.

After West explained what the President was hoping for, Fahd answered that Saudi Arabia could not freeze the prices all by itself at the Opec meeting, that in order to do it he would have to enlist the help of one other major producer, such as Iran.

West said he understood.

The meeting ended with the three royals promising to see what they could do.

Immediately after leaving the king's office, West went to see Yamani. It was literally a matter of minutes between the two meetings. But the first thing Yamani said to West was that he already knew everything about West's discussion with the three royals and had already been ordered by the king to go to the Gulf countries to try and get some support for the price freeze.

West had to be impressed at how fast the news travelled.

But Yamani felt the need to caution him. 'You're making an awful mistake because your economy can stand a 10 per cent rise. However, if you freeze the prices now the dam is going to break one of these days and your economy can't stand that.'

When West sent his report back to Washington, outlining the results of his discussion with the royal family, he also included a couple of paragraphs restating Yamani's feelings.

At the time, the Shah was in the United States on an official visit, talking to President Carter. Within a matter of days, just long enough for West's report to pass through the system at Foggy Bottom and make its way over to Pennsylvania Avenue, the Shah agreed to join the Saudis in freezing the prices.

'I can only speculate about this,' West says, 'but it's the logical conclusion that President Carter's very laudatory statement given on New Year's Eve 1977, you know, that the Shah was an ocean of tranquillity, was at least in part a repayment of the fact that Iran joined Saudi Arabia in keeping the prices down. Subsequently, of course, after the Shah's demise, Yamani's prediction came true. The dam broke and it wrecked our economy. Once again, Yamani had clearly called the shot.'

West doesn't particularly know why Yamani wasn't at the meeting with the king and the two princes, although he's willing to hazard a guess. 'Zaki worked under extremely difficult conditions. During Faisal's time he could make the decisions. But it became quite apparent that when Fahd took over he couldn't.'

However, he notes that Yamani always had his own special way of dealing with members of the House of Saud. 'He can be respectful without bowing and scraping. It's a fairly unique talent. For the most part it served him well.'

Still, West remarks, from the day he arrived till the day he left, there were constant rumours floating around that Yamani was either about to be fired or on the verge of quitting.

'It related back to the time when Faisal gave him full authority over oil policy. It seems after that he never had too much patience for other members of the royal family. Rumours were rampant that Prince Saud, Faisal's son and Yamani's former deputy, would become oil minister. That might have been in the works until the oil job became less desirable than being Foreign Minister.'

The State Department heard the rumours too and they often queried West about them.

'One of the last times they wired me about the rumour I decided to go straight to Zaki and ask him about it. Khaled was still alive then. I said, is it true? He said, no, it isn't. But he said that he didn't want to stay on forever because the job was wearying and it had its difficulties.'

Interestingly enough, during that discussion, Yamani made a point of telling West that he wasn't going to resign under pressure. 'He said he had a good relationship with King Khaled. Everybody knew that he wasn't on very good terms with Crown Prince Fahd, so I always got the impression that he felt his relationship with Khaled was a safety factor or a kind of insurance policy.'

In February 1981, a little more than a year after the Ayatollah's return to Iran, with uncertainty the key word where oil was concerned, Yamani returned to the University of Petroleum and Minerals at Dhahran to make another key speech.

In Arabic, he told the packed crowd of students and Arab oil executives, 'If we force western countries to invest heavily in finding alternative sources of energy, they will. This will take them no more than seven to ten years and will result in their reduced dependence on oil as a source of energy to a point which will jeopardize Saudi Arabia's interests. Saudi Arabia will then be unable to find markets to sell enough oil to meet its financial requirements.'

John West heard about the speech, asked for a translation of it plus a transcript of the question and answer period that followed it, and realized right away that in his own way Yamani had just revealed a key element to post-Shah Saudi oil policy.

Says West, 'Certain Arab leaders, like the ones in Iraq and Libya, often accused Yamani of being too friendly with America. But I never felt he ever prejudiced the interests of his own country. Yamani made that speech at a time when Saudi Arabia was trying to hold prices down and he was personally being criticized for not going along with the other countries who wanted to raise the prices to something like $100 a barrel.'

West says that after Yamani's speech some of the students wanted to know why he continued to go along with the imperialists.

They asked him, why don't you agree to keep production down and let oil prices seek their level.

'Well, he said something like, we have enough oil reserves to continue at the present rate to the year 2050. He said, if I were the oil minister of Algeria or Nigeria or one of those countries that has oil reserves only for another ten years, I would want to get a maximum price. But, he said, I understand western technology and western attitudes. And this was what fascinated me about his speech. He told them, if western technology concentrates on developing alternative sources of energy they can do it in under ten years.'

It turns out that Yamani had hired a team of consultants to determine that, as long as the price of oil stayed below $30 a barrel, it was economically impractical for the oil-consuming states to develop those alternative sources of energy.

He later told West that Iraq had been among the hawks, fighting for price rises, until they saw the results of that survey. Having long-term oil reserves, they suddenly did an about-face and joined the Saudis in trying to hold down the price.

West nods, 'Of course the subsequent facts have proven Yamani out. With oil below the price of $30, every one of our alternate energy programmes is gone and everybody is predicting that the price of oil is going to be very high again before the year 2000. It's amazing how consistently right Zaki is.'

* * * *

John West could get along with Zaki Yamani because he understood that one of the keys to dealing with the Saudis is that they feel more comfortable with a one-on-one relationship.

'The problem', notes another member of Carter's cabinet, 'has always been that Americans don't understand the Saudis. The Saudis are very circumspect. The Americans come crashing in there in a businesslike manner. But the Saudis are Middle Easterners. They don't deal with offices, like the Secretary of Commerce or the Vice President of the United States. They deal with individuals. They either know you or they don't know you. They have to trust you. The fact that you hold an office merely provides you with an opportunity to talk to them. But as far as they're concerned, it's the relationship that's all-important. The formality of the office is much less important. They're also very polite. They beat around the bush. They've got circumlocutions. Americans go out there and don't understand that part of the problem.'

According to James Schlesinger, who also served in Carter's cabinet, one of the keys to Yamani's success was that he could always deal with westerners pretty much on a western basis.

'His behaviour is not exactly the archetypal American behaviour. But he understands the culture. Now mind you, he's a lawyer and a diplomat, so that whatever position he's trying to sell, he's selling consistently, even though he may not believe in that position. In that sense, he's not necessarily giving you all of his innermost thoughts. And, yes, he sometimes takes the oblique approach. But most people who've dealt with him found that he always came to meetings prepared with a degree of candour and frankness that most of the others couldn't achieve.'

Yet in the more abstract world of generalities, the Americans in particular seem to have always had a very black and white view of the Arabs.

Much the way young children can see the world filled with cowboys and Indians or cops and robbers, American foreign policy makers also have an adolescent predilection for pigeon-holing.

Where the Arabs are concerned, the categories are defined as moderates and extremists.

And the Saudis top the moderates' list.

They are, of course, inexorably linked to the United States.

America invented Aramco and turned Saudi Arabia into a petroleum power. America helps to equip and to train the Saudi military. America is the Saudis' largest single trading partner.

At the same time the United States wants to keep Saudi Arabia on the top of the pile because the Saudis hold such a unique political place in the Arab world.

And they know it.

Yamani has often cautioned westerners – especially Americans – not to take Saudi friendship for granted.

He tells them that in order to begin to understand his country they must understand that Saudi Arabia's first priority is self-reliance, and its second is relations with its Arab brothers.

In that regard, the Saudis' huge oil reserves have turned them into the Arab world's pay masters.

Their cheque book however, has never really brought them sufficient muscle to impose long-standing policies on other Arab nations. Or if they've got the muscle, then at least since 1973/74 they've seemed oddly reluctant to flex it.

They've never been able to dictate a settlement in any of the various crises where the Egyptians, Lebanese, Syrians, Jordanians or Palestinians have been concerned.

They haven't been successful in ending the war between Iran and Iraq.

They never stepped in to assume the Shah's role as policeman to the region.

And they admittedly tremble at the thought of the Ayatollah's Islamic fundamentalism spreading to their side of the Gulf.

They are, as it happens, heavily committed to the survival of the previously hostile regime of Iraq's President Saddam Hussein. There is no way they would want to see the Ayatollah win a war that would in turn replace Hussein with a Shi'a fundamentalist. In this case the Saudis have put their money where their ideals are. But financing the Iraqis into a stalemate with Iran has been costly. In the first two years of the war alone, it is believed that Saudi Arabia spent about $10 billion to aid Saddam Hussein. That's not necessarily because they want to see the out-numbered Iraqis win. It's rather that they are committed to seeing the religious extremist Iranians lose.

Still, the Saudis are also very much the glue that keeps the Arab world bound together.

Although Libya is these days treated by the Saudis as if they find Qaddafi too far gone to retrieve, Saudi Arabia was the one to bring Egypt back into the Arab fold after the several cold-shoulder years that followed Camp David.

In 1981 it was Crown Prince Fahd who made the first attempt at an all-Arab initiative which came very close to a de facto recognition of Israel's right to exist.

And, despite ideological differences, the Saudis consider Syria to be such a vital part of the puzzle that today the two court openly.

Much in the same spirit, towards the very end of 1980 and into the beginning of 1981, the Saudis found themselves in the middle of a top-secret deal to try to bring the American hostages out of Tehran.

Washington's intelligence sources had come up with the titbit that it was Yassir Arafat and the PLO who had trained the Ayatollah's personal revolutionary guards.

Ever opportunistic, Carter's people – among them Cyrus Vance as Secretary of State and Zbigniew Brzezinski as head of the National Security Council – looked for some way to use this in a last-ditch attempt to bring the hostages home before Ronald Reagan took office in mid-January.

They felt that if they could somehow pull it off – without informing the incumbent President, who would have had a fit if he'd known – it would give Carter the chance to leave office a hero while severely embarrassing Ronald Reagan in a sort of 'don't get angry – get even' slap in the face for Carter's massive defeat at the polls.

Their hopes lay in the belief that Arafat, for his direct support of the Khomeini regime, must hold a marker with the Ayatollah and could – if he chose to – call it in by asking for the return of the hostages.

Obviously the very notion of such a plan raised several serious questions.

Would Arafat go along with it?

Would the Ayatollah go along with it?

What would Arafat want in return from Carter?

Would Carter be willing to pay the price?

And how would the American public accept Arafat's role?

The last question was answered first.

If Arafat succeeded, it would be Jimmy Carter's success and the end would justify the means. If Arafat failed, no one would ever find out.

Because the White House could never approach the PLO leader directly, Carter's people appealed to the Saudis.

Negotiations were immediately begun between the United States and Saudi Arabia, quickly followed by negotiations between the Saudis and Yassir Arafat.

Within a matter of a few days, a deal was struck.

Arafat, after confidently reassuring the Saudis that he could bring the hostages out, agreed to call in his marker with the Ayatollah. In turn, Crown Prince Fahd said he would send his private Boeing 707 to Tehran to fly the hostages directly to Washington's National Airport. Jimmy Carter said he would be there to welcome them home.

Once everything was set, and that meant once Carter himself said he was willing to pay Arafat what he wanted, the PLO leader went to Iran and Fahd's plane moved into position on the tarmac at Tehran.

The reason the deal never came off was because Khomeini told Arafat, in no uncertain terms, he didn't owe the man anything.

Without any discussion, he flatly refused to hand over the hostages.

However, if Arafat had been successful he would have collected an unbelievable prize.

In exchange for the hostages, Jimmy Carter had agreed that Arafat could accompany the hostages to Washington where, as Arafat stepped off Fahd's plane, in full sight of the world's press, with cameras rolling, the outgoing President would personally welcome him as a hero with a warm and very public embrace.

18

The Ultimate Politician

IN THE 1970s, when the Saudis came into really serious money, they suddenly discovered friends they never knew they had.

Tinkers, tailors, soldiers and accountants.

Doctors, lawyers and Indian chiefs.

Anyone who could smell petrodollars the way a shark can taste long-distance blood set their sights on Saudi Arabia.

As one Saudi put it when he started travelling in the west on a regular basis, 'I'd come home and find letters from the people I'd met on my trip. But no one said how glad they were to meet me. They only wanted to sell me stuff.'

Some of the more clever types took a hint from the Arabs themselves and became middlemen.

We need an agent when we do business in your country, they briefed their prospective clients, so I'll be your agent when you want to do business in this country.

It made sense to the Saudis.

All the more so if the agent had a law degree.

After all, everybody knows you can always trust a lawyer.

Many of the Saudis' new friends were based in Washington DC.

I have contacts with the government, wink wink.

But in the United States, if you're playing at being an agent of a foreign government, you're required by law to register as a foreign agent with a special unit of the Justice Department.

A registered foreign agent is sort of like a consultant. It's legal advice or public relations work or lobbying. It's getting in the middle of deals, introducing people, making contacts, knowing the right journalists.

But to anyone who's ever read a paperback thriller, the whole idea conjures up trench coats, cellar boîtes and ladies with fishnet stockings.

So, Yamani is asked, how about all those people who registered as foreign agents of the Saudis during the 1970s, were any of them spies?

The question amuses him.

Come on, he's chided, what would stop Saudi Arabia from hiring a bunch of lawyers across America, registering them as foreign agents and turning them all into spies?

He shrugs.

So, he's asked, are there Saudi spies in America? You can tell me. Is there a spy network of foreign agents employed by Saudi Arabia prowling around the country, photographing military installations, checking out industrial designs and generally gathering intelligence?

He laughs and his whole face lights up. 'We have to learn somehow.'

* * * *

Sir Julian Hodge is a Welsh, Roman Catholic, multimillionaire financier, dedicated socialist and philanthropist.

Born in 1904, an accountant and banker by trade, he's a man with a square chin and a Kirk Douglas dimple. In 1966, on the 20th anniversary of his mother's death, he formed the Jane Hodge Foundation with a £2.5 million gift. Five years later, seeking a forum to help promote international economic understanding, he established the almost-annual Jane Hodge Memorial Lecture at the University of Wales' Institute of Science and Technology.

Their first speaker was the then Governor of the Bank of England. A year later it was the Managing Director of the International Monetary Fund. Hodge's third guest was David Rockefeller, Chairman of the Chase Manhattan Bank. Next came HRH Prince Philip, the Duke of Edinburgh.

The series' fifth speaker was Zaki Yamani.

He addressed the black-tie group in Cardiff in November 1976, wearing black Arab robes with gold thread sewn through them.

Introduced as 'one of the most powerful men in the world and certainly one of the most exotic', Yamani spoke about the need for energy conservation.

Hodge put Zaki and Tammam up for their overnight stay at his country estate outside Cardiff. He even brought in special household staff to look after them.

Just before the Yamanis arrived, someone pointed out to Hodge that one of his Persian rugs had the symbol of Mecca at its centre. The rug was duly placed in the library, facing east.

The gesture did not go unnoticed.

That night over dinner Yamani made mention of it and then asked Hodge, 'What is the religion of the people of Wales?'

Hodge explained, 'They're Wesleyan, Baptists, Presbyterians, Welsh Congregationalists and Church of England. What I'd call nonconformists. You see, I myself am one of those people who believe in guardian angels, fairies at the bottom of the garden and the goodness of God. I'm a Catholic.'

Yamani paused to think about that, then said to Hodge, 'I don't mind what a man's religion is as long as he works at it.'

Later that night, in casual conversation, Hodge found himself telling Yamani about his old friend George Thomas, a fellow Welshman, then the Speaker of the House of Commons. Upon his retirement from the House in 1981 Thomas would be knighted and become the Viscount Tonypandy.

Thomas's name was mentioned by Hodge just in passing as being someone Yamani ought to meet one day.

A few months after his visit to Wales, Yamani reciprocated by inviting Sir Julian and Lady Hodge to Saudi Arabia.

When Hodge told Thomas that he was going to the kingdom for his holidays, Thomas's eyes lit up. 'Oh,' he said, 'I've never been there, may I come along?'

Hodge rang Yamani and Yamani said, sure, bring him along.

Thomas is a wiry little man, a former Labour MP born in 1909 who seems to have a never-ending fund of enthusiasm. He is regarded by many people as having been the best Speaker at least since the war.

Yamani sent a Gulfsteam jet to Cardiff to bring them to Saudi Arabia.

He met them at the airport, ushered them into his Rolls and drove them to the summer house in Taif.

For Thomas, it was admiration at first sight.

'It was for me an immense experience,' he says in his lilting Welsh accent. 'The humility of one of the most powerful men in the world. This modest man whom I'd never met before jumped to the wheel to drive us himself. He has such a rare flair for drawing people to him. I found there's a magic in him. I can't easily define it but I can feel it. His eyes, his voice, his personality, his consideration for others. He's at peace with himself. With all due respect to him, Zaki could be straight out of the New Testament.'

Early on during his ten-day stay, Thomas and Yamani discovered they shared a common interest, religion.

'I'm a Methodist with a very simple faith,' Thomas continues. 'I never have to wrestle with my doubts. Zaki is in the same happy

245

position. That's what drew us together. He's got a very simple, straight-forward faith. And he doesn't throw it in your face. He has the ability to hold fast to his Moslem faith without being intolerant of people who have different views.'

As so many people do when they talk religion with Yamani, Thomas brought up Judaism. Thomas said he mentioned it 'just to set the record straight'.

Yamani also wanted to set the record straight. 'It's written in the Koran that Christians and Jews are the people of the book. They have a special status in the Moslem world to the extent that we must defend churches and synagogues the same way we must defend mosques. Unfortunately, political events have changed the nature of a once-friendly relationship. It's Zionism we're opposed to, not the Jews.'

The two get along so well that Yamani regularly called on Thomas at Speaker's House when he was in London and Thomas returned some years later for another stay in Taif.

One night at Speaker's House, Yamani mentioned to Thomas that he hadn't yet been able to say his prayers.

'I asked him, why don't you say them here? I suppose in retrospect there's a certain drama about it. But there was Zaki Yamani kneeling in my parlour in Speaker's House saying his prayers.'

Actually it almost didn't work.

Before he began Yamani needed to know where the east was.

Thomas said he didn't know.

There was an awkward moment until the two of them established which direction was south.

The rest was easy.

Another night at Speaker's House, Yamani showed up for dinner with a young, blind Arab poet in tow.

'This young man had become known through the media in the Arab world and Zaki had become his sort of patron. He was clearly making life bearable for this blind young man who could do nothing for Zaki except express gratitude.'

Some months after Thomas's first trip to Saudi Arabia, Frederick Ponsonby, the Earl of Bessborough, visited Yamani in his role as British Conservative Party spokesman on Energy at the European Parliament.

Yamani arranged an entire Cook's tour of the Saudi oilfields for the tall, grey-haired aristocrat, sending his Lordship deep into the Empty Quarter.

When Bessborough returned to Riyadh, Yamani announced they would now be going on to Jeddah.

He drove Bessborough to the airport and pointed to a Gulfstream. 'I will use this one,' Yamani said. 'Of course you're very welcome to join us. Tammam is flying with us. So are the two children with their nanny, my bodyguards and another friend of ours.' Yamani then mentioned that this friend had supernatural powers. Bessborough let the remark pass. 'Or,' Yamani pointed to a pair of Gulfstreams next to his, 'if you don't want to come with us, please go on board either of these and pick the one you like.'

Bessborough naturally chose to stay with the Yamanis for the 75-minute flight.

When they boarded the plane, Bessborough says the first thing that happened was that Yamani's 19-month-old son raced down the aisle from the rear compartment to kiss his father. Then the child kissed his mother. Then the child kissed Bessborough.

Yamani insisted Bessborough take his large seat near Tammam while he sat along the side of the compartment, on a couch that can be flipped into a double bed for long flights.

Lunch was served en route.

Buttermilk, cheese, crackers, apples, oranges and coffee.

Over dinner that night, Yamani spoke about the supernatural, about his clairvoyant friends and about the man with the supernatural powers who'd been with them on the plane. Yamani even promised Bessborough that one day soon he'd see the man with the supernatural powers do 'the rope trick.'

A couple of days later Yamani made good that promise.

The Yamanis were having a huge buffet lunch to celebrate the Prophet's birthday. But it was strictly family. Yamani's mother. Tammam's parents. All the various sisters, brothers, cousins and a few old friends.

After lunch everyone settled down in the big livingroom and Yamani produced a 50–foot nylon rope.

This has always been one of Yamani's most popular after-meal entertainments.

The man with the supernatural powers was a white-robed, medium-sized fellow who Bessborough thought must be somewhere in his mid–50s. He was bound hand and foot. The knots were tied tightly – anyone is always welcome to tie a knot if they suspect Yamani of collusion – and the man was then carried off to a small bathroom.

The door was shut.

Much to Bessborough's suprise, there was less than one minute of loud moaning when, suddenly, the man reappeared.

Ropeless.

Yamani explained that the spirits had freed him of the bonds.

Then the man went into a trancelike state to free himself of the spirits.

He quivered nervously and talked to himself while Yamani sat next to him and gave him glasses of water.

It was a performance worthy of Houdini.

Bessborough returned to London in absolute awe of Yamani. 'He's a man to whom I've become quite devoted. As you know, many people are.'

He discussed his visit with George Thomas and the two of them decided Yamani absolutely had to meet the then newly elected Prime Minister, Margaret Thatcher.

On the next occasion when Yamani gave Bessborough and Thomas sufficient notice that he planned to be in London, a private dinner was arranged by Thomas at Speaker's House.

'I invited the Prime Minister, the leader of the opposition, the major cabinet officers and a group of powerful business leaders from the City. I invited about 40 people in Zaki's honour. And not one single person said no. Everyone came.'

Yamani was there with Tammam, both of them in finely tailored western clothes.

Before long Yamani and Margaret Thatcher had manoeuvred themselves off to the side and were deep in private conversation.

Denis Thatcher kept saying to Lord Bessborough, 'Shouldn't we go over there and talk to them.'

But Bessborough kept Denis away. 'It's sometimes very helpful if leaders like that can talk informally and get to know each other.'

Thomas says he timed the private tête-à-tête at 24 minutes.

'I got the impression they liked each other. And I agree that informal lines of contact can sometimes be exceedingly important. I know that Margaret realized here was a man of integrity and strength and with an open mind.'

As they moved back into the mainstream of the party again, Thomas took a tray and offered them each a glass.

The Prime Minister took one.

And Yamani took one.

The Prime Minister sipped at hers, then bellowed in her now-familiar voice at Yamani, 'What is that in your hand?'

Yamani said, 'The Speaker gave it to me.'

She glared at Thomas. 'George, how dare you?'

He realized the gaff and apologized immediately.

Yamani's whisky was hurriedly exchanged for orange juice.

'He was only holding it,' Thomas says. 'He took it from me and said thank you because he was much too polite to say, you know you shouldn't give that to me.'

As the friendship between Bessborough, Thomas, Hodge and

Yamani was maintained and strengthened, Bessborough arranged to have Yamani speak before the European–Atlantic Group.

Made up of influential members of both houses of Parliament plus business leaders, Yamani addressed the group in the Grand Committee room at the Houses of Parliament on 31 March, 1982.

Yamani warned his audience that these were critical times and that if certain industrialized countries continued to think short term, the results would be devastating for everyone.

Without specifically pointing his finger at Great Britain, everyone in the room – including the then Energy Minister Nigel Lawson – knew who Yamani was referring to when he hinted that some producing countries were not doing everything they could to help stabilize prices.

'Any further drop in the international price of energy will only aggravate the situation. In the area of world oil exploration and production, high-cost oil could be wiped out irreversibly from the market . . .'

That's a direct reference to North Sea oil.

' . . . and further exploratory activities discouraged. Soon the need for greater imports may reappear in many consuming countries to supplement their domestic supplies. With inventories being drawn down to dangerously low levels, the vulnerable position reached by consuming countries as a result can only be redressed by resorting to another round of stock build-up.'

That was on the record.

After the speech the group moved to a nearby hotel for dinner and questions, off the record.

There he told his audience that Britain was putting unfair pressure on Nigeria to lower its prices by keeping North Sea prices so low. 'Knowing the interests of the [British] companies and the flexibilities they have in letting the British Treasury bear the consequences of price cuts, it's unfair.'

Lawson answered later that evening that his government was not being used by the oil industry. 'The British government controls neither the price nor the volume of North Sea oil output. The price which BNOC [the British National Oil Corporation] negotiates has to reflect the realities of the market. It's not the policy of the British government to lead prices down any more than it was our policy to lead prices up.'

It was double talk.

There were political pressures put on BNOC throughout 1982 and they intensified in the spring of 1983. Publicly Lawson said that he preferred Britain to remain a market follower rather than a leader. In the back rooms however, he did whatever was necessary to protect BNOC's place in the market.

Maybe it wasn't the most aggressive of market leaders, but Lawson needed to see that it was at least up there with the front runners.

In spite of his denials, Lawson continued to meet with Yamani. Officially he declined all formal consultations. Instead there were several late-night informal unstructured sessions at Lawson's office, once the press corps was gone for the evening. The way Lawson figured it, the United Kingdom could not appear eager to associate officially with Opec or any of its representatives.

Although prior to the Conservative victory of 1979 and Lawson's elevation to a ministry, Anthony Wedgewood Benn was the Labour Minister of Energy and he actually favoured British membership in Opec.

'Obviously there were links of common interest between all oil producers,' says Benn, who did meet formally with Yamani on several occasions between 1975 and 1979, both in London and Riyadh. 'But although I rather favoured making those links closer, I argued that Britain as a manufacturing country still depended more upon keeping oil prices down, rather than raising them and benefiting in its other lesser capacity as an oil producer.'

The problem with Benn's wish to align Great Britain with Opec was that Opec wouldn't have the UK as a member.

By charter Britain isn't eligible to join. Even if Britain is the world's fourth largest producer, Opec membership is open only to countries where oil is the major economic activity.

'Yamani made no secret of the fact that he was looking to the UK to support Opec's general stance,' according to Richard Johnstone, late of BNOC and now Chief Executive of the entity which BNOC eventually became, called the Oil and Pipeline Agency. 'The purpose of those informal discussions could only have been to try to persuade the UK government to offer that support. BNOC was in fact occupying a formal position of price setter. There were however lots of semanticly based arguments as to what the right word was. We didn't think "price setter" was the right word, but it was really only a question of semantics.'

In January 1983 a secret meeting took place between the Department of Energy and a handful of oil companies, including BNOC. Shell is also said to have been included.

Right away, Nigel Lawson categorically denied that the meeting ever took place.

It was more nonsense.

'I certainly know that the major oil companies were approached by the Department of Energy,' Johnstone confirms. 'But I don't think that Lawson himself got involved. It would have been people getting involved with his blessing, as it were, to see if these major oil companies would continue to support the price at a particular level. And there was an effort to persuade the major oil companies to support the price. But the major oil companies were beginning at that time to be disinclined to support a price which they didn't think made too much sense in the market.'

Johnstone feels Lawson's statement that reports of the meeting were not true can probably be written off to a political half-truth.

'It sounds to me as though it's a sort of reaction to, "Did you have a meeting with Yamani?" If the implication is an official meeting, then the answer is, "No." "Did you meet him for a chat, off the record and informally?" He'd probably say, "No comment", because he probably wouldn't want to field any further speculation. But it was an open secret that the United Kingdom's Secretary of State for Energy did informally talk to people like Yamani.'

In the end the British did not support Yamani's wishes to stabilize prices.

As Viscount Tonypandy put it, 'I got the feeling that Zaki felt let down by some of the things we were doing with regard to prices. That we didn't do enough to help him.'

Perhaps you can point a finger at Lawson for being somewhat cavalier with his public statements.

But you can't blame Yamani for giving it a try.

* * * *

Through the efforts mainly of Sir Julian Hodge and with the strong support of Viscount Tonypandy, the University of Wales conferred an honorary doctorate on Yamani in July 1984.

He'd been holidaying in Spain with his family.

So he and Tammam flew from there in the Gulfstream to the Royal Air Force base at Valley, Anglesey, in the north of Wales.

A formal dinner was planned for that evening. The ceremony was scheduled for the following morning.

They were accommodated overnight at the estate of the Lord-Lieutenant of the area, the Marquess of Anglesey, who by coincidence was also receiving an honorary degree.

Arriving at the Marquess's home, they were greeted by their hosts. After a casual chat they were shown to their bedroom.

Suddenly Yamani realized there'd been a mix-up and that the suit-case with his formal attire was missing.

After some frantic telephoning, they managed to locate Yamani's private secretary who was being put up in a hotel about 45 minutes away.

The errant suitcase was with him.

Now the Marquess got on the phone to the local police. He convinced them that the guest of honour at the University College of North Wales' dinner could not be late, so they dispatched a patrol car with sirens blaring to fetch Yamani's dinner jacket.

They managed the round-trip in half an hour.

In good form that night, Yamani told the audience that he'd heard how Wales was suffering a severe drought. He assured them he understood, as Wales and Saudi Arabia obviously had a lot in common.

Although the Yamanis were to be in Wales less than 18 hours, security measures to protect them were elaborate.

'There were policemen with dogs in the grounds surrounding the house throughout the night,' the Marquess recollects. 'The security was even more stringent than it was for the visit here of the Prince of Wales.'

Yamani received his degree in cap and gown.

He and Tammam then agreed to meet the Hodges and Viscount Tonypandy two days later in Cardiff.

However, they still had one night left of their holiday in Spain and they wanted to see the children. So, immediately after the University ceremony, they flew back to Spain for 24 hours, to officially end their vacation, before returning to southern Wales for dinner.

Through his Welsh friends Yamani learned about some work going on at the University of Wales. They'd run an experimental farm in Saudi Arabia and were now trying to develop a centre for agriculture, forestry and environmental research in association with the semi-arid countries.

A year after that particular trip to Wales, Yamani was approached and asked if he might be prepared to support the development of a centre.

The result was the Yamani Fellowships.

Work now under way includes a project in Mali on pastoralism, the environmental impact of wells and the control of grazing; one in northern Sudan on social forestry; and one in Morocco looking at the utilization of poor-quality brackish water in various oases.

Although the sum has never been disclosed, and although he's since come back with two more contributions, Yamani's initial pledge was £250,000.

19

The Beginning of the Downfall

IF IT was boomtime with oil at $12, just imagine what life was like in Saudi Arabia when oil hit $36.

The Arabs owned the earth.

They bought planes and yachts, Rolls-Royces, Cadillacs, Daimlers and Mercedes, second homes in London, third homes in Paris and fourth homes in Florida.

They bought bricks and mortar on Wall Street, banks in the City and designer jewellery in France.

While a lot of Saudis were trying to find ways of spending money outside the country, Hisham Nazer's Ministry of Planning had its hands full spending inside the country.

If you were running an international construction company, you couldn't pack your best salesman off to Saudi Arabia fast enough.

'It was an incredible sight,' Sir James Craig labels the 1979–1980–1981 version of boomtime. 'When you drove in from the airport to Riyadh, it was almost a cliché. It was one big builders' yard. It was absurd. Wherever you looked you saw a dozen huge cranes, building, building, building.'

The Saudis not only found themselves in the land of plenty, most of them thought they now owned a long lease on it.

Not many Saudis seemed too upset by what was going on.

Says Craig, 'I think most people enjoyed it. There were some who had doubts. But they were the more thoughtful people. Usually the older generation. The younger ones just jumped on the bandwagon and enjoyed themselves. In retrospect, I think the fears of the older ones that it might harm both the economy and the national psychology proved to be justified to a certain extent. But at the time you heard very few doubts about it.'

However, Craig can clearly recall when the first, slight cloud appeared on the horizon.

It was the middle of 1981.

Oil prices had just begun to come down off their peak. No one knew where they'd bottom out. There were rumblings of the severe glut to come.

At one point Craig was talking to the Governor of the Saudi Arabian Monetary Agency and wanted to know, 'If this cloud proves to be only one of many, what will you do?'

The Saudi banker replied, 'There are some of us who won't be very upset. Some of us think the economy is overheated, that a too rapid economic change has put social pressures upon us. We don't need all of this.'

Craig was a bit taken back with the man's candour. 'You don't?'

The banker replied, 'No, we don't. For example, in my family, we have something like seven servants. We could manage perfectly well with two. We have something like nine cars. We don't need more than two.' Then he stopped to pause for a few seconds and a little smile came over his face. 'But I don't know what my sons would say.'

Now Yamani's prediction of a glut didn't seem so far-fetched.

He reiterates, 'It was so clear to me that this would happen. Normally when there's a surplus, you buy for stock to replenish it and when there's a shortage, you draw from stock. What happened here was exactly the opposite. When we had a shortage because of the Iranian Revolution, companies started to buy heavily to stock up. When we had a surplus in 1981, those same companies started drawing heavily from their inventories. This was not a healthy situation. But it was a fact.'

By the middle of 1981 oil prices had eased their way down from around $40 to settle in the $32–36 range, with the Saudis at the lower end of the scale and the majority of Opec at the higher end.

To support those prices, most of the Opec producers cut their production. Only Saudi Arabia pumped at full throttle.

In July, the oil ministers from Algeria, Libya, Iraq, Kuwait and Abu Dhabi came to see Yamani in Taif, hoping to convince him to cut back on production and support the higher prices.

He refused to go along with them.

Iraq's President Hussein even appealed directly to King Khaled for the same cause.

But the king said Saudi Arabia wanted prices down.

The rest of Opec said they wanted prices held high.

A crisis was brewing.

The Indonesian Dr Subroto lobbied the cartel's members,

suggesting an extraordinary meeting to help clear the air. It took Yamani nearly two weeks to agree to the session, but once he did the 13 oil ministers and their staffs descended on Geneva.

At the Intercontinental, panic was the order of the day.

Normally the hotel has plenty of time to prepare for Opec's arrival. This time the management had to make the hotel ready within a few days. Guests already in the hotel were invited to make other arrangements. Reservations for in-coming guests were cancelled. Security checkpoints were hastily set up. Journalists with their ears to the ground got first call on what few rooms were left in town while the ones who heard about the meeting too late found themselves in far-flung digs.

As soon as Yamani arrived the show was off and running.

Early on, in private meetings with selected ministers, he dropped some well-placed and subtle hints that Saudi Arabia might be willing to come up $2 if the other members would meet him at $34.

But the Venezuelan minister, an inveterate politician who even shakes hands with waiters when he leaves a restaurant, insisted his country would stick to its $36 price.

He claimed that a drop in the official price would hurt his country's income.

He claimed it was unnecessary, even under depressed market conditions, to go below present levels as long as everyone else stuck to them.

Saudi Arabia was not prepared to increase prices to meet Venezuela and Venezuela was not prepared to decrease prices to meet Saudi Arabia.

The meeting quickly took on the air of a stand-off between Yamani and the Venezuelan.

In terms of delegates, Yamani was wildly outnumbered.

All of the hawks and most of the moderates, like Kuwait, rallied with Venezuela.

But Yamani could not be swayed.

The strain took its toll early on.

Tempers started to flare.

Hoping if nothing else to ease the tension, Yamani made a traditional Arab peace offering. He sent a basket of dates to all the other ministers. But the message was lost in the heat of frustration as four days and nights of negotiations failed to get either side out of the trenches.

Unable to beg, cajole, push or shove Yamani from his position, a few of the delegates resorted to back-door politics.

At least four ministers cabled home to their head of state requesting that King Khaled be informed directly and immediately.

On the night of 19–20 August, Khaled took calls from the ruler of Kuwait and the Presidents of Iraq, Indonesia and Venezuela.

But Yamani had his bases covered and Khaled's answer was a royal variation on, sorry sir, not my table. The king politely explained to each of his callers that they'd best speak to Fahd.

All right, they each said, put him on the phone.

Unfortunately, Khaled then added, Fahd is on holiday out of the kingdom and cannot be reached.

It served the Saudis' purpose even if it wasn't quite the case.

Fahd was vacationing in Morocco. But Yamani had been able to reach him. He'd briefed the Crown Prince on the situation and Fahd instructed his oil minister not to go above $34.

Dr Subroto, who in his own quiet way had been working for a compromise at $35, visited Yamani in the top-floor suite and made a final plea.

Yamani said he must respectfully decline.

So now Subroto tried to bring the others down to $34.

Algeria, Libya, Iran, Iraq and of course Venezuela said no.

And that was the end of that.

The Venezuelan minister left Switzerland without making any pronouncements.

Some of the other ministers went on record as saying, 'Opec is dead.'

Sheikh Ali Khalifa al-Sabah of Kuwait, whose turn it was to take over as Opec president from Dr Subroto, was stopped by reporters on his way out of the hotel.

They asked him if it was true that Opec was dead.

He mumbled, 'News of Opec's death has been much exaggerated.'

But Yamani was the one the press corps really wanted to talk to.

He faced the press in the sweltering heat of a noisy, over-crowded conference room where air conditioning seemed as scarce as compromise.

'I am not an expert in psychology,' he tried to make the cynical western journalists believe. 'What has happened here was political. We can eliminate this glut if we drastically reduce our production, which we are not going to do. For me, I do not think it is humiliating when I face an economic reality. All important organizations in the world move their prices up and down according to the reality of the market. That is no political humiliation.'

At the State Department they sincerely hoped it was.

Shed no tears for Opec, was the line from several well-placed Reaganites in Washington.

Saudi Arabia also came under the gun.

'The Saudis, as always, are pursuing their self-interest,' wrote Hobart Rowen in the *Washington Post*. 'All the Saudis have been trying to do is force the other Opec nations to cut their prices to the level the Saudis think will best sustain the saleability of the huge Saudi oil reserves.'

His conclusion was that it might be time for the oil-importing nations to take charge.

He said they mustn't be any more bashful in an era of oil surplus than Opec was when there was a shortage.

But the oil-consuming nations hardly had to bother.

The disarray within Opec was already doing it for them.

In spite of the hawks' wishes to keep prices up, the market simply wasn't there.

It was the beginning of a long slide, which gathered momentum as it was further aggravated by barter deals, with Libya, Nigeria and Iran trading oil for goods . . . and discounts, with Nigeria and Iran unofficially offering oil at up to $4 less than their own posted price . . . and non-Opec oil, with Great Britain and Norway pumping away, feeding the glut.

All the time, Yamani kept warning his partners, 'The average price of a barrel of oil may fall below $32 and Opec could collapse if it continues to lose its share of the world oil market.'

Al-Sabah called the cartel together again in late October 1981 and, under the banner of accepting the realities of the market, the 13 agreed to freeze the price at $34 until the end of 1982.

It sounded good in a press release.

In a perfect world it might even have worked.

In reality it was a pipedream.

Within a matter of months the price of spot market crude had slipped below the official Opec level. As a result, the Iranians began dumping more and more oil onto the market to finance their war with Iraq. Then Venezuela and Mexico dropped their prices. And the BNOC cut the price of North Sea crude.

Now spot crude nudged close to $30.

Another emergency Opec meeting was called for mid-March, 1982.

Nigeria opened the session by claiming that so many of their contracts were being cancelled they'd have to get into heavy discounting just to keep in business.

Yamani knew Nigeria was the weakest chain in the Opec link and was worried that any panic could set off a price war. He knew who the villains were, so a not-so-subtle warning went out to the major oil companies. The *Middle East Economic Survey* published a report, citing 'an unnamed senior Saudi official', saying that the oil companies active in Nigeria had better increase their petroleum purchases there or they'd face reprisals from the other oil states.

Royal Dutch/Shell always claimed it did not pay any attention to the *MEES* report.

Mobil, Texaco and Elf tried to give the same impression.

But it's known that both Mobil and Texaco increased their Nigerian purchases and it's reasonably believed that, despite official denials, Shell and Elf did too.

It goes without saying there was never any doubt that everyone knew who the senior Saudi official was!

But that was just a sideshow.

The main problem Yamani had to deal with was how to keep world oil prices from eroding.

The result of the mid-March meeting was an agreement to reduce Opec's overall production from around 20mbd to 18.5 mbd.

Yamani also announced that Saudi Arabia would stand apart from the others in the group and, if the $34 price was still threatened, they would cut back on their own production, playing the role of swing producer.

It was the first time in Opec's history that the group made a decision on production levels.

It was also, some people thought, the first serious indication that Opec was about to collapse.

Daniel Yergin, a Boston oil consultant called Opec's plight 'the biggest crisis since it won control of the world oil market'.

William Brown of New York's Hudson Institute made the pronouncement that 'Opec is 100% dead'.

Bijan Mossavar-Rahmani, an Iranian delegate to Opec until 1978 and now at Harvard University, claimed, 'Forces very much out of Opec's control govern oil prices.'

Petroleum Intelligence Weekly revealed that Saudi oil production was on the way up and that Sheikh Yamani had actually reprimanded some of the Aramco partners for not taking enough oil.

But *PIW* also hinted, 'Saudi Arabia is acting as if it has given up any ideas of defending Opec's $34 marker crude price and may be content to see a substantial reduction.'

Before too long, Yamani would be leading the retreat.

* * * *

Khaled was dead and Fahd was now on the throne.

The king died at the age of 69 of a heart attack on 13 June 1982 at his home in Taif.

Within a few hours Fahd officially named himself Prime Minister. Abdullah became Crown Prince and First Deputy Prime Minister. Sultan was appointed Second Deputy Prime Minister.

Once again, talk spread of Yamani's impending dismissal.

With Khaled gone, the rumour-mongers claimed, there's no one left to protect him.

Even official news sources within the kingdom acknowledged that a ministerial reshuffle 'could not be ruled out'.

Word around town was that Faisal's son, Prince Saud, would be moved from his job as Foreign Minister into the petroleum job. The Foreign Office portfolio would then go to Prince Salman.

When it didn't happen right away, the rumour-mongers promised, but it will.

But it didn't.

The world oil situation continued to worsen, not helped any, as Yamani saw it, by the Reagan administration.

The movie actor president was the sixth to serve during Yamani's years in office. And Yamani suggests that, socially anyway, the White House under Reagan was a pleasant and relaxed place to visit.

'At the end of a formal dinner dance one evening, I was standing in the shadows near the front door waiting for my car. The orchestra was still playing. The President and Mrs Reagan were just saying goodnight to some of their guests. They didn't see me there. They didn't know I could hear them. And after they waved goodbye, Reagan put his arms around Nancy and whispered to her, "Come on honey, let's dance. Now the party can finally begin." '

He doesn't have the same kind words for Reagan's oil policies.

Much to the annoyance of the Saudis, one of the first things Reagan did when he got to the White House was greatly to increase America's strategic reserves.

With prices coming down, the United States was buying for the future.

'Three days after I was sworn in as Secretary of Energy,' explains Dr James Edwards, now head of the Medical School at the University of South Carolina, 'President Reagan told me to go out and deregulate the price of oil. I hardly knew how many gallons there were in a barrel. But I did know that, if we took the controls off, philosophically it was the right thing to do. And all through that period Sheikh Yamani was very friendly.'

However, when Edwards started buying heavily for stock, he says Yamani expressed grave doubts.

'It created a problem for him. As I recall, at our very first meeting he voiced his concern about it. He said it presented a political problem in his country.'

Yamani told Edwards, 'You are taking oil out of the ground in Saudi Arabia, bringing it over here and putting it back into the ground to use against us economically.'

Edwards nodded, 'I understand your problem.' Then he took his best shot at the Saudis' weakest point. 'But what if that big bear [the Soviet Union] came trotting down from the north of you, and occupied your land, and took your oilfields, and cut off the flow of oil from your part of the world to the rest of the world, wouldn't it be good if we had a stored supply of oil somewhere to fuel the tanks and the planes and the ships so we can go back there and retake that land for the royal family and re-establish the flow of oil back to the free world?'

Yamani looked him straight in the eye and said, 'Are you implying that one day you will no longer be a superpower?'

Edwards followed Reagan's orders and went right on increasing the strategic reserves, bringing the stock up from 90 million barrels when he first went to Washington in 1981 to 350 million barrels when he left in 1984.

'That's a lot of oil,' he says now. 'A lot of security. Sure, Zaki could have said, I won't help you fill your reserves. Instead he quietly backed off the position. You see, he understands how the world works. He's got a brilliant mind and I always felt he was a friend of this country.'

Yet, Edwards contends, it was very much a two-way street.

'There was a controversy about giving them AWACs [the airborne early warning and control system that continually patrols the Gulf as part of the Saudis' air defence network]. I knew what those planes meant to Saudi Arabia so I did some quiet lobbying for them. When it was over I rang Zaki on a State Department line to congratulate him on getting the AWACs. That same day he announced that the Saudis were bringing the price of oil down. So I congratulated him on both instances. Do you know that I later learned from some of my friends at the State Department that they were upset I'd congratulated him on fixing the price of oil.'

Fixing the price at $34 until the end of 1982 did not solve the problem. It merely postponed the nastiness that erupted at Opec's December 1982 meeting when Iran accused Yamani of undermining the cartel by not wanting to see prices stay at $34.

There was an odd irony in this as not so long before it had been Yamani who'd fought to keep the cartel together by preaching the inherent risks in allowing oil to climb above $28. He believed that increasing the price would be an historical mistake and create a structural change in the world economy. Yet Fahd was under pressure from

Kuwait, Qatar and Algeria to join them in raising the price from $28 to $32. Yamani argued strongly against it. Cunningly, Fahd waited until Yamani was on his way to Bali before sending Hisham Nazer to Kuwait and Qatar to strike a deal.

History proved Yamani right.

Within a few days, the other Opec countries raised their prices again. Conservation measures clicked into effect. And the eventual collapse of the market was almost certainly more severe than it otherwise would have been.

With oil at $34, the 13 Opec members scrambled to divide up their agreed 18.5 mbd overall production quota. But after 12 of the 13 nations put in their requests, the total stood at 23.5 mbd. And that was without Saudi Arabia as the swing producer.

The meeting broke up in disarray.

To show their displeasure, the Iranians blamed Yamani for the cartel's failure to agree on national quotas.

'With the firm revolutionary stance of the Islamic Republic of Iran,' commented the *Teheran Times* with typical objectivity, 'the fabricated power of Sheikh Ahmed Zaki Yamani would no longer be effective and the United States would have to appoint another agent in his place. The world expansionists, with the U.S. on the top, by their political maneuvers tried to weaken the Opec and bring it to the edge of annihilation. But the Islamic Revolution, with no reliance on political, military and economic means, aborted wicked policies of the U.S. and its lackeys thus achieving a grand success in bringing the oil price to its actual ruling level.'

It just shows what Yamani was up against at some of these meetings.

In late January 1983 Opec tried yet again.

The emergency meeting was held at the Intercontinental in Geneva and the atmosphere was only slightly less ugly than it had been in December.

Eleven of the thirteen states had reconsidered the quotas proposed at the previous meeting and were now willing to accept.

The holdouts were Kuwait and Saudi Arabia.

Yamani didn't necessarily object to the quotas, he simply wanted to include with the plan an adjustment in the differentials between various crude prices. He said he'd go along with the group if the prices of certain cheaper crudes were raised.

It meant the African members, among them Nigeria, would have to raise their prices. But they protested that in a declining market such a move was tantamount to suicide. So the Saudis and the Kuwaitis said no to the proposed quotas. When they did, the UAE and Qatar changed their votes from yes to no and that looked like the end of Opec.

'The conference is finished.' Yamani said leaving the meeting room. 'It was a complete failure. Quite honestly, I don't see a very bright future. In a few days we expect to see the price of North Sea oil come down by $2–3. And that will be the beginning of a chain reaction.'

The press asked what he thought would happen in the months ahead and he answered, 'If I had my crystal ball with me and I looked into it, I would see the British government reducing the North Sea oil prices under pressure from the oil companies. This is the first step. That will pressure the others into further discounting. It's just the beginning. You will have a very interesting month of February.'

Returning home, Yamani confided to the Saudi magazine *Iqra* that there was no alternative but to seek a lower price. He said, if they didn't do it themselves, market forces would do it for them.

He said, 'I can't see any way out of a price reduction. We have lost patience with the Opec members that have chosen a short-term self-interest policy in preference to Opec's and their own long-term interests. This has forced some countries to cut their production to unacceptable levels. Some Opec members who kept to their ceilings found themselves in a financial bottleneck. While others who didn't keep to the ceilings practised radicalism.'

Colonel Qaddafi read that interview and went wild.

It seems he took Yamani's remarks personally.

So he complained directly to Fahd.

Giving in to outside pressure, the king issued an official statement to say that the magazine report was not true.

Except that it was.

Saudi production had reached such a low level that further reductions were just about impossible. And they did up their production in March.

But by then BNOC had cut its prices by $3 to $30.50.

And Nigeria then cut its prices by $5.50 to $28.50.

And Nigel Lawson had triggered a price war.

Opec was looking at $30 oil when it met in London on 3 March.

Eleven brutal days later the group managed to agree to fix the price at $29.

Yamani sternly warned his colleagues that it was no good having an official Opec price if certain nations – he didn't have to name Nigeria – were then going to throw discounts into the deal and bring the prices below the benchmark anyway.

Saudi Arabia, he said, stood almost alone in continually refusing to do discounting deals with the intention of stealing a larger chunk of the market.

The British press reported the Opec meeting in minute detail.

What they didn't know was that during those 11 days 'certain representatives' of Opec had struck an informal deal with Nigel Lawson, exacting a promise from the British to help support the price by keeping production down to 2.1 mbd.

At his press conference after the meeting Yamani promised, 'Opec will be in the driver's seat again.'

From the back of the over-crowded main ballroom in London's Intercontinental Hotel a crusty, 75-year-old, New York oil trader named Harry Neustein heckled Yamani with, 'Sure, tell me about it.'

Yamani let the remark pass. He tried to continue.

But Neustein had ideas of his own. 'Oil is becoming a rag trade again,' he shouted at the Saudi oil minister. 'The small traders are back in where they belong. We are the new oil ministers.'

If nothing else, Neustein's antics did reinforce the idea that the oil market was out of control and that even if Opec knew what to do it might not be able to pull it off.

Nigel Lawson, the man who didn't have official talks with Yamani, was suddenly concerned enough to go to Riyadh.

For unofficial talks of course.

'The oil market now has a healthier tone,' Lawson acknowledged. 'We will definitely get an increase in the demand for oil.'

But not that week.

Or even that year.

Nigel Lawson was named Chancellor of the Exchequer and Peter Walker took his place at Energy.

By the end of 1983, with discounting still going on and pressure on prices to come down, Yamani again appealed to Britain to cooperate in keeping prices firm.

Yamani asked Walker not to increase North Sea production.

Walker responded that Great Britain did not plan any increase on its current production, which was then running at 2.4 mbd.

That was already 300,000 barrels a day more than had been informally promised.

In August 1984, on his way to Wales to accept his honorary doctorate, Yamani stopped in London for a secret meeting with Peter Walker.

The speech he'd written for Wales asserted that a new round of price cuts would induce serious problems in the world banking community, damage sterling and could mean the shutting down of some North Sea fields.

In the private session with Walker he made the very same points.

Yamani said that, should the price of oil fall below $25, Venezuela and Mexico would have trouble repaying their debts to American banks.

That would undoubtedly cause havoc in the foreign exchange markets and damage the pound.

He reminded Walker that North Sea oil was expensive enough to produce and that declining prices could fatally damage the British oil industry.

He pointed out that all of this would surely reverberate badly in the City.

Evidently, Walker got the message.

The next day, under Walker's instructions, the Department's number two, Alick Buchanan-Smith, wrote a secret letter to BNOC's eight major customers begging them to respect the formal price levels set by BNOC.

It was an unprecedented step.

But then Yamani had found the government's weak point.

There was no way that Mrs Thatcher, Nigel Lawson or Peter Walker wanted to risk a crisis which would threaten sterling.

Of course the Department of Energy denied any 'understandings' with Opec or Yamani, or that anyone from the Department sent letters with lightly veiled threats to BNOC's clients.

At least temporarily, Yamani's visit to Walker had paid off.

Spot prices held steady.

What worried Yamani was that, deep down, he knew it was only temporary.

* * * *

Before the year was out, British North Sea production was up to 2.6 mbd. The market was flooded and yet some countries were still overproducing. Frustrated, Yamani felt he simply had to drive home the message that it was in everyone's interest to keep oil prices stable.

He went to Cairo and met with President Mubarak. Egypt is too minor a producer to be an Opec member. But that didn't mean Yamani cared to look the other way when they dropped 50 cents off their crude and dissociated themselves from the cartel's policies. More significantly perhaps, this was the first formal meeting of an Egyptian President with a Saudi cabinet minister since the Camp David Agreements in 1979.

He also went to Malaysia, Indonesia, Mexico and Australia.

Nigeria announced a $2 cut in prices, so he rushed off there to try to convince the military regime that they were playing with fire – that they could trigger a price war which might be fatal.

They didn't believe him.

Neither did the Norwegians, as Statoil followed the Nigerians by knocking $1.50 off its North Sea oil.

'He came to Oslo for two days,' says Kaare Kristiansen who was the Energy Minister at the time. 'He was always stressing that oil-producing countries should stand together and show solidarity to each other. He also thought we should in some way be connected with Opec. But that wasn't our policy at all because we are associate members of the IEA and you cannot be both.'

Yamani desperately wanted to make the Norwegian minister realize that the $1.50 price cut was unnecessary.

But Kristiansen wasn't any easier to persuade than the Nigerian generals.

'The problem was that our buyers knew the formal price in Opec was not the real one. They weren't willing to pay our state oil company a higher price than they were willing to pay other producers.'

The way Kristiansen saw it, Opec brought these hard times upon itself.

'By using mixed oil grades and netbacks and barter deals, they'd undermined the pricing system themselves. We in Norway have no possibility of making such tricks so we have to put the real price on our long-term contracts. We cannot hide that the real price is lower than the formal price.'

Yamani wasn't prepared to agree with his opinions of Opec, although Kristiansen did discover they had at least two things in common.

God.

And dried fish.

'He's a very easy going man,' says Kristiansen, 'and rather pious. As I'm a believing Christian and he is a believing Moslem, we exchanged opinions about that. There he seemed to be very understanding. Two believers, even if they believe in different religions, share a great deal.'

As for the fish, Kristiansen had picked Yamani up at the airport to bring him to a government guest house. On the way into town, Yamani asked his host about a Norwegian delicacy called dried fish. It's a heavily salted cod fish that is specially dried on the mountains along the sea. He said that as a boy he'd eaten such fish in Saudi Arabia and that getting some now would be a very nostalgic experience. Kristiansen promised to see what he could arrange.

He dropped Yamani at the guest house and gave him some time to settle in.

When he returned a little while later Yamani wasn't there.

He'd already asked the guest house staff if they knew where he could get some dried fish.

They told him.
And so he went out alone to buy some.

* * * *

The Saudis were slipping deeper and deeper into trouble.

Fahd's 1983/84 budget listed cuts unilaterally across the board. Defence, down 18.5 per cent. Manpower development, down 12.8 per cent. Social development, down 20.1 per cent. Transport and communications, down 23.3 per cent. Economic resources, down 40.1 per cent. Infrastructure, down 18.1 per cent. Municipal services, down 27.3 per cent. Administration, down 5.5 per cent. Lending institutions, down 14.5 per cent. Domestic subsidies, down 19.2 per cent.

The country was simply not earning enough to pay for all the ambitions they had when the world was oil dry.

And in Saudi Arabia, turning back those spending programmes meant losing face. It also meant political discontent among people who had grown accustomed to having their raised standard of living expectations met.

In the middle of May 1983, Fahd began a reshuffling of his cabinet.

A rumour leaked out of the closed-door palaces of the Al Fahd that Yamani was to be replaced as oil minister.

Out of respect for his 21 years of service he would become a special adviser on foreign affairs.

A Beirut newsletter, the *Arab Report and Memo*, said that his replacement would be Hisham Nazer.

When it didn't happen right away the rumour-mongers promised, it will.

It was the closest they'd come so far to being right.

In April 1984 the Saudi Health Minister, Dr Ghazi al Gosaibi, was fired.

Often referred to as one of the most efficient technocrats in Fahd's cabinet, he was also sometimes referred to as one of the most powerful non-royals in the kingdom.

Gossaibi was a reformer who didn't hide his feelings about corruption in the government. For example, he didn't like the way Prince Sultan doled out defence contracts and he said so.

Then he published a poem in a newspaper criticising the king.

He was history within hours.

He only learned of his firing when he heard about it on the radio.

Privately, Yamani had been saying for years that all government officials should be required to make an annual declaration of wealth. He felt that might slow down some of the kick-backs and commissions that come out of deals finagled by so many people in Saudi Arabia simply by knowing how to work from within the kingdom's labyrinthine bureacracy.

But such disclosures would never sit well with the Saudi royal family. After all, they get their percentage of the action too. So Yamani was, at various times, quietly reminded that he had enough to worry about with the oil business.

All the more so now that the oil business wasn't so good.

The Saudis were in trouble.

And so was Yamani.

20

The Firing – the Inside Story

HIS DAYS were numbered.

And he knew it.

In July 1985, without saying anything to anyone about it, Yamani began to remove all of his personal papers from the ministry.

He took his personal files and set up three private offices.

There's one in Jeddah to handle his affairs in Saudi Arabia.

There's a small office in Geneva, staffed by just a couple of people, to look after his bills, his expenses, staff salaries and a few investments.

And then there's a larger office in London.

He says it handles 'research and servicing' of his various projects.

By July 1985 he was already planning his exit.

The royal family never said so in public, but everyone in Saudi Arabia and everyone in the oil business and everyone with any banking connections in the Middle East knew what King Fahd and his brothers were telling each other when they were alone.

The country was on the verge of going broke.

The way they reckoned, Yamani should be able to get them out of these difficulties. All he has to do is tell the other members of Opec that Saudi Arabia is demanding a larger cut of the action. All he has to do is say, as of right now Saudi Arabia is upping its oil production and upping its oil prices and, just like that, with a wave of Yamani's magic wand, the good times will roll again.

What worried Yamani was that the real world doesn't work like that.

He desperately wanted to keep Opec together, but under the stress of the oil glut the already splintered 13–member cartel was visibly cracking at the seams.

His prophecy of doom was coming true.

Time and time again, ensconced behind closed doors, Yamani

restated his case that Opec's only chance of survival was a united front. That as a group they simply had to cut back on production. That they had to sit tight until the glut dried up. That any country not abiding by its imposed production quota was doing so to the detriment of the group.

But too many of the members were in desperate economic shape. They needed money, and oil was the only way they had of getting it. Then again, only some of the ministers could grasp Yamani's argument that, in this case, less is more. That, in this case, the only sure way to higher revenues was through lower production.

The ones who didn't understand accused Saudi Arabia of not caring about the rest of Opec because Saudi Arabia could best afford to wait out the glut.

Yamani kept his cool.

Not everyone else bothered.

At one meeting the oil minister from the United Arab Emirates lost his temper and openly accused the Nigerians of cheating on their quotas. The Nigerian minister shouted back. The other ministers took sides. Insults were exchanged. Yamani begged for some calm. That's when the UAE minister shoved himself back from the table, stood up, bellowed at the Nigerian minister, 'You are stabbing Opec in the back', and stormed out of the meeting.

It was left to Yamani to clean up, to stand in front of the television cameras and newspaper reporters and news magazine writers who covered his every word and looked for nuances in his every grin. 'This is not the first time that we have not been unanimous,' Yamani mumbled, in gross understatement, putting on a brave face. 'And it will not be the last.'

Prices continued to fall.

So did confidence in the market.

The official Opec ceiling was 16 mbd, and each member had an agreed quota. But agreements inside Opec aren't always worth the paper they're printed on.

Nigeria was desperate for income and even if it was willing at this point to sign $28 a barrel contracts on the table, it was also fast to do deep-discount deals under the table. Nor was Nigeria alone. The spot markets were alive with discounts from Algeria and Libya. There was plenty of bargaining room too with Iraq and Iran, both of whom needed oil revenue to continue their extremely bloody war of attrition.

In addition, the world was still awash with discounted non-Opec oil from England, Norway and Mexico.

As each barrel came onto the market below the official price, Saudi Arabia slipped deeper and deeper into financial trouble.

When the price of oil nudged down to around $27 a barrel, Yamani telephoned his fellow ministers and he went to see them and he lobbied them one by one. 'If we increase production, prices will start dropping. But don't think that they will come down to $26 or $25. They will not come down gradually. Prices will drop sharply to something below $20. There will be no limitation to the downward price spiral. The urgent problem is discipline.'

Despite his pleas, only Saudi Arabia seemed to be playing the game by the pre-established rules.

It was a buyers' market in the purest sense. The oil companies were fat enough that they could afford to sit around, waiting for prices to fall further. And everyone knew they would. Yamani couldn't even talk up the market the way he was able to in the old days when a word from him or a subtle wink could bring about a price movement.

He tried by telling some reporters, 'The world crude oil market cannot worsen further. We will not allow prices to go down any more.'

But before long Norway cut its prices and so did Britain, and the Nigerians continued to produce over their quota and the Libyans and the Iranians and the Iraqis did too.

He tried again with, 'I think the possibility of improving the situation is much better now than before.'

Nobody believed him this time either.

The buyers stayed at home.

Downward pressure on the price increased.

Now Yamani came up with another tack. By his own count there were two million barrels per day too many pouring onto the market. To support the $27–28 price, he knew he had to get that excess oil off the market. But cutting back that much on his own production would in effect take Saudi Arabia out of the oil business. So, he decided, if production can't be cut to create a price, then prices have to be cut to support production. In other words, the price of oil has to keep coming down if Saudi Arabia is going to sell any of its own. He knew that wouldn't make him very popular with the Opec members who were overproducing to keep their own economies afloat. But it would teach them a lesson. And, he was convinced, teaching some of them a lesson was long overdue.

His message to his Opec partners was simple. 'If you do not fall into line with agreed production quotas, Saudi Arabia will abandon its role as the swing producer.'

The cheaters went right on doing their own thing.

In August, Yamani put the cartel on notice again.

Again, nothing much happened.

With his own credibility severely on the line, Yamani turned to

Aramco and the 'netback' – a complicated way of arriving at the price of crude. Instead of pricing oil in the usual manner – by supply and demand in the open market the day the oil comes out of the well – netbacks established a price based on the aggregate weighted value that a basket of refined products would fetch 40–50 days after the crude is lifted from the ground, minus various costs such as transportation and refining. These netback deals produced an attractive market-related price for Saudi oil, the Saudis guaranteed supply for at least six months, and Yamani's refiners could count on a guaranteed margin of profit regardless of the volatile market. The Aramco partners could buy oil at discounts of up to a couple of dollars per barrel. And the Saudis increased their share of the market without resorting to the threatened production increase.

Yet Yamani's threat was still on the table.

He promised to make good on it if he was pushed too far.

A price war was in the offing and everybody knew it.

No one could deny that Yamani and the Saudis were acting entirely in their own national self-interest. They had cash reserves then of an estimated $100 billion. But, sticking to 2.3 mbd at $27, those reserves would disappear in about three years. They were better off, by simple mathematics, selling, say, 4.3 mbd at $20.

Word went out around the oil and banking communities of the west, 'The Saudis are for real this time.'

One American oil analyst put it even more bluntly. He said, 'Yamani has simply run out of room to manoeuvre.'

The market believed him this time and in very real terms he'd succeeded in talking up the price of oil. By the sheer force of his personality and with the power of Saudi Arabia behind him, oil prices started rising.

At one point they hit $29.

But Yamani, of all people, knew how fragile the situation was.

Yamani knew the oil market could collapse at any time.

As it happened, it was sooner rather than later.

* * * *

In November 1986 Yamani tried to intervene in a barter deal with the British.

Saudi Arabia's Defence Minister, Prince Sultan, had hoped to buy 132 military aircraft – 72 Tornado fighters, 36 Hawk trainers and 24 turbo-prop trainers – plus spares, hangars and pilot training, from Great Britain, paying part of the £3–4 billion price tag with oil.

Yamani argued with Fahd and Sultan that dumping so much excess oil onto the market would have an adverse effect on prices.

He must have made his point because a few days later he announced to the press that oil would 'most probably' not now figure in the deal.

It was the right thing for his country.

However, by not minding his own business he stepped on some Sudairi toes.

After all, the middleman's 15 per cent commission on £3–4 billion is £450–600 million.

Yamani won't discuss this.

But other people will.

According to a very senior oil company executive in London, this transaction was not exactly a straight barter deal. The British government, anxious for the sale, pressured BP and Shell to lift enough Saudi crude to pay for the planes. The Saudis then turned those funds over to British Aerospace.

Based on information that a London source has provided, together with information from a non-Saudi Middle Eastern oil executive and information obtained under the Freedom of Information Act from Washington, it turns out that voicing his opinion about the deal for British fighter jets was not the first time Yamani got in the Sudairis' way.

In 1984, with the oil market already glutted, Prince Sultan, as aviation minister and chairman of Saudia Airlines, was forced to accept 10 new Boeing 747s with Rolls-Royce engines.

Petroleum Intelligence Weekly revealed that the king ordered Yamani to open the pumps and deliberately exceed their Opec quota by enough oil to pay £1 billion for the planes. *PIW* then quoted Fahd saying to Yamani, 'And don't tell Opec.'

In Fahd's mind, obviously, the jumbos wouldn't actually cost anything. It wasn't as if they were paying for the planes with real money. It was only oil that would otherwise have stayed in the ground.

Yamani's objection was that 34.5 million barrels of extra oil would be floating around the marketplace, feeding the glut and helping to depress prices even further.

Except that in this instance, Fahd knew exactly where the oil would go. In a rare exception to the traditional oil barter deal, instead of letting Rolls-Royce and Boeing sell the oil to anyone they wanted, Saudi middlemen stipulated that it would have to go to buyers they'd name. It was, the middlemen said, to protect Rolls and Boeing from taking too big a risk on the price of oil. It was, more likely, because the middlemen were cut in on that side of the deal too.

When news reached Fleet Street that a barter deal was in the works,

UK Energy Minister Peter Walker warned his staff that no one was to say anything to anyone, on or off the record.

Nor were many 'inside' details forthcoming from Saudia Airlines, Rolls-Royce, Boeing or the middlemen.

Regardless of the fact that the 10 new Boeing 747–300s doubled the size of Saudia's jumbo fleet overnight and that they didn't actually need the planes in the first place, Rolls-Royce made out, Boeing made out and so did the Saudi royal family.

According to a very reliable source with heavyweight connections to Walker's former ministry, the agents for the deal were Fahd's favourite brothers-in-law, Abdul Aziz and Khaled – the bin Ibrahim boys – whose father was Governor of Bal Jourashi in the Western Province and whose sister is Fahd's main wife.

Also according to that British source, the bin Ibrahims have a very special silent partner.

The way the story goes – and this has now been confirmed in documents filed with at least two US government agencies and obtained under the Freedom of Information Act – the bin Ibrahim pair are merely front men for the business interests of Fahd's (and their sister's) teenaged son, Prince Abdul Aziz.

At 15, the boy is easily the wealthiest high schooler in the world.

Thanks to the middlemen skills of his two uncles, and the near-neurotic doting of his father, he might even be a candidate for the richest man in the world.

As middlemen in the 747 deal, the Ibrahims were entitled to a legitimate 10 per cent commission.

That comes to $100 million.

By setting up the companies to buy the bartered oil, and by keeping it secret long enough for those companies to move 34.5 million barrels into an already flooded marketplace before anyone realized it, the likelihood is that the bin Ibrahims were cut in there as well.

How much of that they were allowed to keep for themselves, no one outside Fahd's immediate family will ever know. Or if they do know, they'll never say. But the largest share of it went straight into the bank account of Fahd's son.

One version of the story, popular around the Boeing Corporation, is that the teenager netted as much as £400 million in commissions on the deal. And that doesn't include the gift of a 50-metre (165 foot) Boeing hydrofoil boat. That same source at Boeing suggests that, when Prince Sultan objected to the 747 deal on sound commercial grounds, saying that Saudia didn't need the planes, the young Abdul Aziz had very little trouble convincing his father to overrule his uncle.

273

What is known to everyone who had anything at all to do with the deal is that Yamani was vehemently against it.

In fact, word around Opec is that Yamani objected so strongly that the bin Ibrahims prudently waited until he was out of the country before doing it.

Yamani's objections, it must be said, had nothing to do with who got what kickbacks. That's all part of business in the Middle East and Yamani would understand that's how the game is played. He was simply disturbed that all this oil would be coming onto the market at exactly the wrong time. On top of that, he didn't appreciate the fact that the national Treasury would not benefit by even a single rial in exchange for $1 billion worth of oil.

Another knowledgeable source, this one in Washington, confirms, 'Yamani fought them on that 747 deal. He understood that if you pay out a lot of oil for airplanes and dump that oil onto the market, it's got to have an effect on price. But Fahd and his brothers wouldn't be able to make that connection. You see, the Saudis are very odd from a rational, western, business standpoint. They don't comprehend that there's always a connection between this and that. Yamani was opposed to all of these barter deals. Fundamentally he cared for the market, about which he was arrogant enough to think of himself as the chief pundit.'

As it happens this wasn't the first or last time that Fahd and his family had circumvented the Treasury.

A few years ago Fahd worked out a deal with his pal John Latsis.

As a Latsis associate delicately explains, the king wanted a new refinery and some new ports. Latsis agreed to take oil in lieu of cash. The only problem was that Latsis did the deal when oil prices were high. He got caught red-handed by the glut. Since doing the deal he's been forced to store expensive oil until he can somehow recoup his very serious losses.

Nor was the 747 deal the first or the last time Prince Abdul Aziz made any money.

When the king visited Great Britain in the spring of 1987, his son came with him. It was revealed in the British press at the time that Prince Abdul Aziz had just received a cash gift from his dad of $300 million.

At almost the same time, it was discovered, dad came up with an even more unique gift.

He gave his son a hospital in the heart of Mecca, across a corner from the Grand Mosque.

But hospitals have got to be small potatoes to the teenaged businessman. Especially when the source at Boeing insists that Prince

Abdul Aziz might have made as much as $1.6 billion in commissions on the Tornado deal with British Aerospace.

If that's true, it would easily stand alongside the largest commissions in history.

However, because certain members of the family objected, the Boeing source adds, the teenager is believed to have split one-fourth of his commission with two of his cousins (both Sultan's sons) – Prince Bandar, who is the Saudi Arabian Ambassador to the United States, and Prince Khaled, Chief of the Saudi Arabian Air Force.

And still those deals are only the tip of the iceberg.

Some time in the late 1970s, explains a well-respected Egyptian journalist, an engineering professor at the University of Petroleum and Mineral, named Nassir al-Rashid, and a Lebanese accountant working in Riyadh, named Rafiq Hariri, formed a company called Rashid Engineering. They soon joined forces with a French construction company called Oger and created a new entity known as Saudi-Oger.

Their first important deal was the construction of the Al-Massara hotel in Taif. It was so successful that Messrs al-Rashid and Hariri were able to buy out their French partners. Once they did that, they went about building government hotels, office complexes and palaces. Oddly, none of the work they got was ever put out to tender, as is government policy. The Egyptian journalist contends it was always negotiated directly between Saudi-Oger and King Fahd.

Someone formerly associated with the French company before it joined forces with Hariri and al-Rashid explains that, on paper, Saudi-Oger is 100 per cent owned by Hariri and merely has a working relationship with al-Rashid. In reality, when a project is implemented it's on a cost-plus basis and the profits from Saudi-Oger projects are divided this way: Hariri 20 per cent, al-Rashid 20 per cent, Prince Abdul Aziz 60 per cent.

Again, none of the teenager's business dealings especially concerned Yamani, except that so many of the deals were being bartered with oil.

Because they took place during the glut – known in more proper terms around the kingdom as 'the cash-flow crisis' – most of the young prince's barter deals were tied into defence projects so they could then be explained away as 'strategically necessary'.

Enter here a disgruntled member of the Saudi royal family who feels the time has finally come to speak out.

'The lower national budget has meant that for these activities, which all come above stated government finances, their strategic flavour has to be accentuated. Speed in these deals is of the essence, especially when it comes to recouping the commissions. The use of oil is most important as it confuses the real contract values and enables the kingdom to pay for these projects while stalling other less-important creditors in Saudi Arabia.'

Yamani must have known what he was doing when he took on the role of main adversary to these glut-period barter deals.

It has been suggested by some people in Saudi Arabia that Yamani argued with the king that barter deals were ruining the economy, that cheap oil was flooding the market, that none of the money for this oil was going into the Treasury and that this sort of business was going to bankrupt the country.

The royal Saudi confirms that on several occasions Yamani is known to have told Fahd and Sultan that he simply could not be party to any of this. 'King Fahd grew increasingly displeased with his oil minister as Yamani consistently opposed these barter deals. King Fahd did not need a minister who would interfere in so-called "vital strategic" matters. Anyway, the king was believing less and less in Yamani's price war policy which meant more oil was being pumped to reach the same targets in the barter deals. In other words, Yamani was becoming a nuisance.'

By mid-1985 the king decided Yamani had to go.

Everyone in Saudi Arabia knew that Fahd liked the idea of making Hisham Nazer the oil minister.

Everyone in Saudi Arabia also knew that Nazer wanted to be petroleum minister ever since he'd first started working as a secretary to Abdullah Tariki in 1958.

Two years younger than Yamani, he's a handsome man with a thick black moustache, a bright smile and a Master's Degree in Political Science from the University of California at Los Angeles.

Until now he'd always been in Yamani's shadow.

The Minister of Planning could never be in the same league internationally as the Minister of Petroleum.

What's more, Fahd knew, Nazer wouldn't raise a stink about barter deals or get involved with the Sudairi Seven's family affairs.

As importantly, Nazer carried with him the stamp of approval of all the right people.

According to a highly reliable western intelligence source, and confirmed by that member of the Saudi royal family, there is in the kingdom today a Masonic-like organization known as Fataa Nejd.

Supposedly not unlike the Italian P–2, which had strong links with the Vatican and found itself tied to the Banco Ambrosiano scandal which left Roberto Calvi hanging dead under Blackfriars Bridge across the Thames, this group is centred around powerful men from the Nejd – the Riyadh area – who share strong views with the king.

Again according to these two sources, the de facto leader of the group is Aba al-Khail, Fahd's Minister of Finance.

Over the past ten years, al-Khail has reconstructed the kingdom's financial bureaucracy by installing a 'financial controller' in every government ministry.

This 'financial controller' happens to be a lodge member.

The result is that the Fataa Nejd wields the final veto over the Saudi government by controlling the money that makes every ministry work.

Or, more simply stated, al-Khail has made it his business to see that every branch of the government, including certain aspects of the kingdom's banking system, has in effect become a sub-ministry of the king's purser.

The only office that seems to have escaped this reorganization was Aramco.

The reason for that, says the royal Saudi, is because Yamani wouldn't have it.

'By getting in the way of the Fataa Nejd,' he goes on, 'Yamani not only upset Fahd who had approved it, he also ran up against a secretive, influential force of men from the Nejd who wouldn't necessarily care to see a Hijazi impede their plans to seize and hold the ultimate rule of Saudi Arabia.'

And all this time Hisham Nazer was known to be acceptable to the Fataa Nejd.

So Fahd, Sultan and Salman plotted to get rid of Yamani.

Of course Fahd could have simply fired Yamani and no explanations would have been necessary.

But Sultan and Salman came up with a better idea.

Salman had recently purchased a group of Arab periodicals published in the west. The most efficient way to eliminate Yamani, they decided, would be to discredit him in the world press. It would make his 'holier than thou' attitude a national joke.

According to that royal Saudi, the three Sudairi brothers spent over a year trying to get something on Yamani, trying to come up with anything at all that could ruin him.

By the autumn of 1986 they gave up.

Despite all of their resources and all of their efforts, they found nothing.

*   *   *   *

Once oil dropped below $27, it sank like a stone.

The momentum was incredible.

The world's most important commodity lost two thirds of its value in under nine months.

There was nothing any one person could do to stop it.

Yamani tried and failed.

By the time he got to the Opec meeting in October 1986, he knew he might not be attending too many more.

Increased production and $18 a barrel.

Not even a royal decree could make that happen.

Throughout the meeting Yamani made statements which Fahd, at home in Riyadh, then contradicted.

Increased production and $18 a barrel.

Yamani insisted it was impossible.

Fahd believed his minister should be more enthusiastic in advancing the views of his king.

Ever talkative, Fahd is reported to have said in a meeting of the Council of Ministers in September 1986 – as related by a minister who was there to an American friend – 'Instead of Yamani coming to me with oil policy, trying to convince me and let me say yes, I have to go to him, to try to convince him, and he says no.'

More than a month later, the king himself admitted to at least one person outside his most immediate circle that during the October Opec meeting he'd sent a cable to Yamani. He wanted Yamani to sign a statement proposing to fix the price of oil at $18 and to allow the Saudis to up their quota.

Yamani refused.

According to a US State Department source with several years experience in Saudi Arabia, Yamani said he would issue the statement with the king's name on the bottom of it if the king insisted, but that he would not put it in the name of the petroleum ministry.

As it happened, the policy Fahd was advocating was the very same one he'd worked out with Agazadeh, the Iranian oil minister.

Yamani repeated that it simply couldn't succeed.

A fellow Opec minister who saw Yamani daily throughout the gruelling 16–day October session and claims to have seen the cable from Fahd, adds that Agazadeh then poured salt onto the wound by pointing out to King Fahd that his own minister wouldn't do what he was being ordered to.

Fahd evidently agreed that this was just one more instance where Yamani had gone too far.

The Opec meeting broke up on Wednesday, 22 October.

Yamani returned to Saudi Arabia and, it was reported in the press, met with Fahd on at least two occasions over the next seven days.

278

The nature of their discussions at that point has never been revealed.

But on Wednesday night, October 29, the announcement was made on Saudi television that Yamani had been fired.

What happened that night, how Yamani heard the announcement and his reaction to it, instantly became a favourite topic of conversation around the dinner tables of Riyadh.

The story goes like this.

Yamani was playing cards.

And he was losing.

He seemed distracted and kept turning around to watch the television set, almost as if he was waiting for something to happen.

Then the evening news came on.

Some people in the room were said to have been shocked by the announcement.

But Yamani is said to have sighed deeply, as if a great weight had finally been lifted from his shoulders.

He went right back to his card game.

And now he started winning.

The story hit the front pages around the world over the next few days.

In the United States, someone who knows Yamani well sums up what happened.

'Zaki clearly understood that all of these other oil producers had to be taught a lesson. Well, he taught them half a lesson before his departure. But the king wasn't prepared to lose that much revenue in order to indulge in pedagogy. He didn't understand at all. The king is totally confused. He doesn't grasp that there's a relationship between price and quantity. He thought the reason prices had fallen was because Zaki was talking them down.'

Another aspect of Yamani's problems with Fahd, he feels, had to do with his own self-confidence.

'He was not as inclined as most Saudis are to grovel before the king. It was partly Zaki's self-confidence, but in this case it was compounded by the desire of the Iranians to get him. They went to Riyadh twice, once in July when the king arranged for the position that Yamani ultimately accepted in the Opec discussions. And once in October. Fahd sent that cable and Yamani wouldn't sign it. We now know that Agazadeh went back to the king and said, this is one fine representative you have there, he won't even accept your words. That was the end. He was effectively fired the next day.'

Calling Yamani 'the most independently minded of the technocrats', the American says it's easy to see what the world can expect from Yamani's successor.

'The job is not one that warrants a lot of independent statements on the part of ministers. Hisham Nazer hears the king saying "the low oil price is over and it's Zaki's fault and I want $18 a barrel". But he's not going to say, "Look Mr Fahd, we knew each other before you became king, when you were a playboy in Paris and I want to tell you this is more complicated than you think." First of all, that would remind the king of Yamani. Secondly it requires a good deal of guts. So what does he do? He says, "Right, I'm going to get you the $18 price." And he did. But it depended on cutting their production by 1 mbd. And who knows if he even told the king he had to cut production to get it. It's kind of lost in the tall weeds. The king wants revenue and he wants a high price but he doesn't want to sacrifice production. So they tell him he's getting it, even if he isn't. Nobody comes along and says, "Your majesty, come off it." Yamani did and he got fired.'

Within a few weeks of Yamani's firing, word leaked out of Saudi Arabia that he was under virtual house arrest.

The king had instructed the Ministry of Interior to make certain that Yamani did not leave the country. All the border posts were alerted.

At first there was even trouble when Yamani tried to fly from Riyadh to Jeddah. But a phone call at the airport to a high official in Riyadh quickly solved that. The rule was, Yamani would be allowed to travel freely inside Saudi Arabia, but Fahd wanted to be certain he didn't leave. Presumably Fahd didn't want Yamani bad-mouthing Saudi oil policy.

Not that he necessarily would have.

He is still, to this day, totally silent when it comes to discussing his personal relationship with Fahd, his last few years in government and his firing.

No amount of prodding, coercing or even begging can get him to open up.

But when the story broke in the west that Yamani was denied the right to travel, that too hit the front pages.

Fahd is a man who can't stand up to public criticism, so when he saw those press reports they were quickly amended with the news that, 'This is not true. Sheikh Yamani is perfectly free to travel as he wishes.'

The restriction was hurriedly rescinded.

Yamani spent part of that winter at the ski resort in Switzerland before getting himself used to the fact that 28 years later it was all over.

'In some ways I guess,' says Sir John Wilton, 'Yamani became a victim of his own media. The royals are always worried about the overmighty subject. Or about anybody thinking he's indispensable. Which of the brothers actually got him? There's no way of really knowing because nobody is present when the family takes decisions of that sort. When Sultan or Salman finally decides it's time to put the knife in and goes to Fahd and tells him, nobody else is there.'

Some people say Yamani's pro-western stand was the reason he got fired.

But not Wilton. 'They pick on the westernization of Yamani as the excuse. You always must find something to complain about. But no, Yamani didn't cease to be the oil minister because some chaps objected to women lawyers in his office. It was a question of oil policy. I'm not contesting the view that his public image was bound to provide pretexts for burying him one of these days. Charles I didn't get his head chopped off because of his little idiosyncracies. He got his head chopped off because the policy was unacceptable.'

Other people think Yamani simply hung on too long. That a quarter of a century in the same job is too much.

At the same time there are those who believe that Fahd should have at least given Yamani the chance to retire.

One person who admits to being very surprised at the firing is the man Yamani replaced, Abdullah Tariki.

'Yes, I was surprised. I felt that after 24 years as the oil minister he should be made oil minister for life. But I don't think he was a very good minister, because he was a yes man. He was the type that suits the government.'

Obviously he didn't suit King Fahd's style of government.

And the Kuwaiti petroleum minister, Sheikh Ali Khalifa al-Sabah, says he will be missed.

'He is an exceptional man. As far as Opec is concerned, of course we miss him a great deal. We are talking about a man of foresight, of wisdom, of great diplomatic tact and of experience. He contributed to the long-term strength of the organization.'

One of America's foremost independent oilmen, Oscar Wyatt of Coastal Corp, agrees with al-Sabah.

'Prior to Fahd taking a position in oil, Zaki was probably the most important man in the Middle East. To me, he represented a degree of stability. I consider the loss of Zaki Yamani from the world oil scene as a pretty serious happening.'

So does James Schlesinger.

'He was the smart one. He looks at the world and learns from experience. Why did the power of the cartel weaken? Because the cartel overshot its goals, over the protest of one Zaki Yamani. Prices would never have been $35 a barrel if he'd had his way.'

So does James Nasmyth of *Petroleum Argus*.

'Many Arabs feel they have some sort of divine right, or that they've been done some sort of cosmic injustice, and that the west owes them. But Yamani was never like that. He was the exception. He understood the marketplace. He was always able to state his mind clearly. He was always to the point. Many of the others are just a lot of hot air. Yamani was always the exception.'

And so does Ian Seymour at the *Middle East Economic Survey*.

'He leaves a gaping hole.'

Obviously he does and Opec hasn't been the same since.

Of course the show will keep running.

But it probably won't get the big reviews any more.

It probably won't be a standing room only affair the way it used to be.

Not now.

Not any more.

The star is gone.

21

An Epilogue

THE ESTATE in Surrey, about an hour's drive from London, is well hidden from the road.

If you don't know where to look it's easy to miss the big, heavy gates.

Even if you do know where they are, they only open automatically when you're expected.

And then, as your car pulls along a shrub-lined gravel driveway that winds a good distance up to the house, one or two of his bodyguards casually step out of the gate-keeper's cottage just to make absolutely certain you are who you said you were.

It's a Tudor, sixteenth-century mansion that the Yamanis fully restored to the period, then added a modern wing on to the rear.

They bought it in 1978 for £500,000.

There's a vast diningroom with a huge open hearth, and a large livingroom that shows their preference for French furniture, and smaller rooms off the narrow, low-ceilinged hallway – a television room and a book-lined study where he has an antique desk and some antique chairs and a stack of papers waiting to be read.

But the place where he and Tammam and their children and their guests spend most of their time is at the end of the hallway in the new family room that's something like their livingroom in Taif – a large open space with an indoor swimming pool.

It is, they both believe, the most beautiful of all their homes.

Yamani is wearing an open-necked shirt, sitting on the couch next to Tammam, in front of the television set, with his daughter Mai and her husband and their children and a collection of family friends. The video runs an American sit-com. Someone pours more tea and offers a plate of cakes. Everyone is talking to everyone else.

Except Yamani.

He's fiddling with a small portable shortwave radio that he carries with him wherever he is in the world.

First he listens to the hourly news on the BBC World Service. Then he plays with the digital frequency selector to get the news in Arabic from the Middle East.

Once that's over, he excuses himself to move into his study.

Now, leaning back in the chair behind his desk, with one foot propped up on a cushion, he talks about the subject that has been his life . . . oil.

'In most cases, when anyone makes a forecast about the future, the present situation reflects itself in that forecast. When there's a surplus in the market, you tend to see the future in that light. When there's a shortage, it's perhaps understandably difficult to talk about a surplus in the future without facing a barrage of disbelief.'

Putting the shortwave radio down, he toys with a silver-topped wooden cane.

'Some time in mid-1978 I said that we did not think that we would ever face a shortage in the supply of oil. But the shortage in the supply of oil was with us by the end of 1978 because of a political event. In 1979 we thought that we would never see an over-supply situation, that there would never be a surplus in the supply of oil. And therefore when I said at the end of 1979 that there would be a surplus in the supply of oil, someone said that I was out of my mind. But just look what happened.'

He raises his eyebrows to make his point.

'So I think we should not be really so relaxed right now and think that we will never again have a shortage in the supply of oil.'

These things are after all, he says, cyclical.

There's a natural cycle. In this case call it the petroleum variation of the corn-hog cycle. First you get a crisis. Then prices are posted up. Then you have a recession and a receding of demand and everyone says, oil glut. Then governments decide, we'll never let it happen again. Subsequently, because there's a glut, people get relaxed and demand builds up towards the capacity level and you set the stage for the next energy crisis.

And the next energy crisis, he promises, is less than ten years away.

'There will be a shortage. There's no doubt about that. How serious a shortage and the magnitude of it depends on the next three years. It may already be too late for the west because the west is always happy for the short-term benefits of low-priced oil. The glut has helped the western economies, this is true. But the ultimate results of short-term thinking will come later on and they will not be pleasant.'

An Epilogue

New York oil analyst Walter J. Levy believes Yamani is right.

'There will be a third crisis in the 1990s, for sure. By then the Arab oil producers will be in the driver's seat again. Production in the non-Opec world will be considerably less. And the only readily available huge source of new oil production will be in the Middle East. What's more, America is not doing much to prepare for this and that is scary. In the States we've been talking about a free market price for oil. But oil prices cannot be left to a completely free market. The price of oil should be at such a level that non-Opec countries can afford the cost of exploration. Personally I doubt that King Fahd knows anything about oil. I'm sure he thinks he knows but doesn't actually know what he's doing. At the moment things are going reasonably well so we don't know how much Yamani is missed. If and when the world becomes more in need of Arab oil, they could bring the prices back into the stratosphere, which could easily happen by the mid–1990s.'

Edward Fried at the Brookings Institute agrees.

'A third oil shock is possible but I think it will take a different form from the first two. It won't be quite as drastic, although any large supply interruption would cause fairly large short-term responses in the oil market. And a substantial short-term supply interruption could arise. Like another war or some drastic turn of events in the Middle East. After all, the majority of the world's oil reserves are held in a very few countries whose politics are uncertain, to say the least.'

But, he says, 'Don't misunderstand me. A number of things are different now than they were during the first two oil shocks. Firstly, we know a lot more. A lot of the damage that was done then was a result of our own policies. There was a scramble for supplies and almost all of the countries that tried it then were, almost by definition, unsuccessful. That is, they got supplied by paying higher prices. So we've learned. Second, there is a substantial amount of emergency stocks now, which we didn't have at all in the early '70s and damn little of it in 1979–1980. Third, the major oil producers have learned a lot too. Particularly moderates like the Saudis. They understand that the price of oil is elastic. By that I mean that, if prices rise sharply, there will be responses in demand over three to five years. This is a much more sophisticated game as played by both sides. They're much more knowledgeable.'

James Schlesinger isn't quite as optimistic.

'Today the United States has a de facto energy policy, which can be called "Growing Energy Dependence". By around 1990, according to current trends, we shall be importing nine million barrels a day and have reached for the first time in our history the 50 per cent dependency level. In the middle 1990s we shall require as much as 13 mbd of imports, if it is available. We are now sowing the seeds of the next energy crisis.'

And he, too, is well aware of the change that is about to come over Opec. 'By the early 1990s, we shall see a world oil market dominated by an "inner cartel", fewer in number than the present Opec, consisting of the principal Persian Gulf producers. Were Iran to crush Iraq, that inner cartel might itself be dominated by Iran. We're actually witnessing a curious race. Between the restoration of Opec's power over oil pricing and the erosion of America's oil production capacity. This is an entirely unsatisfactory situation.'

Yamani says this is absolutely true.

'I am concerned about the impact of a decline in the US oil industry. Considerable damage has already been done. It must stop. Otherwise America will be forced to rely on the Persian Gulf, which is a part of the world, I assure you, that you do not want to allow yourselves to rely upon. Some day, maybe as soon as the 1990s, Americans will look back and curse the officials who allowed this to happen.'

* * * *

There has not been a Soviet delegation stationed in Saudi Arabia since 1938 when Stalin ordered his ambassador home and had him shot.

Then again, oil wasn't as important to the Russians in 1938 as it's about to become.

'The Russians are right now sending something between 1.5 mbd and 2 mbd to the satellite countries. They will continue to produce and to export, but by the middle of the 1990s the satellites will require more than Russia can supply so the group as a whole will be net importers.'

The way Yamani reads the situation, although the Soviets are building coal and nuclear resources which could save them up to half a million barrels a day, their Eastern bloc allies are becoming a serious drain on their resources.

'The Russians only do barter deals with the satellites because the satellites can't get enough hard currency to buy oil any other way. It puts the Russians in a politically strong position over their allies. But while they certainly have enough oil for themselves, as long as they keep supplying the satellites, they will have to go looking for more oil at the very same moment that there will be a net shortage in the world. They will become net importers of oil just when the third oil crisis happens. That's why they're interested in the Gulf.'

He credits Gorbachev with being an intelligent man who came to power realizing that, by the mid-1990s, the Soviet Union could be bankrupt.

'Their defence budget is far too high. It's out of proportion with the rest of the economy. And, until Gorbachev came along, all of their best scientists, all of their best engineers, all of their brightest young students were being put to work in the defence industry simply to keep up with the arms race. If they were working on planes and missiles, they could not be working on factories or building a strong manufacturing base or helping to create a solid economic infrastructure to support the country in the years ahead.'

So Gorbachev needs to get his scientists and his engineers and the bright young students out of the missile factories and into other industries.

That, Yamani says, is what *glasnost* and the arms reductions deals are really all about.

'It is very clear that the Russians have to cut back spending on arms and get out of the arms race or they risk going broke by the mid-1990s when they have to import oil to support the satellites.'

That, says Yamani, opens up two dangerous possibilities.

'First, if Gorbachev's policy of moderation leads to an arms control treaty which makes the Europeans and the Japanese less fearful, then their need for a strong leader, i.e. the USA, will be gradually reduced. If at the same time Russia can become economically strong, then before long you might see a one-superpower world.'

Yamani's second worry is that, just in case Gorbachev can't turn the country around fast enough, the Russians are already starting to take a serious look at the Gulf.

He points out that, even before their occupation of Afghanistan, the Soviets built a road from Kabul straight down to Baluchistan, heading directly for the Arabian Sea.

It was constructed at enormous expense, cutting through largely uninhabitable and hostile terrain.

It's there, Yamani is convinced, for the express purpose of moving Soviet troops through Afghanistan to the mouth of the Gulf at the Hormuz Straights.

'Russian ambitions have not changed. They want to rule the Gulf. And because by the mid-1990s they will need oil for their satellites and because there will be an oil shortage in the world which could reach a crisis point, they will have no choice but to try to put an oilfield under their umbrella. What they want is to buy oil for roubles rather than dollars.'

They are, he goes on, already working hard at trying to increase their influence in the area. They are specifically moving closer to Iran by building stronger economic ties, which he says can reasonably be expected to lead to a stronger political relationship.

They have also cast a flirtatious eye towards Saudi Arabia.

In 1985, when King Fahd's son Faisal was in the Soviet Union with a Saudi Arabian soccer team, he was approached by Russian officials who told the prince, 'We have lost the key to our legation in Saudi Arabia. Might you have another?' It was their way of diplomatically saying, isn't it time we thawed the ice.

In January 1987, the newly installed Saudi oil minister went to Moscow to speak with the Russians. Hisham Nazer was there ostensibly to see if the Soviets could be persuaded to work with Opec in trying to get oil prices higher. But he also met with the Soviet Prime Minister, Nikolai Ryzhkov, and spent over two hours with the Foreign Minister, Edvard Shevardnadze.

He left with the Russians agreeing to a token cut in crude oil exports as a show of solidarity with Opec.

A month later in London, the Saudi Ambassador hosted a dinner for the Soviet Ambassador.

That was followed by the appearance of three Soviet diplomats at a London reception hosted by a Saudi magazine.

None of these things had ever happened before.

Since then, the Soviet Deputy Foreign Minister has made an official visit to Kuwait, the UAE and Oman.

Playing off the fall of the Shah, reminding the Gulf state leaders that the United States cannot be counted on to protect you should Iran win the war against Iraq, the Soviets are overtly romancing the Arabs.

They are also Iraq's biggest ally, having supplied it with billions of dollars worth of arms and aid.

And Yamani finds all this very worrying.

'The west is underestimating the threat. The simplest thing for the Russians to do when they get desperate for oil, which they will by the mid-1990s, is to conquer an oilfield. And if that happens, if they get a foothold in the Gulf, they will soon control the Gulf. We're now talking about World War III. So it is for the west to counter the Soviet's influence now. The oil-producing states cannot do it themselves. The Soviet threat makes even more urgent the need for a settlement of the Arab-Israeli conflict.'

* * * *

Henry Kissinger was coming to speak at Harvard and there was some sort of a protest group who planted a bomb but took the trouble to warn everyone that it was there.

'You understand,' Yamani says, 'there are a lot of Democrats who go to Harvard.'

The bomb went off in the empty hall before the speech and no one was hurt.

But the force of it blew down the false ceiling.

And some bundles crashed to the floor.

No one knew who put them there or how long they'd been there.

Inside was a huge collection of old photographs.

At first glance it was determined that they'd been taken in the Middle East, some time before the turn of the century.

But then they were studied more closely and experts at Harvard's Semitic Museum decided the photos were scenes of Jeddah, Mecca and Medina.

Yamani, who has always been intensely interested in supporting the Semitic Museum, was told about the photographs.

'I heard about these old photos, and realized they might be the earliest photos known of those three cities. So we had them printed using modern techniques. And to my absolute amazement, in one of them, we found that people were recording sound. These were very early photographs and the idea of recording sound at that point in time was fantastic.'

Obviously the photographer of that particular photo was long dead.

But Yamani decided it was worth a try to find any surviving members of the photographer's family.

So he encouraged the museum to embark on a worldwide search, which eventually led to Holland and the photographer's grandson.

As luck would have it, the grandson had some of these sound recordings.

And now Harvard University is convinced that they are the earliest recordings of sound known to man.

* * * *

If and when the third shock comes, the oil weapon could be rolled out again.

'Opec will be changed by then,' Yamani notes. 'By the mid-1990s it will be a different organization than it is now. Some members will disappear as exporters of oil. The bulk of Opec's oil will come from the Gulf. The Arab oil producers will find themselves in a very powerful position. Oil as a political instrument has already been used once with success. This time no one would have to use it. They would just have to talk about it. The west has not forgotten.'

Nor have the Arabs forgotten that there is still a dispute going on with Israel.

And that the Americans continue to support Israel.

And that the Al Aqsa mosque in Jerusalem is still denied them.

'There are two kinds of oil weapons,' James Schlesinger says. 'People keep mixing these things up. One kind of oil weapon is the economic oil weapon. To extract more money from the west. One is, will prices rise again? Will we have to be more deferential to the oil-producing countries than we are in this loose market? Will the Arabs ever again attempt to deny oil to the United States, to punish the United States? I think that oil weapon is dead. But as an instrument of subtle power it's going to come back.'

He feels that the west, and in particular the United States, didn't take Faisal and the Saudis as seriously as they should have in that early period in 1973.

'This was just another king, another head of state, we could well have brushed him off. Today we take them even less seriously than we did in the 1970s. That's partly because of the personalities. Partly because Faisal was a much more impressive man than Fahd. And partly because of the widespread belief that there's a glut and the glut is going to be around forever so we don't have to take them seriously. Much of this is encouraged by the American Jewish community and they are quite mistaken. They're pooh-poohing the return of the general oil problem. It helps them short term in what they want to do. They don't realize that the more we pooh-pooh the oil problem today, the greater is going to be the oil problem in the 1990s and the greater therefore will be the bargaining power they will have to contend with on behalf of Israel. I think they're quite shortsighted. But the tendency in the Jewish community is that it's over with.'

More important, Schlesinger and Yamani both agree, is the American-Israeli relationship in the period of oil glut.

The two countries have become especially close for a variety of reasons. High on the list is that George Shultz, who is reputed to be pro-Arab because he'd dealt with them when he was at the head of Bechtel, got so angry at Syria's President Assad during the Lebanon crisis that he turned a lot of his attention towards Israel.

Says Schlesinger, 'One of the consequences of that has been a lessening of our interest in the Saudis and a distancing of the Saudis from us – partly because they must and partly because they want to. I say they must. Cosying up to the Americans when the American position is synonymous to that of Israel is very difficult for Arab leaders.'

Surrounding that, Yamani sees another, potentially more dangerous, problem.

'Over the next several years the number of Arabs in the occupied territories and inside Israel itself will continue to grow. You merely have to look at the birth-rate statistics to see that one day the Arab population in Israel will exceed the Jewish population there.'

And, he senses, only two things can possibly come from that.

'Either the Arabs must be given the rights of citizens, allowed to vote and to take part in the affairs of the country, which will change the character of the Jewish state. Or the Arabs living there will forever be relegated to being second class citizens. The problem here becomes one where you have a repetition of apartheid, the way you find it in South Africa. The Arabs will make up the majority of the population and yet they will have no rights.'

He believes there is only one solution.

'It is time that Israel recognized, for it's own security and well-being, that they must open a dialogue with the Arabs and help secure a homeland for the Palestinians. There is no other solution possible.'

Yet distrust runs deep.

The Arabs don't seem to understand that 5,000 years of Jewish paranoia is not easily overcome. The Israelis don't seem to understand that answers which might have been workable in 1948 may no longer be viable today.

But it might be different for both sides if they each knew who they were dealing with.

A report on Yamani, filed at an agency in Washington, reveals that while he was studying at Harvard the then Israeli Ambassador to the United States, Abba Eban, was friendly with one of Yamani's professors.

Eban was a frequent visitor to Harvard.

And Yamani met him there on several occasions.

In the Arab world, at least around the Gulf, Yamani will for many years to come enjoy senior statesman status.

He also has what so few other Arab statesmen have. He commands great respect in the United States yet maintains a direct line of communication to the moderate Palestinians.

Eban enjoys that senior statesman status as well, and also carries respect in the United States.

If Anwar Sadat could talk to Golda Meir and at least begin to melt the ice formed by two wars in seven years, it's just possible that a well-prepared Yamani – Eban dialogue could be a positive step towards a negotiated and lasting peace.

But would Yamani be willing to sit down with Eban and try to work something out? And would Eban be willing to sit down with Yamani?

Given time to prepare the way, given the chance to create the right sort of forum and given the proper political support, it's hard to see how either could refuse.

* * * *

Every morning, early, he's on the phone, talking to people in the Middle East where it's two to three hours ahead of Europe.

He says he always tries to ring his mother twice a day from wherever he is. And if his children aren't with him, he always speaks to each of them every day too.

From mid-morning until well into the early evening, the phone seems to ring near him every few minutes as business slows down for the day in Saudi Arabia and begins in North America.

Then, late at night, when it isn't ringing because most people think he's asleep, he's back on the phone talking to people in the States.

Much of his telephoning is just keeping in touch with old friends, he says, and he obviously spends a great deal of time and money doing that. So many of his old friends are in awe of the way he maintains relationships.

The rest of those phone calls are business.

Business, he's asked, or just interests?

He says, business.

But surely, he's told, you don't have to work for a living if you don't want to.

He looks a bit surprised that someone should say such a thing. 'Yes, of course I do. I can't just let my investments slip. You know, it costs me a lot of money to live.'

That it must.

At the same time, Zaki Yamani is not the kind of man who could ever really retire.

He has too many aspirations.

He's formed a private publishing company to produce high-quality books of historically important Islamic manuscripts.

He continues teaching on a part-time basis, lecturing on various aspects of law, sometimes on Islamic law, sometimes on the business of energy.

He takes an active role in his law firm.

And he's also set up some important charitable trusts.

But he won't talk about that side of his life. He says his benevolence is his own private affair, and anyway, 'Once such activities are widely publicized, you lose some of the self-satisfaction and the pleasure that comes from trying to do some good.'

Then there's the energy centre he's established in London.

'We've built a very unique energy centre in the west which cooperates with the top universities and institutions in the world. I created it because I felt it's necessary to have objective studies for energy problems which deal with the matter from a global point of view.'

But again, that's all he wants to say.

'I don't like to talk about these things. I'm supporting them with my own money for my own reasons. I prefer to go about doing these things quietly. I am not doing it to get headlines. I am doing it because I believe in them.'

When he was in government, Yamani calculated that he spent half the year in Saudi Arabia and the other half in his plane.

These days it seems that hasn't changed.

'So far we find that we continue to spend half a year or so at home in Saudi Arabia. But never in one stretch. Sometimes it's a month, like for Ramadan. Sometimes it's only a week. The rest of the time we travel.'

When he's travelling, he spends the majority of that time in Europe, although, having now firmed up his Harvard connection as a guest professor, he's a regular visitor to Boston.

In many ways, the little boy who once wanted to emulate his father and become a great teacher has grown up to do just that.

It's hardly a surprise to hear that when he left government the phone didn't stop ringing with offers from friends in the oil business.

He could have made it onto the main board of any number of major multinational corporations.

With very little effort he could have set himself up as the world's premier oil consultant.

But he chose to busy himself with his own projects instead.

Still, a friend of mine figured, that might not stop Yamani from doing a little freelance consulting work in a spare moment.

My friend rang one night to say, do me a favour and ask the Sheikh what I should do. Tell him I want to take a position in the market. Go ahead, please, find out what he thinks about the price of oil.

It was a personally embarrassing thing for me, to ask for this advice as if I was trying to get a movie star's autograph.

'I keep telling you,' Yamani said, now aiming the silver-topped wooden cane at me to make his point, 'I personally always think long term. I'm too cautious by nature. The future's market is too much like gambling and I'm not a gambler.'

'It's not for me,' I insisted. 'It really is for a friend.'

'Well,' he said. 'All right. Tell your friend if he wants to gamble to go short. But tell him I said he's not investing, he's gambling.'

Yamani

I did. I told my friend, 'Sell.'
And the price of oil promptly went up.

Index

Index

Index

298

Index